Playing in Time

Playing in Time

Essays, Profiles, and Other True Stories

CARLO ROTELLA

The University of Chicago Press ✳ *Chicago and London*

CARLO ROTELLA is the author of *Good with Their Hands: Boxers, Bluesmen, and Other Characters from the Rust Belt*; *October Cities: The Redevelopment of Urban Literature*; and *Cut Time: An Education at the Fights*, the last also published by the University of Chicago Press. He writes regularly for the *New York Times Magazine*, *Washington Post Magazine*, and *Boston Globe*, and he is a commentator for WGBH FM in Boston.

The University of Chicago Press, Chicago 60637
The University of Chicago Press, Ltd., London
© 2012 by Carlo Rotella
All rights reserved. Published 2012.
Printed in the United States of America

21 20 19 18 17 16 15 14 13 12   1 2 3 4 5

ISBN-13: 978-0-226-72909-1 (cloth)
ISBN-13: 978-0-226-72911-4 (e-book)
ISBN-10: 0-226-72909-5 (cloth)
ISBN-10: 0-226-72911-7 (e-book)

Library of Congress Cataloging-in-Publication Data

Rotella, Carlo, 1964–
    Playing in time : essays, profiles, and other true stories / Carlo Rotella.
        pages ; cm
    Miscellaneous essays.
    ISBN-13: 978-0-226-72909-1 (cloth : alkaline paper)
    ISBN-10: 0-226-72909-5 (cloth : alkaline paper)
    ISBN-13: 978-0-226-72911-4 (e-book)
    ISBN-10: 0-226-72911-7 (e-book)
    I. Title.
    AC8.R644 2012
    814'.6—dc23
                                                                    2011050360

♾ This paper meets the requirements of ANSI/NISO Z39.48-1992 (Permanence of Paper).

Contents

FOR MY BROTHERS, *Sebastian and Sal*

Introduction: The Lefty Dizz Version

ON THE WALL BY my desk I have mounted a photograph of a confrontation on the sidewalk outside the Checkerboard Lounge, at 43rd and Vincennes on the South Side of Chicago, in 1982. In the picture, the great bluesman Buddy Guy, who owned the Checkerboard back then, faces off against a young man in a hat who has his back to the camera. The young man, ejected from the club after some kind of beef, had stormed off to his car and returned wearing a jacket, with one hand jammed menacingly into one of its pockets. Guy and a crew of his supporters are lined up shoulder to shoulder to bar the way to the door, each privately calculating the odds that the young man really has a gun and would use it. Backing up the boss, from left to right, are Anthony, Guy's aide-de-camp and security man; L. C. Thurman, who managed the club; and Aretta, who tended bar and waited tables. Standing with them, although he seems more observer or bystander than participant, is Lefty Dizz, a bluesman from Osceola, Arkansas, who hung out at the Checkerboard and hosted its Blue Monday jam for years.

Unlike the others, who strike appropriately forbidding poses—Anthony with drink in hand, Thurman with cigarette balefully pasted in mug, Aretta with hands on hips in iconic disapproval, Guy front and center with his whole being concentrated in the hands-down, shoulder-forward, head-cocked ready position that indicates a willingness to go all the way—Dizz seems bemused, even distracted. He's the only one not fixing the troublemaker with a grim stare, and he's holding something soft and bulky in front of him with both hands, probably a balled-up towel, presenting it with palms inward, like an offering or talisman. The others' body English says, "Mess with me and you'll regret it." Dizz's says, "Life is complex and filled with contingency; this would be a good time to step within for a taste of Old Grand-Dad."

I like to look at this picture, to which attaches a fugitive whiff of the South Side tavern bouquet of my youth: menthol cigarettes, Old Style beer, and hair treatments made by the Johnson Products Company. And there's the pleasure of seeing familiar faces, people with whom I exchanged friendly words on big nights out in my teens, which means it's going on 30 years since I used to see them all a couple of times a week. But I also keep the picture around as a reminder to take second and third looks, to revisit scenes and characters and stories that I thought I knew well.

Marc PoKempner, a longtime photographer of the Chicago blues scene, happened to pull up at the curb outside the Checkerboard on his motorcycle on that summer night in 1982 just in time to shoot a sequence of pictures of the confrontation. I used a different shot from his sequence in a book called *Good with Their Hands*, published a decade ago. That one was taken from an angle farther around behind the young troublemaker, so that he almost entirely obscures Dizz. Guy has stepped more prominently forward in that one, Aretta's not in it, and Thurman (who later wrested control of the Checkerboard from Guy) looks off to the side, all of which has the effect of making Guy seem isolated as he attends to yet another problem that an egregio virtuoso should be able to leave to his underlings. I put it in the book to evocatively illustrate Guy's account of how difficult it was to run a club on the South Side in the 1970s and 1980s.

The Lefty Dizz version may not be a better picture in the conventional sense—yes, the poses are more dramatic, but the troublemaker's free hand is blurred, and Dizz, too, is not quite perfectly in focus—but it has an added valence that matters. Guy was the marquee name, the guitar hero whose ownership of the Checkerboard gave it a reputation as the capital of Chicago blues and attracted fellow greats like Muddy Waters and Otis Rush, insiders' favorites like Fenton Robinson and Magic Slim, and rock stars like the Rolling Stones and Stevie Ray Vaughan, who dropped by the Checkerboard after playing sold-out arena gigs. Dizz, the only person I've ever known who bore a close resemblance to the Cat in the Hat, was by comparison a minor figure, a local character known for a couple of novelty songs—"I'm sitting here drinking my eggnog, but there's nobody to drink with me /

It's the 25th of December, and I'm sad as a man can be"—and for his gift for orchestrating a good time. He had a serviceable voice and a droll showbiz manner, and he was a distinctive, if limited, guitar player. He did a great deal of one-handed playing, part of a large repertoire of onstage gimmickry, but he wasn't all tricks; he had learned a thing or two about propulsive grooves from the blues-party juggernaut Hound Dog Taylor. Thanks to the quality of local talent and in great part to Dizz, an ideal emcee, the Checkerboard's Monday night blues jam was a cut above all others. It usually started out in desultory fashion but built in intensity as musicians, patrons, smoke, inebriation, and sound accrued in the narrow, low-ceilinged room until some magical fission point was attained. On Tuesdays, still lost in the previous night's music, I'd go around in a daze at school—more of a daze than usual, that is.

Dizz, whose given name was Walter Williams, was the most approachable of the Checkerboard's notables. A generous fellow and a natural-born enthusiast, he showed a particular affection for the kids from my high school who hung out there. Dizz, who had studied economics at Southern Illinois University, enjoyed playing the downhome blues sage as much as we enjoyed playing at being barflies and connoisseurs. Each indulged the other. I liked to ask technical questions: "How do you make a song yours when other players already made it famous?" He liked to drop aphoristic advice on whippersnappers: "Take your time and listen. Don't be all in a rush to play fast and blow everybody away. Take your time, and you'll hear that note in that song that nobody else has heard." He played an annual gig at my school, staying up all night with his band, the Shock Treatment, to make the early-morning assembly in the gym, where, bleary-eyed in his third-best suit, he played a short set of his old reliables: "Baby, Please Don't Go," "The Things I Used to Do," "Never Make My Move Too Soon," "Bad Avenue," "Somebody Stole My Christmas."

When I showed up at the Checkerboard with my friends, he'd purse his lips and give us a mock-serious nod from the stage, and between sets he'd stop by to shoot the breeze. (The drinking age was eighteen, but a thirteen-year-old with cash in hand had no trouble getting into the Checkerboard and ordering drinks.) In good weather, we held our between-set colloquies outside the club on the sidewalk, standing around with drinks in hand in the desolation of 43rd Street, a once-thriving business strip that had fallen upon hard times. A mile to the west, the dark towers of the Robert Taylor Homes marched off along the expressway. They're gone now, taken down by Daley the Second (who will, I think, edge out his mighty father in the all-time rankings of Chicago's political bosses), but back then the massed high-rise projects seemed like an immemorial feature of the landscape. I suppose the glaciers seemed equally permanent, back when the Laurentide ice sheet covered the upper Midwest.

Dizz is gone, too; he died of cancer in 1993. When I look up from whatever I'm writing and gaze for a while at the picture on my wall, he comes back to me.

I think of this book of selected pieces—some new, but most published over the past fifteen years in a variety of magazines, quarterlies, and other publications—as a kind of Lefty Dizz version, a second look from a different angle that allows what was obscured and implicit to emerge into view and change a scene's texture of meaning. When I come back to these pieces and read them together (and together with the new ones), removed from the immediate context of assignments and deadlines and editorial demands in which they were written and published, the altered setting brings out new resonances. Putting them together here also returns the pieces to their most original context; that is, they're all about things I'm interested in, and in many cases they're about things I've been interested in for a long time. Seeing them lined up shoulder to shoulder like this gives me new insight into the sustained interests that brought me to these various particular topics and to the ways in which I wrote about them.

In the pieces that follow, blues, boxing, pulp fiction, movies, my old neighborhood, and other people's old neighborhoods recur frequently among a broader range of topics that includes jazz fantasy camp, gambling, ghosts, dogs, what it's like to run a movie studio or megachurch, and fear of clowns. I do go all over the place, which is one of the joys of writing nonfiction; people are up to all kinds of things, and the writer and his readers get to tag along. But I also see some unifying throughlines in this book.

First, most of these pieces are about city life in one way or another. There's a certain kind of child of the middle class who finds himself attracted to both the street and the library, and who fashions a life out of exploring the relationships between them. Such people form a tribe, and among its members are some of the writers whose work has made the deepest impression on me—Émile Zola, A. J. Liebling, and Jack Vance, to name only three. I already knew I was a member of the tribe, but rereading this selection of pieces reminds me just how forcefully this identity has shaped what calls to me and how I explore it.

Second, if I have a meta-subject, it's how creative people give form to inchoate inspirations by pouring them into the vessels available in a particular time and place: genres and styles like Chicago blues or space opera or the stick-and-move technique of the master defensive fighter; institutions like the Checkerboard Lounge or a publishing house or a boxing gym or a government agency. And along with the possibilities for giving form to a creative impulse come the limitations on creative possibility that often supercharge art, sport, and other endeavors with meaning. There's a story in this book about a fight between Larry Holmes, a 52-year-old former champion still looking to pad his all-timer's résumé and make one more payday, and a barnstorming strongman known as Butterbean, who yearned for the legitimacy and subsequent purses he could earn by making a fine showing against Holmes. That fight's meaning was almost entirely a product of the strictly limited circumstances under which an old man and a fat man—both inspired, both gifted in ways that most observers did not credit—practiced the fistic arts. That's one of the lessons I think I've learned about creativity: it begins to have human import, to take recognizable signifying form, to the extent that it's constrained by the conditions in which it's made.

Third, looking back over these pieces reminds me just how powerfully my own inspirations and interests have been shaped by having been poured into the vessels available to me: magazines and quarterlies, the academy and the commercial writing trades, the profile and the essay, assignments, deadlines, travel budgets, house styles, word counts and per-word pay rates. In my early twenties I tried repeatedly to just sit down and write, on my own, in a vacuum, and nothing came out. After a while I figured out that I needed less freedom and more useful constraint: craft training, clearly defined jobs of work to do, editors. Much of what I know about writing I've reverse-engineered from what editors did to my drafts, and editors have paid me for my words and sent me to Las Vegas, New Orleans, and Rochester, to WrestleMania in Orlando and a fencing academy in suburban Atlanta and the Harvard-Yale football game, to polka joints and casinos and a nighttime water-and-fire ritual on the river in downtown Providence, and to many of the other places that turn up in the pages that follow.

(Editors are important, and I've been lucky to work with several superb ones, but they're not *always* right. I have revised some of the published pieces that follow. I didn't attempt to bring them up to date, change verb tenses, or otherwise uproot them from the historical moment in which they were written, but I did touch them up here and there to sharpen the focus of my Lefty Dizz version. I have also occasionally restored a line or a quote that got cut the first time around, undoing editorial decisions that were guided by considerations that I no longer have to take into account.)

I see one more principal sub rosa unity in many of the pieces that follow. They give you a pretty fair notion of what I liked when I was thirteen, or at least of enthusiasms that have lasted: not just for the music of Lefty Dizz and Buddy Guy but also for the writing of Vance and other masters of genre fiction; for the fights and other embodied sorts of knowing; for crime stories, cityscapes, the virtues and mechanics of working at a craft, and the traffic between school and subcultural scenes. As I point out in my profile of the 92-year-old Vance, who was bowled over in early adolescence by the pulp magazine *Weird Tales* and whose own writing similarly bowled me over at that age, you may never again lose yourself so entirely in a work of art as you can when you're thirteen. I think of thirteen as the intellectual age of consent, the moment when the hot wax of a formative sensibility takes perhaps the deepest permanent impressions. It was at that age that I began to recognize in myself the twinned attractions to library and street, and to search—vaguely, at first, but with greater purpose as the years went by—for vessels in which to pour that interest and give it lasting form that could also serve as craft and calling.

It was at that age, too, that I began to realize how libraries and schools were like gyms and music clubs, all of them institutions where specialized knowledge is ordered and passed along, where one can begin to see how people get good at things. Every library is a local incarnation of the Master Library of All Time and Space. Every school, from kindergarten to research university, is a branch office of that world-spanning enterprise, Big School. Every bar, whether it offers live music or not, is a touchingly imperfect copy of the One True Universal Bar. The Mystical Body of Boxing Gyms can manifest itself in a strip-mall storefront with a duct-taped heavy bag hanging in the corner or in a converted industrial loft just big enough for a sparring ring. In my early teens I began to see such permutatively recurring places as my natural habitat, structural elements of the world I wanted to live in, and to realize that the lessons to be learned in them were the lessons I wanted to know more about.

I tend to be most comfortable at ringside, on the close margin, inside the scene but ceding center stage to headliners like Buddy Guy and the troublemaker in the hat with his back to the camera. But I do recognize that there's a kind of self-portrait between the lines of this book, and that returning to these scenes and stories and reading them together brings that self-portrait into clearer view. And I have to admit that the character somewhere between observer and participant who emerges into view in this Lefty Dizz version, the figure whose presence is always implicit even when obscured in the pieces that follow, is me.

Craft

The Genre Artist

JACK VANCE, DESCRIBED BY his peers as "a major genius" and "the greatest living writer of science fiction and fantasy," has been hidden in plain sight for as long as he has been publishing—six decades and counting. Yes, he has won Hugo, Nebula, and World Fantasy awards and has been named a Grand Master by the Science Fiction and Fantasy Writers of America, and he received an Edgar from the Mystery Writers of America, but such honors only help to camouflage him as just another accomplished genre writer. So do the covers of his books, which feature the usual spacecraft, monsters, and euphonious place names: Lyonesse, Alastor, Durdane. If you had never read Vance and were browsing a bookstore's shelf, you might have no particular reason to choose one of his books instead of one next to it by A. E. van Vogt, say, or John Varley. And if you chose one of these alternatives, you would go on your way to the usual thrills with no idea that you had just missed out on encountering one of American literature's most distinctive and undervalued voices.

That's how Vance's fans see it, anyway. Among them are authors who have gained the big paydays and the fame that Vance never enjoyed. Dan Simmons, the best-selling writer of horror and fantasy, described discovering Vance as "a revelation for me, like coming to Proust or Henry James. Suddenly you're in the deep end of the pool. He gives you glimpses of entire worlds with just perfectly turned language. If he'd been born south of the border, he'd be up for a Nobel

Original publication: *New York Times Magazine*, July 19, 2009.

Prize." Michael Chabon, whose distinguished literary reputation allows him to employ popular formulas without being labeled a genre writer, told me, "Jack Vance is the most painful case of all the writers I love who I feel don't get the credit they deserve. If 'The Last Castle' or 'The Dragon Masters' had the name Italo Calvino on it, or just a foreign name, it would be received as a profound meditation, but because he's Jack Vance and published in Amazing Whatever, there's this insurmountable barrier."

The barrier has not proved insurmountable to other genre writers—like Ray Bradbury and Elmore Leonard, who have commanded critical respect while moving a lot of satisfyingly familiar product, or like H. P. Lovecraft and Raymond Chandler, pulp writers whose posthumous reputations rose over time until they passed the threshold of highbrow acceptance. But each of these writers, no matter how innovative or poetic, entered the literary mainstream by fully exploiting the attributes of his specialty. Vance, by contrast, has worked entirely within popular forms without paying much heed to their conventions or signature joys. His emphasis falls on the unexpected note, the odd beat. The rocket ships are just ways to get characters from one cogently imagined society to another; he prefers to tersely summarize battle scenes and other such potentially crowd-pleasing setpieces; and he takes greatest pleasure in word-music when exploring humankind's rich capacity for nastiness. For example: "As he approached the outermost fields he moved cautiously, skulking from tussock to copse, and presently found that which he sought: a peasant turning the dank soil with a mattock. Cugel crept quietly forward, struck down the loon with a gnarled root." While Vance may play by the rules of whatever genre he works in, his true genre is the Jack Vance story.

His loyal readers are fiercely passionate about him. An inspired crew of them got together in the late 1990s to assemble the Vance Integral Edition, a handsome 45-volume set of the great man's complete works in definitive editions. Led by Paul Rhoads, an American painter living in France (whose recent critical appraisal of Vance, *Winged Being*, compares him to Oswald Spengler and Jane Austen, among others, and anoints him the anti–Paul Auster), the VIE volunteers painstakingly compared editions and the author's drafts to restore prose corrupted by publishers. Hard-core Vancians also created *Totality* (http://pharesm.org/), a website where you can search the VIE texts, which is how we know that he has used the word "punctilio" exactly

33 times in his published prose. It was an extraordinary display of true readerly love—a bunch of buffs giving a contemporary genre writer the Shakespearean variorum treatment on their own time.

Vance, who is 92, says that his new book—a memoir, *This Is Me, Jack Vance!*—will definitely be his last. Also arriving in bookstores this month is *Songs of the Dying Earth*, a collection of stories by other writers set in the far-future milieu that Vance introduced in some of his first published stories, which he wrote on a clipboard on the deck of a freighter in the South Pacific while serving in the merchant marine during World War II. The roster of contributors to the collection includes genre stars and best-selling brand names, among them Simmons, Neil Gaiman, Terry Dowling, Tanith Lee, George R. R. Martin, and Dean Koontz. It's a literary tribute album, in effect, on which reliable earners acknowledge the influence of a respectably semiobscure national treasure by covering his songs.

Right about now you might be thinking, Well, if Vance is as good as Simmons and Chabon and Rhoads say he is, and if he refused to give in to the demands of the genres in which he worked, then maybe he would have done better to try other forms that better rewarded his strengths. Isn't it a shame that he confined himself to adolescent genres in which his grown-up talents could not truly shine? But I think that question would be wrong in its assumptions: wrong about Vance, about genre, and about what "adolescent" and "grown-up" mean when we talk about literary sensibility.

———

When I was fourteen or so, in the late '70s, I knew an Advanced Boy, a connoisseur of all that was cooler than whatever his classmates were listening to, smoking, or reading. I was impressed with myself for having graduated from Tolkien to E. R. Eddison and Michael Moorcock. "Kid stuff," said the Advanced Boy. "Try this." He handed me a paperback copy of Vance's *The Eyes of the Overworld*. On the cover a giant lizardlike creature was tipping over a rowboat containing a man in regulation swords-and-sorcery attire and a buxom woman in regulation dishabille.

I can remember the exact lines on the second page that sank the hook in me for keeps, a passing exchange of dialogue between two hawkers of sorcerous curios at a bazaar:

"'I can resolve your perplexity,' said Fianosther. 'Your booth occupies the site of the old gibbet, and has absorbed unlucky essences. But I thought to notice you examining the manner in which the timbers of my booth are joined. You will obtain a better view from within, but first I must shorten the chain of the captive erb which roams the premises during the night.'

'No need,' said Cugel. 'My interest was cursory.'"

The feral, angling politesse, the marriage of high-flown language to low motives, the way Cugel's clipped phrases rounded off Fianosther's ornate ones—I felt myself seized by a writer's style in a way I had never experienced before. Vance didn't even have to describe the "captive erb." The phrase itself conjured up rows of teeth and the awful strength of a long, sinewy body surging up your leg.

Cugel soon finds himself in Smolod, a village whose inhabitants wear magical eye cusps that transform their fetid surroundings into apparent splendor. The cusps are relics of the demon Unda-Hrada's incursion from the subworld La-Er during the Cutz Wars of the Eighteenth Aeon. "I dimly recall that I inhabit a sty and devour the coarsest of food," one elder admits, "but the subjective reality is that I inhabit a glorious palace and dine on splendid viands among the princes and princesses who are my peers." It's a typical Vancian setup: a few bold conceptual strokes, ripe descriptions, and evocative names combine to fully realize a weird place that feels real—because the meatiness of his language endows it with presence, but also because every reader lives in a place sort of like it.

Cugel manages to steal a single cusp before fleeing Smolod ahead of an angry mob. It's merely the first stop on his journey across the Dying Earth, a realm of cynical wonders in which the last exemplars of human civilization go about the age-old business of lying, cheating, and stealing to satisfy base desires as the enfeebled sun falters toward final darkness.

I read the book in a kind of rapt delirium and went looking for more. In addition to picaresque fantasy, Vance has written high fantasy, science fantasy, planetary romance, extraterrestrial mystery, revenge sagas, and less-classifiable speculative adventure tales on scales ranging from the short story to the multivolume chronicle. For good measure, he wrote eleven mysteries under his given name, John Holbrook Vance, and three more under the floating pseudonym Ellery Queen. He had a brief stint early in his career as a writer for the Captain Video television series, and over the years several of his stories have been optioned, but Hollywood has not snapped up his work as it snapped up, say, Philip K. Dick's. Part of Hollywood's lack of interest in Vance can be traced, I think, to an oversimple reading of him as a baroque stylist whose writing depends mostly on language to achieve its effect, rather than on plot, character, or high-concept premise.

Vance believes that the musical flow of language is all-important to storytelling—"The prose should swing," he told me more than once—but some social or cultural problem always moves beneath the action, inviting the intellect to pause and consider. *The Languages of Pao*, for instance, develops the proposition that language can be transformed to make a people more warlike; "The Dragon Masters" pursues an analogy between genetic manipulation and aesthetic sophistication. He will also mute or undercut the action with a well-struck psychological grace note. After hunting down one by one the evil geniuses who slaughtered his family, the hero of the Demon Princes cycle becomes so subdued that his companion asks if he's all right. "Quite well," he answers in the closing lines of the fifth and final novel. "Deflated, perhaps. I have been deserted by my enemies. Treesong is dead. The affair is over. I am done." *Deflated, perhaps*. Rarely has a science-fiction hero reached the finish line with so little fanfare.

Intricate plotting is not Vance's forte, but he artfully recombines recurring elements: the rhythms of travel; the pleasures of music, strong drink, and vengeance; touchy encounters with pedants, mountebanks, violently opinionated aesthetes and zealots, louts, bigots of all stripes, and boyishly slim young women with an enigmatic habit of looking back over their shoulders. His stories sustain an anecdotal forward drive that balances his digressive pleasure in imagining a world and the hypnotic effect of his distinctive tone, which has been variously described as barbed, velvety, arch, and mandarin.

Reading Vance leaves you with a sense of formality, of having been present at an occasion when, for all the jokiness and the fun of made-up words, the serious business of literary entertainment was transacted. And it teaches a lasting lesson about the writer's craft: whatever's on the cover, you can always aim high.

It turns out that mine was a common reaction to a first encounter with Vance's prose at an impressionable age. Some of the celebrated fantasists who contributed to *Songs of the Dying Earth* told me similar stories.

Dan Simmons was twelve when his older brother let him read "The Dragon Masters" and he suddenly found himself in the deep end of the pool. Neil Gaiman was twelve or thirteen when he stumbled across a Dying Earth tale. "I fell in love with the prose style," Gaiman said. "It was elegant, intelligent; each word felt like it knew what it was doing. It's funny but never, ever once nudges you in the ribs."

Tanith Lee told me that in her early twenties she was "a great misfit, unhappy in my heart, and I knew I wanted to write." Her mother bought her the first Dying Earth book, which invested Lee's then-mopey existence with writerly possibility. "I loved the black humor, the elegance, and I loved the sheer viciousness. And when I got to Cugel, I loved him. He was a lifeline." After we talked, she e-mailed me one of her favorite lines from Vance: "I would offer congratulations were it not for this tentacle gripping my leg."

Michael Chabon, who did not contribute to the tribute volume, was twelve or thirteen when he read "The Dragon Masters." He places Vance "in an authentic American tradition that's important and powerful but less recognized. It's not Twain-Hemingway; it's more Poe's tradition, a blend of European refinement with brawling, two-fisted frontier spirit. I picture this sailor in his blue chambray work shirt, his jeans, and a watch cap sitting on the deck of a ship in the South Pacific, imagining a million years in the future, this elaborate world going through its death throes. The prose isn't just rarefied and over-ripe. Vance has the narrative force, the willingness to look very coldly at violence and cruelty, to not shy away."

Chabon contrasted Vance with Tolkien and C. S. Lewis, British dons who shared a grandiose "impulse to synthesize a mythology for a culture. There's none of that in Vance. The engineer in him is always on view. They're always adventure stories, too, but they're also problem-solving puzzles. He sets up these what-ifs, like a syllogism. He has that logic-love like Poe, the Yankee engineering spirit, married to erudite love of pomp and pageantry. And he has an amazing ear and writes a beautiful sentence."

Most of these writers were adolescents when they first read Vance, who awoke in them an appreciation for the artistic possibilities of language. When applied to literature, "adolescent" does not only have to mean pedestrian prose that evokes the strong feelings of emotionally inexperienced people. "Adolescent" can also mean writing that inspires the first conscious stirrings of literary sensibility. So, yes, Vance worked exclusively in adolescent genres—if under that heading we include the transformative experience of falling in love for the first time with a beautiful sentence.

————

Vance lives in the Oakland hills, in a house he tore down and rebuilt over the years in idiosyncratic form. He has a reputation for reclusive crabbiness, and encounters between strangers in his stories are often instinctively truculent. (A specimen exchange between a customer and a clerk: "'Your methods are incorrect. Since I entered the chamber first, you should have dealt first with my affairs.' The clerk blinked. 'The idea, I must say, has an innocent simplicity in its favor.'") As I climbed the steep driveway on a gray afternoon last winter, a large dog barking at my approach, I tried to banish the irrational expectation that Vance and I would exchange Vancian dialogue. Me: "Why did you persist in writing hurlothrumbo romances of the footling sort favored by mooncalfs?" Him: "The question is nuncupatory. I grow weary of your importunities. Begone."

But he was gracious and regaled me with stories about his adventures in the South Seas. He sat in a rocking chair at his desk, bundled up against the chill in windbreaker and watch cap, with a blanket around his shoulders and a heater by his slippered feet. Old age has stooped and diminished him, but his deep voice still carries a rasp of authority. He spends his days at his desk, listening to mysteries on tape (he has been blind since the 1980s), talking on the phone when somebody calls, listening to or playing the traditional jazz he adores. At one point during my visit he pulled down a baritone ukulele from the rack of stringed instruments behind him and strummed it with abandon as he sang a forceful little ditty about pitching woo. He also plays—or played—harmonica, washboard, kazoo, and cornet.

Unlike many of his characters, who are forever puffing themselves up ("I am studied in four infinities and I sit as a member of the Collegium"), Vance presents himself as a down-to-earth, practical fellow. He deflected my questions about the fan letters in his file cabinets from the likes of the young Ursula K. Le Guin, the software zillionaire Paul Allen, and the game designer Gary Gygax, whose Dungeons & Dragons borrowed heavily from Vance, but he was happy to explain how he once raised a sunken houseboat using an air compressor and eight 50-gallon drums.

Vance never got rich, but he made enough to support his wife,

Norma, who died last year after 61 years of marriage, and their son, John, now an engineer. They traveled often to exotic locales—Madeira, Tahiti, Cape Town, Kashmir—where they settled in cheap lodgings long enough for Vance to write another book. "We'd hole up for anywhere from a couple of weeks to a few months," John told me. "He had his clipboard; she had the portable typewriter. He'd write in longhand, and she'd type it up. First draft, second draft, third draft."

That he could make a good living as a genre writer was supremely important to Vance, who was born into a San Francisco family that fell on hard times during his early childhood. Growing up during the Great Depression on his grandparents' farm on Little Dutch Slough in the waterway country east of the city, he came early to his love of sailing, self-reliant handiness, and genre fiction. He admired Edgar Rice Burroughs's tales of John Carter of Mars and, he said, "I waited at the mailbox every month with my tongue hanging out for the latest issue of *Weird Tales*," the pulp magazine that featured seminal fantasy writers like Lovecraft, Robert E. Howard, C. L. Moore, and Clark Ashton Smith. Vance attended the University of California, Berkeley, but his practical education as a writer came from reading the pulps and other entertainments: L. Frank Baum's Oz books, the mannered yarns of Jeffery Farnol, the light comedy of P. G. Wodehouse, his literary hero.

Other than mastery of tonal effects and a penchant for creating formidable matrons of advanced middle years, Vance would seem to have little in common with Wodehouse, least of all in his view of human nature. Vance's characters tend to share a dark, grasping quality, and cruelty comes easily to them. In *Araminta Station*, the first novel in his ecopolitical Cadwal trilogy, Vance mock-cites *The Worlds of Man*, a study by the galaxy-spanning Fellows of the Fidelius Institute: "In our journeys from one end of the Gaean Reach to the other and, on occasion, Beyond, we discover nothing to indicate that the human race is everywhere and inevitably becoming more generous, tolerant, kindly and enlightened. Nothing whatever." Vance told me that he and his family always found good treatment and good company in their travels, eating and drinking well and filling up their eyes with the beauty of the world. So what, then, inspired the pandemic interpersonal nastiness in his writing? He declined to speculate, but his son told me, "I think that came from when his family lost its money, dealing with the people he had to deal with. Times were tough, people were rugged. My guess is that pattern comes from his experiences in his early days, in California and in the merchant marine."

Vance takes pride in his craft but does not care to talk about it in any detail, going so far in his memoir as to consign almost all discussion of writing to a brief chapter at the end. Jeremy Cavaterra, a composer who lives in an apartment attached to Vance's house and helps look after him (and who was recruited as a lifelong fan when he read *The Eyes of the Overworld* at age fourteen), said of this reticence, "Part of it is that he feels like it's the magician telling you how the trick works, and part of it is that he writes by feel and doesn't interrogate it."

Vance's lingering distaste for talking about himself as a fantasist may also go back to his own adolescence, when he arrived in high school very young after skipping grades. The character of the awkward youth with a made-up world in his head recurs in his writing, as does the scene of popular kids tormenting a loner. The most prolifically homicidal of his strange dreamers is probably the Demon Prince Howard Alan Treesong, who speaks in the voices of imaginary avatars and terrorizes a school reunion. Norma used to say that her husband was Treesong. John told me that his father prefers to think of himself as a less dastardly Cugel. Put them together, Treesong the dreamer with streetwise Cugel, and you get Vance, whose long labor at his trade grew from a youthful discovery: you can turn idle dreaminess into purposeful art, and you can turn art into a paying gig.

Now Vance has begun to lose words. When he made a little show of waving me toward his bar and said, "Go get yourself a drink of single-malt scotch," he laughed and added, "There's a word I can't remember to describe that. It has a sense of aesthetic mastery, of command, but also a sense of thinking highly of yourself." His old favorite "punctilio" came to mind, as did "hauteur" (sixteen listings on *Totality*), but neither seemed quite right, so I didn't say anything. During our conversation he had already summarily dismissed several people, including two celebrated science-fiction writers I grew up reading, as a jackass or a show-off. Volunteering the wrong word might qualify me as both. I went to get my drink, leaving him to consider the exact shape of the hole the lost word had left behind in his mind. It might not be lost forever, though. It could well turn up in Michael Chabon's prose or that of the contributors to *Songs of the Dying Earth* or in Ursula K. Le Guin's. Maybe even in mine.

The Year of the Blues

THE UNITED STATES SENATE — An august body, yes, but not widely regarded as authoritative when it comes to lamenting in song a mean mistreater's offenses or bending a guitar note so fiercely that the high and low E strings kiss—has designated 2003 as the Year of the Blues. It has been exactly one century, the Senate's resolution reminds us, since W. C. Handy, the first great popularizer of the blues, had a life-changing encounter at a train station in Tutwiler, Mississippi, with a rag-clad stranger who played slide guitar with a knife blade and sang about going "where the Southern cross the Dog." Handy may well have embellished that dramatic episode of discovery, but it has passed into musical mythology as the moment when the blues caught the ear of the nation and began to exert its far-reaching influence on American culture and the whole world's musical habits. A year-long series of well-funded, high-profile celebrations has been arranged to mark the blues centennial—at Radio City Music Hall in New York City, at the Kennedy Center in Washington, at Experience Music Project in Seattle and other museums to which EMP's blues exhibit will travel, and on public television and radio stations across the country.

All very nice, and thanks for the overdue recognition, but Washington-area blues gigs are hard to come by these days, and Linwood Taylor has a living to make. With almost all of a long three-set evening of work still in front of him, Taylor, one of Washington's leading blues guitarists, is playing the opener of "Crosscut Saw." Flanked by

Original publication: "Linwood Taylor's Blues," *Washington Post Magazine*, August 24, 2003.

bass player and drummer, he stands on a small triangular stage in the corner of the cozy front room of the Sunset Grille, a roadhouse-style bar and restaurant set among the minimalls, chain stores, and subdivisions that line Columbia Pike in Annandale, Virginia. Forty or fifty people are listening, drinking, dancing, having a good time. The average age looks to be at least 45, and pretty much everybody except Taylor and the drummer is white. "Crosscut Saw" is the second tune of the band's first set, which opened with an uptempo Freddy King instrumental. Before the band came on, the Sunset Grille's customers listened contentedly to a recorded mix of songs by ZZ Top, the Who, Eric Clapton—well-ridden warhorses of classic rock.

Taylor's a lean, knotty fellow with prominent cheekbones, a soul patch beneath his lower lip, and a wolfish smile. When dressed for a show, all in black and hung with extra adornments at the wrists and ears, he looks like a friendly pirate. Bluesmen, like novelists, are "young" until they're 50. He's 47, and eight years have passed since he was recognized by the magazine *Living Blues* as one of 40 musicians under 40 to watch out for. It's getting to be time for Taylor to either break big in the blues world or prepare to settle for his current status as a local figure in a city not known as a blues capital.

The Sunset Grille's patrons, of course, don't know or care much about any of that. They're already warmed up and loose, partying with the unfrantic ease of people who've been doing it for decades and can handle both their booze and their hormones. A Colonel Sanders–looking white-haired dude in sporty hat and red suspenders, identified by a passing waitress as "the house sweetheart," dances with all the ladies. A still-youngish blond cutie in faded denim cutoffs has been draining cocktails at the bar at a giant-slaying rate, but she makes her way without staggering to a clear spot in front of the stage and does a curiously modest shimmy, all smiles.

Two fifytish men—sneakers, jeans, T-shirts stretched over pooched-out guts, mustaches—are leaning forward and nodding briskly along with Taylor's playing, each holding a draft beer in his right hand in the traditional incurve-wristed keg-party posture that brings the beer up close to his chest. One turns to the other and says, "The thing I like about this guy is he takes care of your guitar fix right away, doesn't he?"

He sure does. Taylor plays a great deal of strong, fluid, nimble guitar, displaying command of a variety of blues styles as he inventively reassembles their familiar components. Having opened the set with a burst of instrumental virtuosity, he's settling into the evening's work, pacing himself to get as much as he can out of each musical idea before moving to the next. It's 9:15, and his playing will still sound fresh at the end of third set, well after midnight. He used to be faster, wilder, but maturity as a guitar player has brought a sharper feeling for the melodic and expressive qualities of the music. He's not just repeating licks and wailing on guitar, although there's plenty of wailing to go around, enough to satisfy the two men with the draft beers and all the other patrons of the Sunset Grille.

Guitar heroism can take you a long way, but if you aspire to be a first-rate bluesman, and not just another hotshot sideman, there comes a time when you have to sing the blues. When Taylor chokes off a lick, steps close to the mike, and sings the first lines of "Crosscut Saw," his first vocals of the evening, there's the slightest hitch in the audience's response, a collective, not-quite-conscious "Hmm." Taylor freely admits that he's not a great blues singer, or even a very good one. He gets by well enough when chugging along at speed, playing guitar chords and fills to frame the lyrics he barks out. But the stiffness in his singing, the lack of blues fluency, still comes out at the ends of lines, where a blues singer should hold and bend a note. And on a slow blues his voice feels badly exposed. You can hear that he's often talking and shouting through a song, artfully relying on his guitar playing to carry his voice. The Sunset Grille's patrons never stop moving to the music or calling out encouragement, but every once in a while when he sings, another almost imperceptible echo of that "Hmm" ripples through them. They seem slightly relieved whenever he takes a guitar solo.

————

At least for the next few hours, the Sunset Grille, of all places, is the home of the blues. It's Saturday night, and middle-aged white baby boomers have gathered on their suburban home ground to hear their music. Some would say that the blues isn't supposed to belong to these people, that it's supposed to belong—if you accept that a cultural form can belong to anybody at all—to the black working class. But to deny that white enthusiasts exert a decisive influence on the sound, the business, the future, the very meaning of the blues today is to deny the roundness of the earth. Much of the black blues audience moved on to R&B and soul music in the 1960s; today, black blues fans tend to be concentrated in the audience for a smooth-groove subgenre, soul blues, purveyed by singers like Tyrone Davis and Denise LaSalle who are well known mostly in the South. Since the 1960s, the blues-influenced rock of the Rolling Stones, Clapton, Led Zeppelin, et al., has recruited white fans who dominate another, much more powerful constituency within the blues audience. They typically like their blues guitar-heavy and rocking, and rough enough to be recognizably descended from folk music (which satisfies them as to its authenticity), à la Muddy Waters or Buddy Guy.

The blues-rock aesthetic holds sway at the Sunset Grille, and the restaurant's "off-white-collar crowd" (as a manager described it) has cohorts in high places. Taylor says, "I play where the guys who work for roofing companies come, and I play for the guys who own the roofing companies. Doctors, lawyers, bankers, all kinds"—all kinds of baby boomers, that is, who share a belief that the blues matters because it's roots music. The most powerful members of this far-flung tribe of blues lovers—contemporaries in Congress, the software and movie industries, and the big-money end of the culture business—are in a position to institutionalize that shared belief.

They're busy doing just that. The Year of the Blues campaign is an initiative of Experience Music Project, the museum founded by Paul Allen, who made his billions as Bill Gates's founding partner at Microsoft. EMP and the corporate backers it has recruited—led by Volkswagen, which, thanks to the memory of the Beetle, enjoys a permanent association with Sixties nostalgia—have made a serious commitment to the Year of the Blues, supporting and publicizing an integrated year-long campaign kicked off by the Congressional resolution and a once-in-a-lifetime gathering of living blues talent and their celebrity admirers at Radio City Music Hall in February. On September 7, the Kennedy Center, in a major departure from its previously casual attention to the blues, will devote its Open House Arts Festival to "Celebrating the Year of the Blues." In addition to an impressively varied lineup of performers, there will be how-to sessions on singing the blues and playing harmonica. If all goes well on September 7 and at other scheduled blues shows on the 17th and 18th, the Kennedy Center plans to start programming the blues on a regular basis.

The live shows prepare the ground for the Year of the Blues campaign's other features, most of them scheduled to appear in an attention-getting cluster in the fall. The centerpiece is PBS's set of seven 90-minute blues documentaries, overseen by Martin Scorsese and directed by an honor roll of moviemakers that includes Scorsese, Clint Eastwood, and Wim Wenders. The campaign also features a traveling

Chicago blues exhibition created by EMP, a radio series produced by Public Radio International, a companion book, CDs and DVDs, and a nationwide push to get the blues into the high-school curriculum.

The mastermind behind this convergence, Bob Santelli, is the CEO of EMP, a happily cacophonous museum of popular music housed in a Frank Gehry building in downtown Seattle. Santelli, a strapping, friendly fellow of middle years who used to be an academic but looks like he'd rather be snowboarding, had the idea of getting Congress to declare an official Year of the Blues. The declaration itself doesn't actually count for much—it's not like the Senate was voting to waive taxes for anybody who can sing "Stormy Monday"—but it helps to get the word out, and it demonstrates that people in high places are taking the blues seriously.

"I want this music to thrive," Santelli says. "The blues is the bedrock of American popular music. As most of its legends and stars grow old and die, this musical form needs a shot in the arm to allow it to compete with other forms. I grew up in the Sixties, so thanks to the Rolling Stones and Cream, I got into Muddy Waters. But young people today haven't been exposed to it." For the blues to thrive, somebody has to recruit listeners. Santelli doesn't aspire to capture the attention of every kid in the classroom, but he needs to reach one or two in the back, the more adventurous and independent-minded consumers who are inclined to find their musical pleasures in a slightly esoteric niche market like that for the blues. Santelli's long-range goal is to build just such a younger constituency to succeed boomers like himself, who are beginning to age out of that phase of life in which one steps out regularly to hear live music and keeps up with the genre by buying new recordings. The Year of the Blues campaign's effort to inject blues into the schools may ultimately be its most important element.

"EMP can't teach anybody how to sing the blues," Santelli says, "but we can educate people, and the hope is that if we put the music and information in front of people they'll take it from there."

———

It's early afternoon on a Wednesday, typically the busiest day of Linwood Taylor's week. Seated on a wooden chair in the music room of a small white house in Wheaton, Maryland, he intones, *Mee meh mah moh mooooo.* Guitarless, Taylor uses his hands to feel the action of his diaphragm and to keep his jaw from dropping open; when he sustains a note he spreads them to either side, palms up, and closes his eyes. Alison Leadbetter-Hines, his voice teacher, sits facing him, straddling a piano bench and tapping out pitches on the piano with her right hand. Bookshelves filled with sheet music line the room. On the wall above the piano is her framed diploma from the Shenandoah Conservatory of Music in Winchester, Virginia. Classically trained, Leadbetter-Hines also sings show tunes, jazz, and church hymns. She readily admits that she's no blueswoman, but she knows all about singing.

Right now, she's taking Taylor through vocal exercises to improve his mechanics. They've been doing these exercises together every week for fifteen years. Taylor concentrates on using his diaphragm to pump air up into the resonating chamber of his head, focusing the note "on the bone," as Leadbetter-Hines says, which means getting it to ring most intensely at a spot just above where the bridge of the nose meets the skull. "You want to connect from here to here," she says, putting one index finger below her navel and the other between her eyes. When Taylor does it right, his voice seems to leap out of him and fill the room. When he does it wrong, he strains and falls off-key.

On this day, some extra urgency animates the lesson's familiar routine because Taylor recently had a rough singing night at Bangkok Blues in Falls Church, Virginia. His voice started to get ragged, which used to happen to him all the time before Leadbetter-Hines improved his technique. Between exercises, they discuss Taylor's various theories about why his voice gave out. He'd had gigs on consecutive nights, and the new guitar player who sat in played too loud. Also, he forgot to drink his protein shake the day of the show, and his trainer has been beating up his abdominal muscles with esoteric medicine-ball workouts at the gym. Taylor and Leadbetter-Hines agree that his rough night was probably a one-time occurrence, not part of a larger backsliding crisis, but they'll be alert for any other signs of trouble.

Leadbetter-Hines doesn't want Taylor to get too anxious about his voice, though, since that will only choke him up. "You already think too much," she tells him, kind but firm, big-sisterly. "You have to let the air make the sound. You stop and start the air with your gut, and just let the pitches tumble." When she sings along with him, the music seems to rise up from deep inside her of its own volition; she lets it out, rather than pushing it out as Taylor does. Even his dedication can work against him. When he pushes too hard, eager to get it just right, his technique falls apart.

That Linwood Taylor sings the blues at all is a testament to his ambition and discipline. When he began getting serious about the blues in the early 1980s, he saw that playing the guitar wouldn't be enough. In part, it was a practical recognition. "When I went to blues jams it quickly became obvious to me that if you sang you stayed up longer," he says. "There would be twenty guitar players, and only three of them sang." But the respect accorded to singers at the jams pointed to something deeper than practical necessity. The call to sing the blues goes to the heart of the music because the genre's seemingly inexhaustible power comes primarily from the stories it tells about being caught up between sorrow and joy. Even the most guitar-obsessed noodler must concede that, and even the most soaringly virtuosic blues solos proceed from and refer back to the human voice singing simple phrases freighted with complex feeling. Being able to play fast or mimic old recordings note-for-note is not at all the same thing as being able to tell a blues story.

Taylor would not settle for being anything other than a frontman, the guy who sings and gets the lion's share of the glory, and he was resourceful enough to squeeze the most from his modest vocal potential. After observing the importance of singers and impressing everyone with his guitar playing at his first two blues jams, he went home and learned Willie Dixon's "I'm Ready" so he could sing it at the third. "Not being a tuneful kind of person," he says, "I did the best I could." He didn't have any traditional blues vocal training—he had not learned to sing in the black Protestant church, nor had he served an apprenticeship to an experienced blues singer—but, having assessed his own limitations and noted the examples of blues-influenced diseurs like Jimi Hendrix and Bob Dylan, he sought out recorded models of conversational blues singing. "I listened to Muddy Waters, John Lee Hooker, Howlin' Wolf. They're basically singing like they talk. They're not always that tuneful themselves, you know. They actually talk a lot." He doesn't remember how "I'm Ready" went over the first time he sang it at a blues jam, "but I know it was horrible and I know I knew I would get better."

He also knew he needed help. Eventually, he found Leadbetter-Hines. "I had a lot of bad habits to get out of," he says. "Not using my diaphragm, overblowing. And I have asthma. I had to build up endurance and stop straining." She helped him make himself into some kind of singer, if not exactly a great blues singer, and they still work hard at it.

Asked to describe Taylor's progress, she says, "He's my poster child of progress. When he came to me, he could not match a pitch on the piano. He couldn't sing a melody. He couldn't sing 'Happy Birthday.'"

She had friends who, when they found out she was working with Taylor, said to her, "Oh, God, I've heard him. You're working with *him*?" But Taylor was game, and he had been blessed with other gifts. "He's the most honest person I know, and honest with himself, too," says Leadbetter-Hines. "He didn't lie to himself about what he could do or how far he had to come. And he has a remarkable knowledge of music. He knows a lot of music theory, mostly self-taught on the guitar." When they first began to work together, Taylor could only sing a melody if he was playing each note on the guitar at the same time, George Benson–style. "He's come a long, long way since then," says Leadbetter-Hines, "and he'll keep getting better. His pitch range continues to grow, and the quality of his voice keeps getting better. That's kind of where we are now," she says, summing up their fifteen years together. "Now we can work on things like making his singing bluesier."

Still, though, when they work on a song they start by trying to nail down the melody. "Always, with Linwood," says Leadbetter-Hines, "the first thing is to establish what the vocal line will be." Most blues songs don't have strictly reproduced melodies in the same way that classical, Tin Pan Alley, or even rock songs do. Blues singers develop a set of vocal moves, bits of melodic DNA they can use to improvise a melody while executing swoops, slides, growls, moans—the musical vocabulary, mimicking and elevating everyday speech, that opens up the rich emotional range of the blues. But Taylor doesn't work that way. He figures out a melody for a song with his voice teacher and he doesn't depart far from that line, not even to hold or bend a note in the usual blues manner. In that sense, she isn't teaching him traditional blues singing. "He's not going to be put in a box that's what a black bluesman is supposed to sound like," says Leadbetter-Hines, who is white, and she has a point. The timbre of his voice is not unpleasing, and his approach to melody makes for a slightly more formal vocal style that could actually help him stand out among blues singers. But he has to keep working at his craft, honing it, reinforcing good habits and breaking bad habits.

After spending half of the hour-long lesson on exercises, they turn to a song that Taylor wants to add to his repertoire, Freddy King's "Me and My Guitar," a ditty about getting your woman to be as tractable as your instrument. Taylor unpacks an acoustic guitar and accompanies himself as he runs through the song once to familiarize Leadbetter-Hines with it. Having the guitar in his hands makes him more confident, but it interferes with his concentration on vocal technique. They zero in on one especially awkward line in the chorus, "I'll play the blues for you." Taylor keeps letting the focus of resonance fall away from the sweet spot between the eyes, leaving the two prominent *oo* sounds sounding especially off-pitch and forced. Singing those *oos* is just like singing *moo* in the exercises, Leadbetter-Hines reminds him. "I'll tell you what," she says, "let's do it without the guitar." When he puts the guitar down, Taylor seems paralyzed for a moment. He has to silently hum the guitar intro to himself before he can begin to sing the first verse, and when he arrives at the chorus he's so worried about "blues" and "you" that he seizes up and blows them. But as Leadbetter-Hines patiently walks him through the song, pausing for a quick *mee-meh-mah-moh-moo* to shore up his technique, he relaxes and the sound flows more freely. Finally, at the end of the hour, she lets him use the guitar again and he sings the song through, this time singing the *oos* properly.

"That's a lot better," she says, and it is. "This is everybody's problem," she tells him. "It's not just a Linwood thing. To take what we do in the vocalese and put it in the song, that's the hard part."

The lesson over, it's time for Taylor to switch from student to teacher. He grabs a bite and drives to Bethesda Music to teach guitar lessons in a tiny studio in the back of the store for the rest of the afternoon and early evening. He's been teaching there since 2000, when the Washington blues scene entered its current downturn and he found himself obliged to pick up some extra work to compensate for the scarcity of gigs. He has eight students this afternoon, from beginners to moderately accomplished players. They arrive at thirty-minute intervals, most of them bringing music they want to learn: two Metallica songs; a Billy Joel song; an old Fleetwood Mac song; Clapton's "Badge." None of them shows any particular interest in learning to play blues guitar, but Taylor doesn't mind. He knows most of the songs already, quickly figures out the rest (even a Metallica song in a weird tuning), and sends each student home happy and a few licks the wiser. "My students stick with me," he says, "and they stick around. I make sure they have fun. The coolest thing about teaching is that it put me back into guitar in a new way. It's satisfying because I'm perpetuating what I love, which is guitar."

When he's done at Bethesda Music at 8:30, Taylor drives back to Alison Leadbetter-Hines's house in Wheaton to give an hour-long private lesson to her son Ryan, an easygoing blond, sideburned fellow, nineteen years old, who plays in a reggae-rock fusion band called Catch a Fire. Taylor's back on the same wooden chair in the music room, only now he's the teacher and he has a beat-up Fender Stratocaster in his hands. Ryan sits on the piano bench, holding a white Epiphone. They're plugged into the same amp. Taylor says, "Modes, we got to work on modes," a formal term for different relationships between scales and the chords of a song. "You already know the Dorian mode," says Taylor, "and the Mixolydian, that's Santana, he hangs out there all day. But, like, Phrygian mode, that's how Steve Vai and Joe Satriani play that crazy-sounding stuff they do. Try 'em out, and don't forget to mix in some minor pentatonic blues licks for contrast." He plays a series of succulent grooves, among them Wes Montgomery's "Bumpin' on Sunset" and the Paul Butterfield Blues Band's version of "Work Song," and Ryan works up exploratory solos to play over them. It's obvious that Ryan hasn't studied his modes this week—he says, "Um, remind me of Dorian," to which Taylor responds, "You're killing me"—but he's been playing a lot with his band and he has good ideas as an improviser. At one point, having just played something particularly elegant in Mixolydian and followed it up with an acrid blues phrase, Ryan murmurs, "That's cool, actually." He's getting it.

Taylor rounds out the lesson by playing instructive riffs he reverse-engineered from Lou Reed's "Rock 'n' Roll Animal" almost 30 years ago and stored away in memory, then offers pointers on technique. Finally, some advice: "Don't let other people push you. You do it on your own time, then time stands still. You gotta relax your body. When it's just right, when you have your skills down from practicing, it's like you're leaning against the music." In other words, if you've worked hard and prepared yourself, then you can relax and draw strength from the music rather than feeling as if it will overwhelm you—a lesson for both student and teacher.

———

Linwood Taylor was not born to sing the blues. Growing up in the 1960s in Lanham, Maryland, he lived in a black neighborhood, but from the fourth grade on he attended predominantly white Catholic schools. His father's record collection, an eclectic mix of jazz and R&B, nurtured Taylor's budding musical sensibility, which was transformed by the British Invasion. The Beatles and the Rolling Stones opened up a new vista, then Hendrix gave him a purpose in life. "Rock was what was on TV," he says. "When Jimi Hendrix came along, I'm watching TV and there's this brother playing guitar, with two white guys with afros bigger than mine. Admittedly, part of it was his image. Until then, Booker T and the MGs was my favorite band." Once he'd seen and heard Hendrix, Taylor just wanted to rock, and he wanted to play guitar. He got his first acoustic guitar in 1968, but that didn't really scratch the itch. He washed cars and mowed lawns to earn enough to buy his first electric guitar, a Fender Bronco, in April 1971. Cradling it, he knew he had found his calling.

Taylor's musical career didn't work out the way he thought it would, exactly; but it didn't exactly turn out otherwise, either. "I encountered obstacles," he says, when he tried to make his way as a rock guitar player in the 1970s. He would try out for bands and they'd tell him, "You were great, you were the best, but you just don't have the look we want," or "We don't want to be so close to Hendrix." Taylor thought he knew what was going on. "Look, whatever I play, I'm playing Hendrix," he says, "and being a black guitar player with a rock sound is akin to being a black quarterback in the NFL. Playing Jimi is the kiss of death for any black guitar player." Convention still assumes that black men play the blues and white men rock, even though, as Taylor points out, black musicians in a variety of genres played leading roles in inventing rock and roll. There's also a tradition of black rock guitar heroism, exemplified by Hendrix, and there are black guitar heroes in rock these days—Tom Morello, Lenny Kravitz, Vernon Reid, Prince—but they're still working against the grain of received wisdom. "Most people don't realize that, for instance, Slash, of Guns 'n' Roses, is a brother," Taylor notes, because Slash isn't *supposed* to be a brother.

By 1980, after encountering serial frustration in the previous decade, Taylor found himself following the path of least resistance that led him to the blues. "The blues path became open to me," he says, "and once I started on it the doors kept opening." He started attending open-mike jams and one thing led to another until he had assembled the spare, hustling life of a working local bluesman: gigging at a variety of bars and clubs around Washington, playing the festival circuit in the summer, putting together the occasional string of out-of-town or overseas gigs, making CDs on a shoestring budget and selling them from the stage, teaching guitar lessons, making ends meet. He used to buy and sell guitars, too, but he had to cut that out because he was too much the guitar freak to make money at it. "I was my own best customer," he says ruefully.

Taylor makes his way without benefit of a day job, and that's important to him. In his twenties, he worked construction and other odd jobs until he managed to secure a jacket-and-tie position in the accounts receivable department at Coca-Cola. But the routine wore him down. "Basically," he says, "I got to a point where I was thinking I would be an old man saying, 'I wish . . .'" Twenty years ago, when he was 27, he quit the Coke job, resolving to make a living as a musician. He had to work as a salesman at a music store for a few more years, but he finally broke free of day jobs entirely. He's not the rootless, unlettered drifter in overalls of blues cliché (nor should he have to try to conform to that increasingly ridiculous ideal of unspoiled outsiderhood), but in some ways Taylor does lead a traditionally marginal blues life. "I live cheaply," he says. "I do what I need to do and what I want to do. I never thought to be in the mainstream as much as some other people." At 47, he has few attachments, fewer responsibilities, no health insurance. He keeps his stuff—mostly guitars, cowboy boots, and shirts—at his mother's house in Lanham and at his girlfriend's place. He may not be a star and he may not have much financial security, but he makes a living in music, and he's not punching the clock at Accounts Receivable every day, either.

Taylor, who manages himself, spends a lot of time on his cell phone setting up gigs, scheming with other musicians, working his network. Mostly, he makes his business calls at his girlfriend's place. Without an office to go to or a gig to play every other night, with lessons to teach only two afternoons a week, most of his time is his own. He has to be disciplined to put it to good use, and discipline is Taylor's strong suit.

Keith Federman, president of Mystery Media, the small Maryland roots-music label that put out Taylor's most recent CD, says, "Linwood's the most disciplined, the most committed musician you could imagine. Just in every way. He works constantly at his playing, his singing, his health. He listens to everything—old blues, new blues, rock, reggae, jazz, everything—and he's always growing and making adjustments, musically." Federman, who has known Taylor for twenty years, describes Taylor's musical development as a triumph of rigorous self-fashioning. "When he came out on the scene, he had so much more ability as a guitar player than anybody else, but he was playing a lot of Hendrix—he sounded like his influences." Taylor was fast and raw; loud, too. "I remember seeing him at Krakatoa," says Federman, "and my ears rang for two days. But over the years his playing changed, his tone changed. He stopped sounding like other people. You could hear him becoming himself, and getting more into blues playing. Now, he plays with such authority that he doesn't have to try to blow anybody away. He's still capable of ungodly speed, but that's not what it's about anymore."

For Taylor, pursuing a career in the blues entails sustaining all sorts of balances, the principal one being between the two sides of the delicately split personality he must cultivate. The ambitious dreamer in him won't give up on hitting it big. What qualifies as big? "Hey, man," he says, "B. B. King. Lenny Kravitz. Big." Even becoming semi-big, rising to high levels of blues success that still fall well below King's position at the pinnacle, would be a signal accomplishment. A steady national and international touring schedule, headlining regularly at festivals, recording for a prominent blues label like Alligator or Evidence—that constitutes making it for a bluesman, and Taylor aims to make it. But the practical scuffler in him, the part of him that's just happy to be playing music for a living, must be prepared to settle for the far more modest status of a respected local musician. The dreamer and the scuffler have to sustain a working truce. He can continue to think big, but "in order to protect myself," he says, "I have to have a sense of 'I'll believe it twenty minutes after it's happened.'"

Federman ranks Taylor among the top blues guitar players of his generation. Federman is Taylor's friend, and he's talking up one of Mystery Media's recording artists, so he can be pardoned for exaggerating, but he's not completely out of line. Taylor's a magnificent guitar player. So why is he still a local bluesman and not a national figure? Could the disparity between his singing and his playing be holding him back? Federman loyally refuses to entertain the notion. "Every CD is better, every CD progresses. He keeps improving, he keeps working on the presentation. If he keeps it up, he'll come into his own. If he continues to search and change, he's gonna shoot and it's gonna hit something." But even if Taylor's singing proves to be good enough, the current state of the blues business may stand in the way of his advancement. "Some of it is up to the fates," says Federman of Taylor's career trajectory, "but some of it is up to the national blues scene. Right now, record sales are down, performance revenues are down. The baby boomers are getting socked economically in the last couple of years, and just when they're getting old enough where they're not wanting to spend the same amount of money on music that they used to." This may not be the best time for Taylor to be coming into his own as a bluesman.

So, more balancing acts. Pushing ahead in search of his big break may oblige Taylor to pick up and move on someday—if, for instance, a prominent blues singer or band needs an ace guitarist. "You have to be ready to leave DC to make it," says Taylor. "You have to. There are tons of great musicians who used to be from here, but they had to move to make any kind of headway." Moving away would mean separating from the local network of friends, family, and musicians he has built up—really the only form of security he can count on—but if the opportunity is big enough, he'll have to risk it. While he looks for his break, though, he has to earn his keep in Washington, and that means he often has to scramble. There used to be more local places to play the blues, reliable sources of gigs like City Blues and Smokeless, but some have closed and some now book other kinds of music. He can still rely on a few venues, like the Sunset Grille, or the Ebb Tide in Annapolis, Maryland, or Murphy's Pub in Charles County. (He was playing at Murphy's on February 7 while B. B. King, Buddy Guy, and other blues titans shared the stage of a jam-packed Radio City Music Hall with members of Aerosmith and the Allman Brothers, Bonnie Raitt, John Fogerty, Macy Gray, India.Arie, Chuck D, and a score of other blues-loving pop stars recruited by the Year of the Blues campaign.) Most of the time, Taylor's a long way from the blues world's big time, but he makes periodic visits to it. His guitar playing earns him invitations to join big-name touring acts onstage, and he has played with greats like Albert Collins, Luther Allison, and Johnny Copeland. The next such chance to impress could come along at any moment, but in the meantime he has to attend to the smaller-scale business of living. In the afternoon before his Sunset Grille gig, for instance, he was supposed to play a biker rally in Rehoboth Beach, Delaware, that his cousin lined up for him, but it rained hard and the gig fell through. The money he expected to make there has to come from somewhere else: find another gig, give some more lessons, sell a guitar, something. "My thinking is it's a cycle," he says. "I've seen it happen before, that the blues scene went down and it came back."

A few years ago, during the last up-cycle in the local blues scene, he was playing all the Washington-area gigs he could handle—up to fifteen a month, as opposed to four or five now. He doesn't miss those days. As comfortable as he was in terms of week-to-week cash flow, constant gigging wasn't getting him any closer to a big break. He's content, for now, to "float, contemplate, regroup. I'm sort of pondering my own artistic direction. Teaching lets me even say no to a gig I don't want to play." What he really wants to do is record another CD and get it distributed more widely than his previous three, two of which he put out himself. And he'd like the new CD to be funkier, with his rock-inflected guitar set against popping bass and hip-hop drums. "Blues was originally a dance music," he says, "which has kind of gone away as more, you know, white people got into it. I want to bring that back. And I think I could be a lot more free as a singer in that style." It would be one more ironic turn in the stylistic road for him: to move back toward "black" music because it's easier to sing.

Taylor is not bitter about being pushed from rock toward the blues, even though at times this musical direction seems to be carrying him away from a shot at celebrity. "It's a waste of energy to worry about it. That's the way it is. They haven't beaten me. I ask, how am I going to get around the way things are? That's what you learn in Catholic school: there's the way things are, and you try to get around them best you can." After a pause, he adds, "I play all the rock I want now," meaning that there's enough rock in his blues to satisfy the impulse awakened in him long ago by the British invasion. "The sound [of the blues] changed, in large part thanks to Hendrix and Clapton. A lot of the young black blues players wanted to sound like that."

Maybe Taylor's guitar playing is so compelling because it tells his story: the tale of a brother who just wanted to rock; the devious-cruising path, by way of the blues, on which that impulse launched him; the balance between his musical desires and those of his audience. The story has an epilogue: inside Linwood Taylor the bluesman, locked away in a dungeon but with spirit unbroken, the Linwood Taylor who wants to be Eddie Van Halen (rather than, say, B. B. King) broodingly awaits a chance to break loose and crank it up. "Hey, man," Taylor says, leaning close and nodding slowly for emphasis, "I still have my Marshall half-stacks"—stored away, he means, but not forgotten. The Marshall stack is the iconic hard-rock amplifier setup, the distortion-crunching sonic Armor of the Gods worn by Hendrix, Van Halen, and countless others, including Slash, when they stormed to rock stardom in a welter of feedback and bombast. They're all brothers-in-arms that way. Linwood Taylor, too.

————

The romantic myth of the natural bluesman, that outsider in overalls inspired to sing the essential folk truths of his people as he sits on the porch with bottle and guitar after a day in the fields or on the street corner, is mostly sentimental claptrap founded on facile assumptions about race and identity. The myth, which has had a long run in American culture, contributes to the enduring popularity of musicians of the 1930s like Robert Johnson, who is reputed to have sold his soul to the devil at a rural crossroads in the Mississippi Delta, and Huddie "Leadbelly" Ledbetter, a sophisticated fellow with eclectic musical tastes and a fondness for fine suits whose handlers obliged him to perform a narrow repertoire of folk and blues songs while wearing prison stripes, acting the part of a paroled savage. The myth of the natural bluesman contributed as well to American culture's forgetting of the great early blueswomen, who were mostly too cosmopolitan and polished to fit the myth's requirements, and to the revival in the 1960s of a taste for the blues among rock fans looking for cultural bedrock on which to ground their pop preferences.

The myth obscures the simple truth that the blues, as a musical form, is a craft and not a birthright or an existential condition. And these days, most people who play and listen to the blues have to work their way into it via other, blues-derived music. If even the bluesman Linwood Taylor traces his musical lineage from the guitar heroes of rock, where do you go to find a character who doesn't come to blues without first passing through the veil of another genre? If even the bluesman Linwood Taylor needs Alison Leadbetter-Hines to teach him to sing the blues, where do you go to find a character who claims the blues as an inheritance? It turns out that you don't even have to leave Washington: you go to Capitol Hill.

Senator Blanche Lincoln, a 42-year-old white Democrat from Arkansas, was the Year of the Blues proclamation's crucial supporter in the Senate. Bob Santelli and his associates rallied other senators to the cause, but Lincoln was its most active and passionate advocate. "Blues is part of my heritage," she asserts boldly, her Arkansas accent rounding the edges of her voice. "I grew up in Helena, in the Delta. I come from a seventh-generation Arkansas farm family. We'd been in the area for a long time. My dad was a farmer, and he had a business office in a bank building where KFFA was, the oldest blues station in the country. I used to go up and hang out at the studio. Sunshine Sonny Payne, the deejay, was a contemporary of my parents. I can remember my mother picking me up at kindergarten and riding to my dad's office, and hearing blues there. It was just part of my life." In Helena in the 1960s and 1970s, with rock and soul already dominant in young people's culture, the blues "wasn't a pop thing. It was a part of your basic diet, your daily normal life, a mainstay. It's always been such a large part of our lives in the Delta. Like grits 'n' greens, it's a mainstay for us, even if it's a novelty or an art to others."

When the Year of the Blues campaign came to her looking for support, Lincoln jumped at the chance not only to celebrate "the way blues has reached out to people around the country and around the world" but also to remind everybody "where it comes from." As she sees it, the blues can only thrive to the extent that it continues to flour-ish in places like the Delta. "The blues is still alive in the Delta," she says, allowing to float in the air the implication that it's perhaps not so alive in other places. "Blues came from heavy labor and discrimina-tion and poverty, and the Delta is still impoverished."

Lincoln has made encouraging economic development in the Delta one of her principal legislative concerns (even though, to follow the logic of her own argument, success in that endeavor might well cut into regional production of authentic blues by lowering the incidence of hard times). Looking out for the region's material well-being dove-tails with her personal desire to see her hometown music properly honored. "Blues certainly matters culturally," she says, "and we want to preserve and highlight it, but without a doubt it's also an economic tool. I've been beating my brains out up here trying to convince the administration and others that the Delta is impoverished and needs help, like Appalachia got 40 years ago. And this blues history is an important part of bringing people and interest to the region."

She goes on to tout annual festivals in Memphis and Clarksdale, Mississippi, elements of a larger regional effort to exploit economi-cally the cultural charge of the blues. Drawing on the example of New Orleans, boosters and preservationists in Memphis and the Delta region—and Chicago, in the North—have begun to theme these places as homes of the blues. They want to attract tourists and conventioneers looking for the roots of rock and soul, a sense of con-nection to cultural history, or, more often, just a passable facsimile of a down-home good time. This kind of packaging of blues experiences (which often includes retailing the myth of the natural bluesman) can seem as lamely contrived as the logo-emblazoned goody bags designed to resemble little cotton sacks handed out to the press and corporate ticketholders at the big Radio City show in February, and the produc-tion of blues-under-glass for tourists doesn't promise to inspire musi-cians to breathe new life into the genre. But if the blues presents an opportunity to attract business, then hard-pressed communities will exploit that homegrown resource. A genre that has survived both the neglect and the love of the American people can probably survive a little cut-rate imagineering.

––––––––

Most people think they know the home of the blues when they see it: a bare-bones juke joint or a cropper's cabin in the Delta, the low-rise brick kitchenette buildings and hole-in-the-wall lounges of Chicago's South Side. It requires a mental stretch to see Capitol Hill, the Kennedy Center, the spanking-new EMP building in Seattle, or PBS and NPR stations as homes of the blues. But they are, and the expectations and aesthetic preferences that hold sway in such places help to define the state of the blues as it enters its second century.

You can see and hear the blues-rock aesthetic in action at the Sunset Grille, another unlikely home of the blues, as Linwood Taylor plies his trade. After "Crosscut Saw," he delivers a set built around more standards—"Dust My Broom," "I'll Play the Blues for You," the inevitable "Sweet Home Chicago." He sings Hendrix's signature slow blues "Red House," too, by request. He doesn't mutter "That's all right, I still got my guitar" when he gets to the solo, as Hendrix did, but the sentiment can never have been more appropriate.

To close the first set, the band kicks into "Drivin' South," a Hendrix instrumental that owes a debt to Albert Collins and the Texas shuffle. The rhythm section settles into an eight-cylinder groove, and Taylor goes for an excursion into the blues-rock territory traversed and defined by Hendrix and Clapton and an army of guitarists that has followed their examples. Liberated to go long, his guitar lines extend and wrap around themselves to form lyrical tangles from which new melodic figures emerge, climbing up and out. His noise range expands into rock's buzz and crunch, and even a typical pose of the big arena rock show makes an appearance when he executes a downward run terminating in a power chord and then raises his picking hand skyward to let it ring out. In the middle of the tune, the musical ideas flowing out of him one after another, he detours through the Allman Brothers' endless "Mountain Jam" and raises an echo of the closing frenzy of Santana's "Black Magic Woman" before making his way back, discursive but purposeful, to Hendrix.

By letting the guitar do the singing, he has broken through from competence to inspiration. He's telling a story that matters deeply to him, a founding myth of classic rock: how Robert Johnson, Muddy Waters, and B. B. King placed the ax Excalibur in the stone, and how it was drawn from the stone by Hendrix, Clapton, Duane Allman, Carlos Santana, and other rock guitar heroes, who conquered the world with it; how these heroes and their successors built the kingdom of rock and, within it, a new home for the blues, a sacred shrine to the roots music that made rock possible. It's obvious from the near-ecstatic response to "Red House" and "Drivin' South" that this story is charged with special passion and meaning for the Sunset Grille's clientele. They are, in that sense, Taylor's people.

As the evening lengthens into the second and third sets, he sings many more blues standards and samples the rock songbook, doing his best with the vocals and playing ever more thunderous guitar. During the second set he leaves the stage mid-song and executes a bar walk, playing flurries of notes as he proceeds. The excursion has a ginger quality—he has some difficulty moving customers out of the way so he can get safely up on the bar; he makes sure not to kick anybody's drink while he's picking his way along, ducking down so as not to brain himself on the ceiling; and he carefully dismounts with a movement that says "Let's not turn an ankle here" rather than "Rock on!" But the crowd loves it. The Sunset Grille's patrons will go home satisfied, and only an authenticity snob would begrudge them that satisfaction.

Still, you don't have to be a snob to recognize that the blues is somehow diminished when it becomes junior partner in a merger with rock. His typical audience, Taylor admits, is "clueless" when asked to venture beyond, "you know, Muddy Waters-to-the-Rolling Stones," a tightly delimited canon of heroes, songs, and reasons to care about the blues. He knows that the regulars at the Sunset Grille expect plenty of hot guitar licks from him and not much else, but he still tries to strike a balance between satisfying them and "showing some growth and restraint" as a bluesman in ways they might not notice or appreciate. For better or worse, though, they're his core audience, and his business is to make them happy.

Maybe the Year of the Blues campaign will help to recruit a new audience for Taylor. The Year of the Blues is only going to matter, he thinks, to the extent that "it effects change, gets some young people interested. Put it in the schools. Otherwise, it's just window dressing." Bob Santelli, working hard to create the next generation of blues fans, would agree. The kind of grand-scale institutionalizing and constituency-building that Santelli has undertaken will take time, if it happens at all, and at the moment it's not entirely clear what qualities a new, younger audience might value and reward in the blues it wants to hear. Will such listeners want more rock content or less? More R&B and soul content or less? Will they hear the blues as black music, white music, neither, or both? Will they come to the blues as roots music? Folk music? Proto-hip-hop? American "world music"? All or none of the above?

In the meantime, Taylor's core audience keeps coming back, although everybody's a little older every time out. Far removed from the big doings afoot on Capitol Hill and at EMP and in other centers of power and wealth, his Year of the Blues is shaping up to look a lot like every other year of the blues he's ever had and those he can foresee in the future. You can see his situation as crisis or continuity, as evidence of contemporary problems in the blues or as evidence of the historically consistent facts of blues life. Taylor, in keeping with his adopted genre's worldview, sees it both ways. And if he's ever disheartened by the historical conditions and personal compromises that have shaped his career and brought him together with his audience at the Sunset Grille, he can always seek consolation in what matters most: that's all right, he's still got his guitar.

The Professor of Micropopularity

ON A MONDAY EVENING in September, James Schamus and a dozen students in his graduate seminar in film theory at Columbia University were discussing the dialogues of Plato. Each participant who spoke called on the next speaker, and Schamus gave the group plenty of leeway to tussle with the text, but every once in a while he raised his hand and intervened to guide the conversation. The course was called Seeing Narrative, and the discussion centered on Plato's skepticism about the ability of any visible thing to represent ideal truth—a skepticism that, say, a bunch of beautiful images strung together in a movie could communicate the perfect, invisible idea of Beauty.

Schamus, in bow tie and jacket, his mobile face alight with intentness, said, "In Plato, the philosopher's job is to love knowledge, *logos*, but it's always corporealized, and the body fools your senses, your perceptions. The soul is invisible and doesn't change, and it wants to connect to other such invisible, unchanging things"—including Truth and Beauty in their ideal forms—"but it's trapped in a body that's always taking it to visible things that are never the same."

During a break at the midpoint of the four-hour seminar, Schamus checked his BlackBerry. There were, as usual, lots of messages pertaining to his other job: for the past nine years he has been CEO of Focus Features, the specialty unit of Universal Pictures. As the head

Original publication: *New York Times Magazine*, November 28, 2010.

of a successful movie studio owned by a giant corporation, Schamus finances, produces, and distributes movies that are "independent" to the extent that that label describes a style, a target audience, a price tag. "They make smart movies for low budgets," as Tim Gray, who oversees *Variety*, put it. Focus's Oscar winners include *Milk*, *The Pianist*, and *Lost in Translation*, among others.

Schamus has also had a prolific career as a writer and producer. He has made eleven films with the director Ang Lee, including *Crouching Tiger, Hidden Dragon* and *Brokeback Mountain*. Along with two partners, Schamus ran Good Machine, a production company that between 1991 and 2002 made and distributed a series of important indie films like *Safe* and *The Brothers McMullen*. Until he got too busy with Focus, Schamus, who is 51, also did uncredited rewrites on the kind of expensive popcorn movies that Focus Features doesn't make (but he wouldn't tell me which ones).

The messages that came in while Schamus taught Plato included a notice that a preview screening of *Hanna*, a thriller to be released next April, had been moved from Nyack, New York, to Paramus, New Jersey. Other messages tracked how *The American* was doing in Europe and how DVD sales of the strange-but-cute documentary *Babies* were doing at Target. The news was good.

Focus was doing remarkably well in a time when the movie industry was still in the midst of an upheaval brought about by the decline of the DVD, piracy, and the general economic crisis, among other factors. After a boom in the late '90s and early '00s, when hedge-fund money flooded Hollywood and the indie sector was riding high, the ensuing contraction had taken out many of Focus's competitors. Paramount Vantage, Warner Independent, and other specialty units were gone, but Focus was hanging on with one of the largest shares of the indie market, exploiting its excellent relationships with distributors around the world.

"Focus has made a profit every year," Schamus told me on another occasion. "Some years it was modest profit, and in some years we did extremely well. But modest profit is not enough. We're part of a big corporation; our margins have to be justified. I'm not particularly a fan of late capitalism in general, but I realize our movies have to make a profit."

With extended speculation in the air that the cable company Comcast would buy Universal from NBC, a deal that could either include Focus or lead to it being sold off as a separate entity, Schamus was under more pressure than usual to have a very good year. So far, so good. *Greenberg*, a slacker romance starring Ben Stiller, did not do as well at the box office as it did with critics, but *Babies* did surprisingly well, and *The Kids Are All Right* and *The American* were breakout successes. With two releases still to go, 2010 was shaping up as a big winner.

There really isn't anyone else like Schamus. There's no precedent for a real academic—he's a professor of professional practice in Columbia's School of the Arts, a teacher and scholar who has served on the editorial board of *Cinema Journal*—to have a first-rate career as a writer, a producer, and an executive in the film industry. As Tim Gray put it, "There have been a couple of film scholars who wrote scripts, but he's the only person in the business I've ever seen who said, 'I can't go to Cannes because I've got to work on my doctorate.' I liked his book about Dreyer, but I understood about a third of it." The book, based on Schamus's dissertation, is a study of the Danish director Carl Theodor Dreyer's *Gertrud*, a film that Schamus has described as "the single most obscure Scandinavian formalist failure."

Schamus makes his home in one of the academy's most cloistered corners, where film theorists, cultural critics, and philosophers formulate critiques of cinema and capitalism from the detachment afforded by an elite discourse that's often impenetrable to nonspecialists. They're usually as far removed from the actual sausage-making of the film industry as they can get, and mostly prefer it that way. But the combination of intellectual enthusiasm, eclectic taste, extremely high executive function, and a roaring appetite for solving complex problems in stimulating company can take a thinking person to strange places.

When the seminar reconvened after the break, Schamus said, "Let's dive into the Meno," a dialogue in which Plato and Socrates consider virtue. "The heart of it is the mathematical proof." He rose from his seat and went to the whiteboard, where he drew figures and scribbled numbers as he worked through the geometry. "You can only get the proof visually," he concluded, stepping back and gazing at it. Plato may be skeptical about the category of the visual, he said, but "you are confronted with a visual proof that gets you back to the idea embedded in visuality."

Hands went up all around. A woman said, "So you can't get to that higher plane without a nudge from daily existence"—and off they went into the Meno, each speaker calling on the next in turn. They got so involved in the discussion that they ended up skipping the film they were scheduled to watch, Ingmar Bergman's *Persona*.

———

"I'm in this weird corner of the business," Schamus told me, "where the capital's just low enough that the only way to succeed is to throw out the focus groups and make a compelling case that our stuff is different."

He rides the subway from his apartment near Columbia to the offices of Focus Features, which occupy multiple floors in a building on Bleecker Street. Focus has branches in Los Angeles and London, but most of its 110 employees are in New York. In Schamus's sunny, high-ceilinged office there are family pictures—he is married to the novelist Nancy Kricorian, and they have two teenage children—and souvenirs from his movies: a *Brokeback Mountain* throw pillow inscribed with "Love Is a Force of Nature"; a green plastic Hulk fist.

Focus Features is known as a director's studio. By controlling budgets and preselling international distribution rights to finance productions, Schamus can position artists to make the movies they really want to make, as long as they want to make movies that don't cost too much and that he can sell. "What we strive for is a genuine alternative voice, but one that speaks *to* people," he told me. "We want to get people who are turned away from the mainstream to turn a bit toward it, and those turned toward it to turn a little away."

In practice, turning a movie toward the mainstream might mean just a small adjustment to the soundtrack. When I was hanging around his office in April, he said on the phone, "They need something to make it smoother. How about a viola, dude?" Or it can mean cutting to conform more tightly to the demands of a genre. Ang Lee told me that after screening an early cut of *Brokeback Mountain*, he ran into Schamus in the theater's bathroom. "It was still too long," Lee said. "James said, 'Ang, that was great, but it was three hankies and two bladders. My goal is four hankies and one bladder.'" Schamus, whose personal tastes tend toward the forbiddingly arty—no hankies and five bladders, à la Jean Eustache's post–*nouvelle vague* navel-gazer *The Mother and the Whore*, would be fine by him—sometimes finds himself working hard to ensure that a Focus production doesn't turn out to be the kind of film he loves best.

But he also nudges filmmakers the other way, a little further from the mainstream. Even the indie-est directors, he said, may internalize the demands of the industry and find themselves trying to make the movie they think a studio would want them to make. "There's so much pressure now, and they get to a point in the process where they start playing defense, worrying too much about trying to be commercial," he said. "So I find I'm constantly telling our filmmakers that it's my pressure, not theirs. Relax, play offense and go make your movie. I have my notes and ideas, and yes, we need movies we can sell, but we need good movies to sell, and fear isn't conducive to good filmmaking."

Playing offense artistically often means letting a film violate some Hollywood expectations, letting it be a little slower or more abstract or bookish or otherwise alien-seeming than what's in the multiplex—in short, weirder. "Weird" is one of his keywords, a crucial element of his business model.

Of course, Focus movies aren't high-art provocations like *Gertrud* or the kind of avant-garde films that Schamus shows in class: Ernie Gehr's *Serene Velocity*, Stan Brakhage's *Window Water Baby Moving*. The indie formula, which can be as narrow as the action-movie formula, calls for just enough weirdness to distinguish a movie from standard Hollywood fare but not so much that it slides out of the realm of commercial cinema and into the margins shared by the art film and mutant bottom-feeding forms of pulp cinema too bizarre to reach a mass audience.

David Bordwell, the distinguished film scholar, says of Schamus, "He's very good at figuring out the sweet spot, that middle range where independent cinema has to be. Ideally you have some stars, strong content, often from good books, and it needs to be offbeat enough to seem fresh, but it has to be still recognizably part of a familiar cinematic tradition, something challenging but not too challenging."

The moderate weirdness that puts a Focus movie in the sweet spot bespeaks an ethos as well as a bottom-line strategy. "There's a certain subversiveness at work in Schamus," Eugene Hernandez, a founder of Indiewire.com, says. "With *Brokeback* and *Milk*, for instance, there's more to it than an acclaimed film that has Oscar potential." In each case, Focus got the most out of a committed gay audience while marketing the film as a widely accessible story with a universal theme. Schamus scrupulously avoided displays of righteousness, but he clearly enjoyed doing great box office and winning awards while putting homosexual characters center stage in otherwise traditional renditions of the Western and the biopic.

Schamus, who is forthright about his lefty politics, discounts any crude ideological intent in making queer movies, or in, say, distributing a road movie about the young Che Guevara (*The Motorcycle Diaries*). Rather, he says, he is drawn—and audiences who think of themselves as outside the mainstream are drawn—to stories of outsiders. "The story of America, of Western culture, is often the story of queer culture, of being Jewish"—Schamus is Jewish—"of being outsiders and refugees who find a place that is the not-place." His personal experience, he says, reinforces his taste for such stories. "I grew up basically covered with psoriasis," he said, "and I skipped grades, so I do tend to gravitate to the kid in the corner, who, incidentally, is most likely to grow up to be one of our directors."

But, he insisted, "if I tried to run a studio on the principle of making movies that had certain gender politics, or any politics, that I approved of, we'd go out of business fast. When I'm here," as CEO, "I'm solving problems in the culture business, cutting trailers and doing promotions and figuring out audiences. I put things together all day. Then, when I go home at night, I can take them apart" as an academic.

There is a middle way; think of it as the moment of perfect overlap at twilight. He said, "If we can make it profitable to use the common language of film, a language that addresses a public, to say something worth saying that was previously unsaid or unsayable, then those things get said." That such movies have to turn a profit in order to exist, a condition of truly public utterance in a capitalist society, just adds another element to the puzzle, one more rule to the game.

———

The son of lawyers, Schamus grew up in Southern California and attended Hollywood High School and a couple of colleges before graduating from the University of California, Berkeley, and going on to graduate school in English there. While working on his dissertation, he moved to New York City and drifted into the movie business, starting out, he said, as "the oldest production assistant on earth."

The dissertation fell by the wayside as he teamed up with Ted Hope to form Good Machine. They billed themselves as the no-budget kings of New York; their motto was "The budget is the aesthetic." Hope, an advocate of radically decentralized media democracy, was the revolutionary; David Linde, who came over in 1997 from Miramax International (and eventually went on to be co-chairman of Universal Pictures), was the business guy; and Schamus was supposed to be the avant-gardist, the intellectual, but his love of solving multifactor problems awakened the manager within.

During his Good Machine period, Schamus also began solving problems for Ang Lee—helping him stretch a grant from the government of Taiwan to make the Chinese-American family drama *Pushing Hands*, fixing lines of dialogue. Schamus was soon producing and writing Lee's movies. "I know he thinks a lot about what's the best for me to do," Lee told me, "and I keep that in mind, even when we disagree. He only acts as much or as little as I need him to."

Lee also began to rely on Schamus for fresh inspirations. "After *Eat Drink Man Woman*, I was out of stories to tell," Lee said. "With *Sense and Sensibility* and *The Ice Storm*, we started taking chances on new things." Schamus told me, "I have to write a script that scares him enough to make trying to make it worthwhile. They're very underwritten, and he has to figure them out as he goes along. So he spends the whole time asking me, 'Why? Why are we making this movie?'"

Schamus also steers his partner through the eternal dance of turning toward and away from the mainstream. Lee recalled, "I was cutting the bamboo sequence," a celebrated fight scene in *Crouching Tiger*. "One night I pick up the phone to talk to James; I was thinking a lot about *Hamlet*, and I was very excited. He said, 'Remember you're doing a movie in the same genre as *Drunken Master*. You're not doing *Drunken Hamlet*.'"

There was another writing problem, in an even more formally constrained genre, that Schamus set himself to solve. When Berkeley invited him to give a commencement address eight years ago, he decided that it would be a good opportunity to finish his incomplete PhD. Dusting off his dissertation, he carved out extra research and writing time from his schedule, pulling all-nighters when he had to. "My dissertation committee was really selfless with their time, but they were tough," Schamus said. He panicked, briefly, when they rejected an entire chapter. "They were right, it was tangential, but my rear end was hanging out. I had set it up so failure was not an option. I had to give the address. My parents were coming. My kids were coming." He got it done in the end and marched with the other graduates in 2003.

———

In early September, Schamus spent a weekend at the Toronto Film Festival, where a Focus Features release, *It's Kind of a Funny Story*, had its world premiere. "What I want to do while I'm here is go see all the films that almost everybody else despises," he told me. "But that's not what my business is." What he did in Toronto, mostly, was sit for two days in a plush hotel suite and receive small groups of executives in the indie trade, many with European accents.

The meetings were occasions for familiar trading partners to renew connections and extend feelers. They all gushed relentlessly about how brilliant and moving their films were and about the genius of the talent in their employ. This can be hard to take after a while, but the indie-movie sector is an enthusiast's business, and Schamus is a natural enthusiast. He can get excited about all sorts of things: the aesthetic theory of the French philosopher Jacques Rancière, *E.T.*, Scandinavian art cinema (in June he gave a talk in Oslo at a symposium on Liv Ullmann and was relieved when Ullmann laughed at the funny parts), the ultragreen house in upstate New York he built in 2000, good food and fine wine and his studio's movies.

Schamus let his visitors crow about their recent successes and current projects, and he took his turn to tout his slate of coming releases, among them Sofia Coppola's *Somewhere*; Cary Fukunaga's *Jane Eyre*; Lone Scherfig's *One Day*, a romantic drama starring Anne Hathaway; Kevin Macdonald's *The Eagle*, a Roman frontier adventure starring Channing Tatum; and Joe Wright's *Hanna*.

Schamus also talked up a film about Fela Kuti, the Nigerian Afrobeat king, that he has in long-term development. "It's not a biopic," he said. "It's experimental in form," with long movements based on Fela's rambling songs. "I don't do passion projects, but this could be a *Battle of Algiers*, on that level." He had lined up the British video artist and director Steve McQueen to direct it, and the Nigerian poet Chris Abani was writing the script while Schamus tried to make the budget work. Filming in Nigeria would give the right look, but Ghana might be easier, and perhaps they could shoot interiors in South Africa. "It's too expensive," he said, "but we'll figure it out."

Schamus accepted a lot of compliments from fellow executives and filmmakers in Toronto. Focus had come to town on a roll, at a high point of its very good year. Creative promotion of *Babies* had paid off, and *The Kids Are All Right*, which Schamus described to his staff as "the third of three sperm-donor movies out there," had just crossed the $20 million mark, the industry's most successful limited-platform release of the year. (A platform release, the opposite of a wide release, opens first in a few selected theaters and then gradually expands to more on the strength of word of mouth, reviews, and judiciously adjusted marketing.)

And *The American*, a coolly meditative spy film directed by the Dutch photographer and music video auteur Anton Corbijn and starring George Clooney, was number one at the domestic box office. "It's a big deal for us," Schamus said. "As of today we broke $20 million, going into its second weekend. Even if the film fell off a cliff into an abyss we'd be way ahead, and it's not doing that."

Schamus was perversely proud that CinemaScore, which predicts how a film will do at the box office on the basis of exit polls of moviegoers, had given *The American* a D-minus. "On our wide releases there's an almost inverse relationship between audience polls and success," he said. "CinemaScore polls at outlying theaters, and it works very well for movies made for the broadest mainstream audience, but it's been proven again and again that the metrics become nearly useless if you make something weird. We take the metrics as no more than a hermeneutic puzzle."

For Schamus, the key to the puzzle was that *The American*, a rigorously formulaic genre movie composed and paced like an art film, was weird enough to provoke strong reactions. While an A from CinemaScore was always welcome, he said, "a B or B-minus is 'eh.' I'd rather have a C-minus or D, knowing that people have strong reactions. It's OK if a lot of people don't like it, as long as the people who love it are spreading word of mouth with passion, getting others excited." Focus can aim to pique the interest of the minority of moviegoers who think of themselves as independent types; big studios like Universal have to please most of the rest or go broke.

The artistic cherry atop the ice cream sundae of happy business news during Schamus's stay in Toronto came when he got word from Italy that *Somewhere*, which opens in December as Focus Features' final release of the year, had won the prestigious Golden Lion at the Venice Film Festival—an honor also won by two Lee-Schamus films, *Brokeback Mountain* and *Lust, Caution*.

The only shadow on the otherwise glorious weekend was that *It's Kind of a Funny Story*, an understated tale of a suicidal teenager's transformative stay in an adult mental ward, seemed too slight to prosper. The premiere was well received, and reviews were kind, but it went on to disappoint at the box office.

———

In Toronto, I asked Schamus, as I had been asking periodically for months, about the relationship between running a studio and being a scholar. As usual, he resisted combining his vocations into one overarching project. He said, "I don't want to be saying, 'My interest in property and privacy informs my work at Focus, and vice versa.' When I'm at the office, I do the job." We were in a car at the time, passing bus-stop posters for *The American* that featured a dark-suited Clooney running with a tasteful little gun in his hand. "The job has to be done under certain conditions, and they're dynamic, and I have to adjust."

It's true, though, that a main element of the dynamic conditions in which he does business is the relationship between art and commerce, which is also a principal focus of his academic interests. "It is all about intellectual property," he conceded: he's all about how ideas circulate in markets. He's interested in the conditions of possibility in which creative people work—from the mechanics of making a living to the philosophical questions raised by setting aside a category of commodities called Art to the prospects for saying the previously unsaid by using the common vocabulary of word and image (which is where Plato comes in).

Usually Schamus shifts from making culture for profit to analyzing the results of process, but there are times when the two roles flow together. One was when Good Machine pitched Todd Solondz's black comedy *Happiness* to studios. As Schamus described the experience, "I would go in there and say, 'It's about subjectivity in late capitalism, the overproduction of desire. We spend about one-third of our GDP convincing ourselves to buy what we make. What Todd's talking about is desire when it's unmanageable within the system, unattached to something you can buy.' It was bought by October Films, which had been bought by Universal, which had been bought by Seagram. They ended up freaking out and giving the movie back to us."

Schamus also employs high theory as equipment for living in a book he is writing, *My Wife Is a Terrorist: Lessons in Storytelling from the Department of Homeland Security*, which will be published by Harvard University Press. There is a government surveillance file on Nancy Kricorian because she is active in Code Pink, a women's antiwar group. Using as his primary text a heavily redacted copy of her file, secured after an ACLU suit, Schamus employs speech-act theory, narratology, and other interpretive frameworks to plumb the meanings of an opaque document consisting mostly of blacked-out pages. Along the way he considers how the culture industry and intellectuals might respond to the state's role as "the most prolific and influential producer of popular narrative."

He did a trial run of this project as an "anti-keynote address" at the London International Film Festival in 2009. Some in attendance were thrilled, some put off, many perplexed. An ironic *explication de texte* that would have fit right in at an academic conference seemed weird in that context, and elicited strong reactions.

————

Between classes at Columbia on a lovely September afternoon, Schamus found a spot in the sun behind Dodge Hall to smoke a cigar. "For me," he said, "the happiest place on earth is a well-run school. If I have a false nostalgia, it's for an ongoing conversation in which anyone can say anything interesting, a conversation you have in public, and that includes people who are dead. To the extent that I have a management style, I try to replicate that environment." His conversations with students and filmmakers have in common a desire to get them to stop trying to please an imaginary internalized Professor or Studio Head and free themselves to say something original, fresh, and useful—something constructively weird.

He realizes that his current arrangement, with one foot in the movie business and the other in the academy, is not necessarily permanent. "I would be happy to run Focus for the next twenty years," he told me in an early conversation, "but I have to be ready for that not to happen." His role model, he told me half-jokingly, is the poet Su Tung-p'o, an eleventh-century Chinese bureaucrat who served faithfully until he fell out of favor and was twice sent into exile. "Some of it is the translation," Schamus said, "but you read him and it feels so weirdly modern, as if he were talking to you today." (Here, for example, is a bit of "On First Arriving at Huang-Chou": "Funny—I never could keep my mouth shut; / it gets worse the older I grow / . . . An exile, why mind being a supernumerary? / Other poets have worked for the Water Bureau.")

As we sat in the sunny quadrangle amid the eternal rhythms of the university, I asked, "If that happens to you, if your run in the movie industry comes to an end, do you come back here?"

He said, "This isn't exile. This is *work*. I don't see the university as a retreat from anything."

The Saberist

AT NELLYA FENCERS, A fencing club tucked away amid cut-rate pharmacies, auto parts stores, and evangelical churches along strip-malled Forest Parkway in suburban Atlanta, two women and two men prepare for a late-morning saber practice. Sada Jacobson, 21, a Yale junior on leave who is currently ranked first in the world in women's saber, and her sister, Emily, eighteen, bound for Columbia in the fall and currently ranked tenth, will both be fencing in Athens in three months as part of the US Olympic team. Matt Zich and Luther Clement, neither on the 2004 Olympic team but both aiming for 2008, have come down from the elite Fencers Club in New York for the week to train with them. Sweating hard in shorts and T-shirts after warm-ups in the humid spring heat, they suit up for fencing: first, the traditional close-fitting white breeches and jacket (under which women wear a plastic chest protector and everyone wears an under-arm protector called a plastron), and a glove for the weapon hand; then a gray metallic-mesh jacket called a lamé, and a cuff made of the same material that fits over the glove.

The sisters' coach, Arkady Burdan, addressed by all as "Maestro," is a short, sturdy-looking fellow with close-cropped gray hair, a modest paunch, a serious Russian accent, and a taste for Marlboros. This morning he has already guided the fencers through warm-ups, beginning with stretches, sprints, lunges, push-ups, and sit-ups, then mov-

Original publication: "Edge of Greatness," *Yale Alumni Magazine*, July/August 2004.

ing on to quick-shuffling weaponless advances and retreats in fencing position—part shadow boxing, part ballroom dance.

Spending significant portions of one's life exercising vigorously in the *en garde* position—weapon arm raised and legs flexed, with the leading foot pointing at the opponent and the rear foot pointing off to one side—produces a distinctive bodily asymmetry. The weapon arm is noticeably bigger than the other arm, and the calf of the rear leg, used for pushing off, is much bigger than the other calf. But the most arresting feature is the lead leg's colossal thigh, hyperdeveloped by years of bearing a fencer's weight, especially when she lunges. Sada (pronounced "SAY-dah"), a left-hander, has a left thigh that would not look out of place on the current governor of California; Emily, a right-hander, has a right thigh nearly as impressive.

Nellya Fencers occupies a warehouse-like shed that used to house a plumbing business. In the main room, a mostly empty gym with seven 40-foot-by-6-foot rectangular fencing strips painted on the floor, built-in fans rattle away on one wall. Three raised shutter-style doors in the opposite wall open onto a concrete loading dock, admitting bugs and a sluggish breeze. Through the open doors you can see a guy on a riding mower trimming the grass in the cemetery next door. "Why do dead people need every day cut grass?" asks the Maestro, who enjoys playing the emigré perplexed by American life: the excess and waste, the indulgence of children, the insistence on sending athletic prodigies off to college when those prodigies should be training full-time. Sada and Emily, who know this routine, exchange a look.

Having suited up, armed themselves with long, flexible sabers, and donned mesh-fronted masks, the four fencers grab extension cords hanging down from the ceiling and plug themselves in at the small of the back. As in formal competitions, each fencer's saber is connected to a body cord that runs up the sleeve of the weapon arm and connects to a reel wire worn around the torso under the lamé. When touched by an opponent's blade, the conductive metal in their lamés, masks, and cuffs will now send an electronic signal to a monitor that registers a hit with a colored light and a buzzer. The fencers pair off for a round-robin of practice bouts.

A bout consists of a series of brief engagements called touches, each touch ending when one or both fencers score a hit. In saber, legal hits can be scored anywhere above the waist and with either the tip or the edge of the blade. The other fencing disciplines—foil and épée, in both of which only the tip is used to score—still carry echoes of duels between gentlemen, but saber is based on the slashing and thrusting of cavalry troopers in a melee. It's faster and dirtier, and strength matters more in saber than in the other disciplines. Opponents often exchange near-simultaneous hits at lightning speed, so a referee must decide who gets the point. (Fifteen points wins the bout.) Determining who has the right-of-way, who initiated the scoring attack, the referee brings sporting order to what the untrained eye sees as a series of brief, incomprehensible spasms of murderous action punctuated by the scoring machine's lights and buzzer. The Maestro, mounted on a high stool, serves as referee for the practice bouts, barking out ritual commands in Russian-accented French: "Êtes-vous prêtes? . . . En garde . . . Allez!"

One duo goes at it in front of the Maestro while the other practices *sans* referee on a neighboring strip; then they switch partners and start over. Both Sada and Emily have to adjust to Matt's long reach when they oppose him. Luther is not as tall as Matt, but he's quicker and trickier. Sada likes to train against men, who use their greater strength and speed to push her up and down the strip, which, she says, makes her work harder. She and Emily hold their own against the New Yorkers, the Maestro occasionally switching from referee to coach to offer advice or praise. When Emily, attacking fiercely, scores a series of points against Matt to draw even in one of their practice bouts, the Maestro calls out to him, "We have *fencers* here. No girls, no boys. Fencers."

Sada and Emily take their turns against each other, too. Watching the sisters fence is like listening to blood relatives sing harmony. A quality of intimacy, of knowing the other all the way to the bone, supercharges the exceptionally close interplay of two characters, two styles, two bodies in motion. Sada is taller than Emily, and she has shed more of the rounded softness of postadolescence, but otherwise when they face off on the strip in matching gear they make a near-mirror image: Sada in a left-handed stance, Emily in a right-handed stance. Both of their lamés have "Jacobson USA" printed in block letters across the back. Their very different styles are almost perfectly complementary. Emily presses long, fluid attacks that show off the elegant lines of her fencing and her surpassing quickness. Sada stymies Emily's advances with crisp defensive moves, disturbing her timing and creating opportunities to score with parry-ripostes.

At first they seem to be playing out an over-familiar formula, running through rote sequences of attack and counterattack, but they become more inspired as they proceed. The engagements extend and grow more heated, the two sabers forming a live-wire tangle of clanking, hissing metal as the sisters contest each touch with increasing improvisational fervor. When they land hits at the same time, they both turn to the Maestro with a wordless shout, each positive that the point should be hers. The Maestro encourages such demonstrations by his pupils—he calls it "giving voice" to show that you feel you won the point—but when serving as referee he seems to shrink a little before their competitive fury, putting aside his normally peremptory manner to explain in detail the logic by which he awards the point to one sister or the other. When he renders judgment, one sister nods, satisfied; the other stares at him for a long baleful moment before returning to the *en garde* position. When he calls out "Simultané!" which means that neither receives the point, both sisters stare him down, temporarily united against this irksome man who keeps interfering with their private duel.

––––––––

Their private duel may well continue in the Olympics—perhaps even in the gold-medal bout, although the Maestro superstitiously refuses to even discuss the possibility. Sada, at the top of her game these days after having taken a year and half away from Yale to devote herself entirely to training, prevailed in their practice bouts on this day. But Emily is one of the strongest female saberists in the world, a formidable opponent, despite having been distracted from training of late by her senior year of high school. The balance of power between the sisters swings back and forth; one will dominate their practice bouts for a few weeks, then the other will take over. They have met four times in official competitions so far this year, and each has won twice.

After practice, and having eaten a carry-in lunch with her training partners and coach (how often do you hear someone say, "Maestro, what do you want from Subway?"), Sada sits on a folding chair on the loading dock and talks shop. "Ideally," she says, "you should have a sense of what you're going to do in every touch. If I did a fast attack last time, then this time I might take a step back, let my opponent fall short. Then the next time, something different." A certain warlike joy lights up her face as she says, "Every once in a while you'll really get someone, you'll have them in the palm of your hand, and they don't know what to do. The smarter fencer should win." This is her mantra. The smarter fencer should beat the technically superior fencer and the better athlete, the merely diligent and the fortuitously gifted.

Her mentors agree. The Maestro, asked to explain what makes Sada so good, says, "Hard work and very good think. She have good memory, too—remember opponent from years ago. Like chess player. She prepare special tricks, play around opponent's action. She play game." Henry Harutunian, Yale's Armenian-born fencing master, says, "She has exceptional athletic ability, but also so strong in the mind." Harutunian, who coached Sada when she won the NCAA title in women's saber in 2001 and 2002, sees her virtues as in part inherited from her father, David Jacobson, who fenced for him at Yale in the early 1970s. "She never want give up," he says. "I can see same thing I remember her father have, but daughter have more drive, more killing instinct."

Sada was already Arkady Burdan's pupil when she came to Yale, and Harutunian tried to gloss rather than revise the Maestro's teachings. "Burdan have his style," says Harutunian, "and I try never to change that style, not to disturb that foundation. I try to give my opinion, my feeling—more lighter, more elegancy, more neatness between rhythm and fencing." But Harutunian recognizes that Sada's main strength does not lie in polished fencing. "Sada winning because of her temper, her power," he says. "Her sister more natural fencer." He looks forward to having Sada back at Yale after the Olympics for one or two more years of college fencing. She could potentially win two more NCAA titles for Yale, but the talent pool grows deeper and the competition stiffer every year. Emily, in particular, fencing for Columbia and training regularly at the Fencers Club, will be tough to beat.

Had they been born a few years earlier, the Jacobson sisters would not have had the opportunity to duke it out for national and world titles in saber; they would have had to content themselves with competing for the unofficial household championship. Only in the last five years has women's saber been completely incorporated into the circuit of World Cup competitions in fencing, and the 2004 Olympics will be the first to include it in medal competition. Like the marathon, boxing, and the military combat arms, saber was long deemed especially unladylike—perhaps because men were not ready to see women excel in the rough stuff. Sada and Emily have come along at just the right historical moment in which to exercise their talent for cut-and-thrust. Sada says, "Women's saber has been around just long enough now that we're starting to see some complexity. It's getting more interesting." And she will probably be around to help it grow more interesting. "In fencing, you peak in your late twenties, so I still have a lot of time." She's in the right place, too. An influx of master coaches from Eastern Europe since the end of the Cold War has turned the United States into a fencing power, finally ready to compete with the European countries that traditionally dominate the sport. "We've never had such a strong US fencing team, especially in saber," Sada says. "I wouldn't be surprised to see anybody on that team take a medal. That didn't use to be the case."

———

Sada's parents did not raise her to be a fencer, and her father believes that if she had not taken up the saber she would have found something else: martial arts, perhaps, or chess, or some other individual competition requiring copious preparation, concentration, will, and a mind capable of scheming against an opponent while anticipating the opponent's scheme, then reacting against the opponent's reaction.

David Jacobson says, "This is a young person who, from the time she was very small, could focus on a task at hand with great intensity. Even when she was two or three years old, doing a puzzle. And she has a drive to excel in all aspects of her life, a powerful desire to be the best in whatever she does." These traits, and an understanding of the importance of hard work, seem to be inborn, impossible for Sada or her family to explain. Before she fenced, she swam competitively, but swimming did not fully scratch the itch for mastery. "She is extremely quick and strong, but she probably never would have been a great swimmer," says her father. "There's only so far technique and desire can take you in swimming. Being a natural athlete built for swimming counts for so much." As a fencer, though, Sada's particular gifts, combined with excellent coaching (which matters more in fencing than in perhaps any other individual sport), have taken her all the way to the top. "Among her level of fencers, she's probably a B athlete," says her father, "but she made herself into an A-plus technician, and she has A-plus intellectual skills."

It's a good thing Sada found fencing—or, more accurately, fencing found her. It began with a visit from Coach Harutunian to the Jacobson household during the Atlanta Olympics of 1996. The two men dug David's old fencing gear out of the closet where it had been stored, untouched, for many years. "We were just goofing around in the driveway for old times' sake," says David. "That was the first time my daughters"—Sada, Emily, and their younger sister, Jackie— "ever saw me fence." Harutunian recalls, "Their eyes were so big, so amazed. They looked at their father completely different." Afterward, he gave Sada a couple of pointers in basic footwork, but it seemed to go no further at the time.

The experience inspired David to get back into fencing, though, and a couple of years later Arkady Burdan, one of the foremost saber coaches in the world, arrived in Atlanta. David began taking lessons with the Maestro, and his daughters followed him to the club. "There was no plan," says David. "The girls gravitated to the club one by one because they were curious. Arkady Burdan is so dynamic, he got them going. They had success early—remember, there weren't that many women in saber at that point, and they moved up fast—and it snowballed from there." Sada remembers that on one of her first visits to the club, "my mom and my little sister got me all dressed up, and then I almost died in warm-up, it seemed so hard. Plus, a guy in the club got hit in a sensitive area, and he was screaming on the ground." The point of this story does not seem to be that the rigor and the frisson of danger gave her pause; rather, she seems to be explaining what made her say to herself, "Now, *this* is what I want to do."

She fences regularly with her father these days, just for fun. He describes the experience as "humbling." David, like Sada a lefty, competes in the over-50 division, and he describes himself as "pretty good, even very good, and I'm certainly bigger than her," but he must fight desperately to keep from being embarrassed by her. "I'm not talking about trying to win; I'm talking about scoring enough points to make it look semirespectable. When she takes a parry, it's like hitting a brick wall. When she comes at you, it's like a freight train. She's a very intimidating opponent, and very frustrating, too, because it seems like she knows what I'm going to do before I do it." The Maestro teaches his charges to crush their opponents' spirit, to demoralize them by defeating their technique and their plans so utterly in the first few touches that the conclusion of the bout seems foregone. Sada can't unlearn this lesson just because she happens to be fencing against her father.

———

Later in the afternoon, having digested her sub and warmed up again, Sada has a one-on-one lesson with the Maestro. They fence "dry," without electricity or the gear it requires. Both wear shorts, T-shirt, mask, and glove. The Maestro, who will be taking all the hits, also wears a black padded sleeve on his weapon arm, the right, and a sleeveless heavy leather jerkin of the kind worn by villainous underlings in swordfight movies. He carries his blade low, tapping a couple of beats on the floor as he advances, then bringing it up as he presses home the attack. The Maestro affects the persona of a lout who rushes in ceaselessly for the kill, only to be sharply rebuffed each time by Sada, who parries and counters, smacking him on the padded arm, the jerkin, the mask. When she lands a hit, he holds his pose so that she can repeat it, to ingrain more deeply the feel of a successful move. The lesson takes on a satisfying rhythm: the Maestro's weapon tap-taps on the floor, then he takes a running step or two and tries to overpower her, she stands her ground and stops his blade, then comes a zing and a smack as she lands the counter, then the same zing-and-smack again, and again. Sometimes the Maestro calls out a particular sequence of moves in code, just like boxing trainers do when they put on the practice mitts for their fighter to bang on, and she briskly obliges.

More fencers have been arriving for afternoon practice. They mill around in the carpeted anteroom that adjoins the gym. A boy of eleven or twelve sticks his head through the doorway into the gym to ask a question of the Maestro, who shouts, "Never more in time lesson you talk to me after today! Okay?!" The boy recedes swiftly from view, his head bitten off. If you're going to have people call you "Maestro," you have to act like one.

The interruption gives the Maestro a chance to stop the action and underscore the crux of today's lesson. He and Sada remove their masks. The Maestro says, "When first time you beat opponent in preparation, he remember you beat him because he slow. So next time he fast, so now maybe you can trap." Sada nods, but then asks, "How do I know he's gonna go for the mask?" If the opponent does not attack the mask, Sada can't spring the particular trap they're working on. "You *make* him," answers the Maestro. "You give no *choice*. Psychology! He try here"—he gestures at her ribs—"but you no let him. Then he try here"—the arm—"but you no let him." He imitates the opponent's frustration. "So, the mask," he says with a shrug, dismissing this imaginary stooge whose own aggression and competitiveness have been turned into agents of his undoing. "Is everything psychology. If somebody stubborn, stupid, you take advantage." You take advantage. This is what Sada does best. She makes her opponents fail, then she makes them pay.

Sada and the Maestro put on their masks and fence for a few more minutes, then the masks come off again, they shake hands, and she thanks him for the lesson. They will fly to France in a few days for a World Cup event, in July they will go to Rome to train with the Italians, then in August they move on to Athens for the Olympics. As Sada stows her equipment in an oversized sports bag, novice fencers come into the gym—boys and girls, white and black, dabblers and aspiring Olympians, all sorts. One or more of the girls may face Sada one day in an NCAA competition, a World Cup event, the Olympics. The Maestro warms them up, his voice trailing out of the gym to Sada as she puts her bag into the trunk of her car. "Run to line and back! Poosh-ops! . . . Stand up! Now, en garde! We begin!"

Sada gets into her car and heads for home, ready to call it a day. Between a training session and a lesson with the Maestro every day of the week but Sunday, five additional sessions per week with a strength and conditioning trainer, and the extra rest required by all this strenuous activity ("I need nine hours of sleep a day now; at Yale I was lucky to get six"), fencing has pushed everything else in her life out of the way for the past year and a half. Back at Yale, her contemporaries in the Class of 2004 are intent on senior essays, graduation, life after college. Sada is thinking about the competition: "There's my sister, of course, and then there's a Russian, maybe three from France, one from China, an Italian, a couple of Germans, a couple of others to watch out for." All of the top-flight saberists have met repeatedly in World Cup competitions. "I know their styles, what to expect. We know each other's technique. So here's where strategy really starts to matter." That means she needs to plan for each opponent, reviewing tendencies and weaknesses, crafting new tricks to go with tactics that have worked in the past. A saber bout can reach fifteen points in a hurry, years of preparation compressed into a few minutes of bewilderingly ferocious action. Sada, as ferocious as they come, aims to be the one doing the bewildering.

Sada Jacobson won a bronze medal at the 2004 Olympics and a silver medal in 2008. In May 2009, having completed her first year of law school at the University of Michigan, she married Brendan Bâby, a former NCAA-champion épéeist, at Nellya Fencers.

A Man of Deep Conviction

WHEN BISHOP GILBERT THOMPSON preaches in the main hall of Jubilee Christian Church, a 1,250-seat room in a converted supermarket on Blue Hill Avenue in Mattapan, he stands so far out on the forward edge of the purple-carpeted stage that he typically has several inches of shoe leather projecting over its lip into space. This seems like a posture that a veteran public speaker would want to avoid, fraught as it is with possibilities for an ankle-spraining pratfall. But Thompson, who takes a little stroll now and again during his hour-long sermon, returns to the edge of the stage or of one of the steps leading up to it almost every time he comes to rest. Sometimes he leaves the front half of one shoe hanging in thin air, sometimes the other, sometimes both. It gives him a sense of momentum, even when he's standing still.

A spare, upright, unlined man of 60, who looks 30 from a distance and not much older than that up close, Thompson has a commanding presence, at once prophetic and managerial. While he insists that he devotes his attention primarily to the kingdom to come, he's on a roll these days right here in the world of things. Thirty-four years after coming to Boston, the native Philadelphian has emerged as a star congregation builder among local spiritual leaders, developing Jubilee, formerly known as New Covenant, into a certified megachurch, one of only seven in the state and one of only two black megachurches in all of New England. (The standard qualifying statistic is weekly attendance of more than 2,000.) Thompson's main hall fills up for all

Original publication: "The Kingdom and the Power," *Boston*, August 2006.

three services on Sundays, with parallel services for children in another room, which means 5,000 souls every week. The number can reach as high as 7,000 on major Christian holidays, and Jubilee's tracking of donations shows that in 2005 more than 18,000 people gave at least $100. Expecting that continuing growth will require more space for worship and richer sources of income, Thompson has also accumulated a handsome real estate portfolio. This spring, Jubilee bought the defunct Our Lady of the Rosary in Stoughton from the Archdiocese of Boston for $3 million. In that well driven bargain could be heard the grinding of tectonic plates labeled Religion, Culture, and Politics.

Thompson's success in building up Jubilee has produced leverage felt well beyond his ministry. Especially in his role as president of the Black Ministerial Alliance of Greater Boston, an advocacy group that claims to represent more than 20,000 congregants, he's often in the news—inveighing against abortion and same-sex marriage, pressuring policy makers to do more to combat violence and poverty in the inner city, giving or denying his blessing to candidates for office. It's all for the greater glory of God, says Thompson. "All my ambitions are for the church. I vote for presidents, but I have a king." But even as he tries "to be in the world but not of the world," Thompson has worked hard to accumulate this-worldly capital in the form of supporters, property, connections, and a public persona to be reckoned with. People don't pay attention to Thompson's opinion of, say, Deval Patrick's candidacy for governor just because they're impressed by the bishop's piety. When Thompson preaches, maybe he plants himself on the stage's edge—a habit of which he claims to be unaware—to remind himself of the fine balance he's striking.

———

On a mildly apocalyptic May morning, the tail end of Boston's great spring monsoon of 2006 buffets the long ranks of cars in Jubilee's lot and the yellow-slickered volunteers huddled around the church's doors. Inside there are more crowd-wranglers, these wearing earpieces and black polo shirts adorned with a shield-shaped Armor Bearers crest over the heart. Flanked by images of himself on wall-mounted screens, Thompson is attired in an episcopal-looking black robe with a fetching shoulder cape, accessorized by a slim ear-mounted microphone. Though it's Mother's Day, Thompson will not be preaching about motherhood. "Neither do I preach resurrection messages on

Easter. 'Cause I recognize that there are people who only go to church on those days, and if you preach the same kind of message, that's the only kind of message they'll think you have."

The protagonist of today's sermon is Moses, "a man of deep conviction and deep passion," as Thompson portrays him. Patient but "explosive," Thompson's Moses is the righteous action hero who slew an Egyptian for mistreating an Israelite servant, and who "said, 'Let the earth open up and swallow you up, not just you but everybody that's in your family.' Moses was *rough*, y'all."

Thompson's a forceful preacher, but he's a teacher rather than what he calls "a whooper and a sweater." He stays close to scripture and he likes to cross-reference his theme; he'll frequently tell his congregants to put a streamer in their Bibles to mark the day's main text while he leads them off to related passages. They stay right with him, some taking notes. They are, for the most part, well dressed, upwardly mobile, middle-class, young (75 percent are between 25 and 45, according to the church's own estimate), and black, though there's also a cohort of Latinos and the occasional white or Asian. During the early phases of the service, before Thompson gets up to preach, some raise their hands and voices or march in place when the spirit moves them. Their responses during his sermon are more muted: applause, amens, calls of *yes, yes, yes*. The house style of worship, Pentecostal enthusiasm tempered by businesslike propriety, reflects Thompson's sensibility.

"Though God may not use us like he used Moses," Thompson says, "he will use us nonetheless. Just like there were people in Moses's life who were in bondage, there are people in my life who—they may not be in bondage to Egypt, but they're in bondage to sin, they're in bondage to hypocrisy, they're in bondage to craziness, they're in bondage to all kinds of . . . *liberal* thinking"—and here there's the briefest collective hitch in the audience's response, which Thompson acknowledges by calling out "A-men" in a way that seems to say *We've been over this before, people, so stay with me here* before continuing—"what we might call *politically correct* thinking, that leads us nowhere because it is powerless."

Preaching about an encounter with the divine leads Thompson to the culture wars waged by political operatives. Preaching about eternal life in Christ will bring him to God's desire for our children to get an education and become doctors and lawyers. An emphasis on moral confidence supplies the binding thread. "If you are to be used by God, you gotta get you some guts." He has them repeat it aloud: *Get you some guts.* "Get some conviction, get some passion," resources they will need in the struggle against militant unbelief. "The ones who are so-called politically correct, they espouse a doctrine. If you withstand them, they'll look at you like you're *crazy.*" He works up to a summation: "You need to believe your beliefs and doubt your doubts."

So what does Thompson believe? "I believe that God created the heavens and the earth. I believe that God created man in his own image. I don't believe I evolved and climbed up out of water, grew me some legs—amen—I had to grow kidneys, I had to grow a liver, and it all took place over millions, over eons of years, all by accident."

He launches into a broad comic riff on the unlikeliness of the first man and woman simultaneously reaching a compatible evolutionary stage, a riff that seems almost willfully ignorant, as if he were going out of his way not to understand the science he's lampooning. And that might be part of the point. Thompson presents himself at stage's edge as a paradox: a shrewd shepherd and steward, a man of consequence in matters of land and money and power who knows many things but for whom it must entirely suffice to know just one thing— the literal truth of a creed that often flies in the face of the practical good sense he possesses in abundance.

———

A few days after preaching his Mother's Day sermon, Bishop Thompson sits in his office at Jubilee, wearing an elegant blue suit and sipping yerba maté—which, he says, contains no caffeine, a chemically debatable point not really worth debating unless you begrudge a mild maté jolt to a man who abstains from strong drink, coffee, soda, fried foods, pork, shellfish, and sin. His cell phone and desk phone ring regularly; underlings stick their heads in the doorway to ask and tell him things. He has eleven associate pastors working under him, 43 full-time employees, 26 part-time employees, and more than 500 volunteers. He oversees mission and charity work, fundraising, a school, three bookstores, a recording studio, and Jubilee's property holdings, which include commercial spaces on Blue Hill Avenue, an office building in Dudley Square, and 25 acres of undeveloped land in Roslindale. He isn't quite running one of those Christian life-malls that the truly giant Sun Belt megachurches offer, the ones that provide yoga and dry cleaning along with salvation, but the bishop's a busy man.

Between interruptions, he talks about Jubilee's growth. Thompson started out in an old church in the South End in 1972, preaching to 41 people. In the 1980s he held services in the Bradford Hotel and the Strand Theater. When he transplanted his congregation to its present home in 1991, it numbered around 600; fifteen years, several renovations, and one name change later, more than ten times as many people attend Jubilee services on Easter Sundays. Sound business practices, not just heartfelt belief, have made it happen. "Follow-up is a keyword," he says. "It starts on Monday night catechism class. We try to get those who made a commitment, who came up to the altar on Sunday, to go. We do basics there, then there's a baptismal class, then Foundations on Tuesday," a "tripod" of pedagogy that steadies a member's devotion. "Another key is teachers I can count on, who have been with me a long time." The associate pastors to whom he delegates important duties include his wife, Yvonne, and two of their adult children.

A pastor cannot win a following solely on the strength of his charisma, says Thompson. "The reason people go to a restaurant is because the food is good. We're scratching where they itch, meeting needs they have. If I was not married, and I was bangin' some sisters"—even this merely hypothetical fornication causes his lips to curl in disgust—"people would not be coming to church to sleep with Bishop Thompson. They're coming because their real needs are being met."

Hearing Thompson rail against gay marriage or Darwin does not rank high on the list of his congregants' real needs. If you look for the heart of his ministry in such issue-mongering, you'll miss it. Look instead at what he consistently teaches about the mechanics of the good life: fiscal as well as moral discipline, an orderly as well as a loving family, success in work, personal efficacy, good health. Thompson, whose church gives financial aid packages to help members get out of debt and educate their children, preaches in favor of home ownership far more regularly and more passionately than he does against abortion.

Thompson promotes the prosperity gospel—sometimes called the "health and wealth" gospel—the God of which tangibly rewards faith with goods and services. While some proponents, including the pastors of many megachurches, reduce it to a crude contract in which believers ante up prayers and tithes to secure late-model cars and svelte physiques, Thompson offers a sober, gratification-deferred variant. Lowell Livezey of the New York Theological Seminary reports sitting in on sessions in which Thompson asked his flock, "How many of you bought a new car last year?" Many raised their hands. "How many bought a house last year?" Only a couple of hands went up. As if calling upon them to abjure false prophets, Thompson said, "Do you know what *appreciation* is? Sell that car and save up for the house." Livezey adds, "Notice how slim just about everybody is at Jubilee? It's like they all just came out of a health club. Ordinarily, you'll see a lot of obese people in church. But not there."

Thompson, who has run the Boston Marathon and describes himself as "a health nut," points out that "when God spoke to the children of Israel in the Old Testament, he gave them dietary laws," and "Jesus taught more about money than he did about heaven and hell." Sipping his maté, he says, "God is not antisuccess. He is the God of the poor, but that doesn't mean, as some believe, that God wants us to be poor." Thompson and his family live well but not extravagantly. Money seems to matter to him to the extent that he can use it to expand his church. If he has a temptress, it's power, not wealth.

Thompson's belief in faith-based self-improvement distances him from the community-mindedness that was central to the civil rights movement. "A community is made up of families, and families are made up individuals, and at some point you help individuals. At the end of the day, I want to see some people helped that I can name, not a line of statistics that says we spent this much money on this program or that one. If that's what's described as conservative, then I am."

Mukiya Baker-Gomez, a veteran Democratic strategist and now chief of staff for state representative Gloria Fox, sees Jubilee as typical of black churches that no longer pursue one of their traditional missions. "Jubilee doesn't do community organizing. Instead, there's a lot more attention to individual development, but I don't think individual development relates to responsibility to the community. When I was coming up, most every church in Boston had a social action committee that engaged people in their community and trained them in political and civic action. That doesn't exist anymore." Although Baker-Gomez characterizes Bishop Thompson as "a star supporter of Romney," she's inclined to view him as largely apolitical. Judged by her standards, "he's been somewhat conservative about getting into politics."

But the nature of a megachurch's mega-ness—the sheer numbers of citizens and dollars and square feet involved, the emphasis on growth as a cardinal virtue—tends to thrust its leader into the public sphere (and, often, to blunt the more uncompromising edges of his theology). Thompson's achievements as a religious leader have pulled him deeper into politics. As president of the Black Ministerial Alliance, a position he has held since 2004, he must get a theologically and politically diverse group to speak with one voice. Charged with representing mainline liberals as well as the conservative evangelicals like himself who have begun to supplant them, the master congregation builder has to match his signature forcefulness with tact.

———

"The whole Northeast is just beginning to deal with the fact of large numbers of evangelicals. They're not tremendously powerful yet here, but their power has been increasing, and in 25 years they will be even more so," says Scott Thumma of the Hartford Institute for Religion Research at Hartford Seminary. The flourishing of New England's first cohort of megachurches has special significance in an era when conservative evangelical credentials command particular political respect. Campaign consultants, the media, and grant-making government agencies all pay serious attention to a minister who can influence several thousand motivated, upwardly mobile, committed voters. And Thompson's coziness with Governor Romney will gain him even greater clout if Romney makes a credible run for the White House in 2008. Put that together with the emergence of the so-called New Boston as a majority-minority city and the decline of entrenched religious powers, and you begin to appreciate how expertly Thompson has picked his way through a social landscape in upheaval.

With his purchase of Our Lady of the Rosary—which is getting an upgraded sound system and rows of folding chairs to replace the pews, thereby nearly tripling its capacity—Thompson seized on an opportunity decades in the making. Though linked in the public mind with the Catholic Church's sex abuse scandal, the closing of parishes can actually be traced to the suburbanization and increasing prosperity of white-ethnic Catholics after World War II. James O'Toole, a Boston College historian and former archivist for the archdiocese, says, "Like most American dioceses, Boston put off for as long as it could facing this problem of big church 'plants' built by and for immigrant populations that had long since moved away." This failure to face demographic facts had political consequences. "The church here did have real influence in the early twentieth century, and could sway voters and turn them out for the polls, but starting in the '50s and '60s, the church doesn't try the direct political approach as much, and it doesn't work as well when it does."

Entrepreneurial Protestants like Thompson have begun to fill the power vacuum. As he makes his move, Thompson has kept in mind the example of his father, who imbibed the bootstrap philosophy of Booker T. Washington as a student at Tuskegee. Like his father, Thompson has made sure whenever possible to own the land he's standing on, which makes the footing a lot less precarious. "Real estate, real property," he says, "is like a part of my DNA."

By carefully attending to worldly as well as spiritual business, Thompson has built an institution on a scale to match his ambitions. His legacy, he hopes, will be "a church without walls," a phrase he says he "heard" years ago while praying. "It starts with the spiritual," he says, "and then out of that comes economic development, social and political strength. Now, I'd part company with my liberal Democratic brethren on how to do it. They look to the government, but I think African Americans need to build strength for themselves, the way the Koreans, the Chinese, the Jewish did it."

In the course of elaborating this vision during the conversation in his office, Thompson brings up two popular movies that, taken together, say a great deal about him. One is *Field of Dreams*, in which a man of stubborn faith heeds a disembodied voice and ends up meeting a need felt so deeply by so many people that he causes a traffic jam not unlike those you'll find on Blue Hill Avenue on Sunday mornings. "If you build it, they will come," says the bishop, smiling a little. The other movie he mentions is *The Godfather*. "When they come to the wedding, they all bring money," and he smiles a little when he says this, too.

A History of Violence

"THIS IS KEN-GAR," SAID George Pelecanos. We were sitting in his car on a quiet, green block of Plyers Mill Road. Bright sunlight warmed a row of modest, well-kept houses facing the old Baltimore & Ohio Railroad tracks.

Pelecanos, one of the most respected crime writers working today, was telling me a story. In the summer of 1972, three white teenagers riding around in a car went looking for trouble in Ken-Gar, a black enclave between Kensington and Garrett Park in Montgomery County, Maryland. "They threw a firecracker" at a group of young people in front of a grocery store. Also, Pelecanos said, they probably shouted a racial slur. "They were blue-collar kids. They'd heard about other people doing it, but they didn't know you were supposed to do it on the way *out*." Big mistake. Ken-Gar, a seven-block triangle bounded by the tracks, Rock Creek Park, and Connecticut Avenue, is a warren of dead ends. By the time the kids in the car realized that Plyers Mill Road was the only way in or out, they were trapped. Angry residents blocked the street. One of them had a gun.

"One kid jumps out of the car, books off down the tracks. He gets away," Pelecanos said. The other two tried to talk their way out of the jam. "The kid who tries to reason with them gets shot in the back and dies. The other kid gets beat up pretty badly. The police locked down the neighborhood." The gunman was convicted of manslaughter and sentenced to ten years in prison.

Original publication: "Crime Story," *Washington Post Magazine*, July 20, 2008.

Pelecanos based his fifteenth novel, *The Turnaround*, which arrives in bookstores next month, on the incident. He read court documents and interviewed longtime residents, gathering material that lent itself to his favorite themes: place, local knowledge, and community; the interwoven dynamics of race and class; masculinity's rites and burdens; and the near infinite resonance of an act of violence. The peculiar geography and history of Ken-Gar, which was settled by former slaves at the turn of the twentieth century, shaped what happened on that August afternoon 36 years ago, and the shots fired and the blows given and taken in the space of a few overheated seconds changed forever the lives of four young men and their families.

Pelecanos, who grew up nearby in Silver Spring and lives there with his wife and three children, was fifteen that summer. "I remembered it vaguely," he said, "and I did my research, and I was interested in what it was like to live there back then, but I didn't want to learn too much about the case itself. I wasn't writing journalism. Having too many of the facts of the case would have gotten in the way."

He went on to explain that *The Turnaround* owes a significant debt to another source that has nothing to do with the Ken-Gar incident. "It also comes from the last scene of *Josey Wales*," he said, referring to Clint Eastwood's post–Civil War western *The Outlaw Josey Wales*. "'We all died a little in that war.' It's about forgiveness."

There wouldn't seem to be much room for forgiveness in hard-boiled crime stories or the westerns they descend from, but emotional complexity and understated resolutions enjoy a rising presence in Pelecanos's work. He has wearied of climactic shootouts, blind vengeance, and other stock formulas of retribution. "I've been struggling with that," he said. "You want to deliver the genre goods, but in the last few books, I've been delivering them more sheepishly. *The Turnaround* isn't even really a crime novel. But you need conflict to make a novel, any kind of novel, and I don't know any other way to do it than crime."

Pelecanos is not the kind of crime writer who sets up a series hero and then regularly cranks out comfortable variations on the same book. He has been described as not only the Raymond Chandler and the James Ellroy of Washington but also its Émile Zola and Theodore Dreiser. His fans include the distinguished novelist Jonathan Lethem, who has described Pelecanos's prose as "full of music and pain," the horror titan Stephen King, who has called him "perhaps the greatest living American crime writer," and Michael Connelly, a best-selling writer of psychologically textured mysteries, who has called him "the best-kept secret in crime fiction—maybe all fiction." Pelecanos's books sell steadily to a loyal audience, but his publisher keeps pushing to raise his profile, to turn a writer often described as a cult figure into a mega-brand like Connelly or Elmore Leonard. There are other ways to measure success, though. Pelecanos enjoys the respect of peers and critics; he played an important part in creating the wildly acclaimed HBO show *The Wire*; and he has branched out into side pursuits, such as writing a war drama for HBO and editing collections of stories set in Washington—the second of which, *D.C. Noir 2: The Classics*, due out in September, features the work of Langston Hughes, Richard Wright, and Edward P. Jones.

Pelecanos, who is 51, told me, "Sometimes I think *The Wire* said it all, and I might as well not write any more crime novels. I can feel my energy beginning to dissipate. One thing I didn't realize about this business when I started was that it could be my job to write a novel a year, but it's also my job to take a walk and think." He owes one more book to his publisher, and the contract specifies that it be a crime novel and that it be delivered by the end of the year, but he's not sure in what direction his writing will go after that. Working in the overlap where the crime novelist meets the literary novelist, Pelecanos has always been willing to push his heroes, his city, and his storytelling craft through difficult changes.

———

In the summer of 1968, when Pelecanos was eleven, he went to work as a delivery boy at his father's diner, the Jefferson Coffee Shop at 19th Street and Jefferson Place NW. He dreamed up serial westerns in his head to amuse himself as he made his rounds on foot. Two months before, the death of Martin Luther King Jr. had sparked riots in Washington, as it had in other American cities. There's a scene in *Hard Revolution* (2004), Pelecanos's novel about that time, in which eleven-year-old Nick Stefanos, who will grow up to become an alcoholic private eye, comes out of Sunday school at his church and hears King's amplified voice, preaching. "That was me," Pelecanos said. "March 31, 1968. I was coming out of St. Sophia, and they had hung speakers outside the National Cathedral, across the street, where he was preaching." King would be murdered in Memphis four days later.

We were standing on the corner of 14th and U Streets in Northwest as Pelecanos, an upright, chesty fellow with a deep voice and a manner composed of equal parts reserve and dry good humor, told the story. "Fourteenth burned from all the way down there to all the way up there," he said, making a sweeping gesture with one arm. "Fourteenth, Seventh, H Street, all burned. I took the bus every day down Georgia Avenue, and I could see the ashes. It still smelled of fire, and you could feel that people had changed. It felt like this thing had been lifted. I could see how people treated each other. They were thinking, 'How do we talk to each other now?' There was a lot of tension. Black people were less deferential toward whites, and, at the diner, white people treated the black employees with more respect."

Looking back on that summer, Pelecanos sees himself launched down the path to his calling. "Working at my dad's diner, that was the most important thing. That summer, the first summer—the riots, the young ladies wearing miniskirts, the music on the radio, it was all there. That's what made me a writer."

Of course, it took more than this original inspiration. For one thing, he had to learn more about the city that would serve as his subject and setting. There's a tendency to assume a mystical connection between a crime writer and "his" city, but close-grained knowledge of a place comes not by inheritance or sentimental osmosis but from curiosity, attention, and sustained effort. Working for his father took Pelecanos down Georgia Avenue into Washington, and, later, so did sports. He played pickup basketball in playgrounds around the city, and he played second base on a rec league baseball team that won the District title in 1973, he said. As he entered adulthood, his interest in punk and go-go music and his appetite for movies drew him to clubs and theaters offering cosmopolitan attractions unavailable in Silver Spring. Then there was work: tending bar and selling shoes, stereos, and appliances in the District gave him copious opportunities to catalogue the speech and manners of Washington's citizens.

Getting to know the city was half the equation; developing the technique to render it in prose was the other. Unconsciously at first, then with a growing sense of purpose as he sharpened his focus on writing crime stories, Pelecanos stocked his authorial toolbox by assimilating various influences.

His earliest appreciation of the storyteller's craft came from the movies. He said, "I had this book, *The Movies*, a big book full of pictures, and I just studied it obsessively when I was eight, nine, ten." Steve Rados, an old friend of his, told me: "When we were just getting into our teens, I'd sleep over at his house, and we'd maybe steal a little liquor and watch movies all night, and he would know the director, he would know where this movie fit into the history of Hollywood. He was already getting more than face value out of watching a movie." Pelecanos ate up the standard guy pictures of his youth— *The Magnificent Seven*, *The Great Escape*, *The Dirty Dozen*, *The Wild Bunch*, spaghetti westerns, blaxploitation movies—and they penetrated into his storytelling DNA. (He listens to Ennio Morricone's operatic movie soundtracks while he writes, and he drives a limited-edition 2001 Ford Mustang GT based even down to its exhaust note on the car Steve McQueen drove in the chase scene in *Bullitt*.) But he also extended his interest into the more eclectic fare offered by the Circle Theatre and other DC repertory houses: classical Hollywood films, European art movies, Japanese and Hong Kong cinema.

He majored in film during an on-again, off-again college career at the University of Maryland, but he had no prospects in the business. "I was just a Greek guy from DC who didn't know anybody," he said. "I wasn't going to make movies." In his senior year, he wandered into a course on crime fiction taught by Charles Mish, who introduced him to a trade he could pursue and master on his own. "I said to myself, This is what I really want to do. I could go sit in a room and do this. I didn't have to ask anybody for anything; I didn't have to sell myself. It changed my life." Pelecanos kept the epiphany to himself. "I was a quiet guy in class. Years later, I wrote to the professor after my first novel came out, and he wrote back, 'Congratulations; I don't remember you.' But I can still tell you what we read: *Red Harvest*; *Lady in the Lake*; *I, the Jury*; *The Blue Hammer*; *Call for the Dead*; *The Deep Blue Goodbye*."

After graduating in 1980, he "read for the next ten years, just to catch up. Crime fiction was changing then. The traditional private eye novel was dying out." He went back to Horace McCoy, Edward Anderson, and other pre–World War II masters of social-realist crime fiction, but he also took note of contemporaries who were stretching the genre. "James Crumley, Kem Nunn's surf noir *Tapping the Source*, Newton Thornburgh's *Cutter and Bone*—they took the form and did something different with it," Pelecanos said. "It wasn't police fiction. It wasn't the detective with the bottle of whiskey in the file cabinet. There wasn't a mystery to solve. It was about people out there, kind of lost after the Vietnam War, a generation knocked off center, and it dealt with that through the crime novel, exploring that world at a street level. I started thinking maybe I can just write about what I know. There are a lot of bars and shoe stores in my early books."

He needed a push, though, to make the jump from reader to writer. He got it from the DC punk scene that flourished around hardcore bands such as Fugazi, Minor Threat, and Bad Brains. He said, "The whole idea was you didn't have to be a musician, you didn't have to have ties to a record company, you didn't have to be somebody's son. You just picked up a guitar and made something—maybe it was art, maybe not." DIY, as the punk motto puts it: Do It Yourself. So, Pelecanos did the writer's equivalent of picking up a guitar and making something.

He worked day jobs and wrote on his own time. In Pelecanos's first novel, *A Firing Offense* (1992), Nick Stefanos, advertising director at an electronics store called Nutty Nathan's, searches for a missing stock boy, a metalhead who has sunk deep into trouble over drugs and money. Pelecanos, who had no agent at the time, sent the manuscript to a single publisher, St. Martin's Press, which bought it and the four that followed. The advances were nowhere near enough to live on: $2,500, $3,000, $3,500. During the 1990s, Pelecanos worked for Jim and Ted Pedas, who had owned the Circle Theatre and other movie houses but had moved into production and distribution. While helping to produce the Coen brothers' early films and distribute John Woo's Hong Kong crime classic *The Killer*, among other tasks, Pelecanos honed his novel-writing chops and began to build a loyal audience. He switched to Little, Brown and Company, receiving a $45,000 advance for *King Suckerman* (1997), a 1970s tale that features a hotly awaited but uniquely disappointing blaxploitation movie. When Miramax bought the rights to the book and hired him to write the screenplay, Pelecanos took a chance and quit his day job. "I told my wife, 'I think I can make a living at this.'" The movie was never made, one of several near-miss attempts to adapt his novels. Unmade screenplays and elapsed options don't improve book sales, but they do produce welcome infusions of Hollywood money.

His book advances kept growing. The latest, in 2004, was $1.5 million for three novels, the second of which is *The Turnaround*. The first of the three, *The Night Gardener* (2006), based on the case of Washington's never-caught serial murderer known as the Freeway Phantom, got a big push from Little, Brown, and made the *New York Times* best-seller list, a first for Pelecanos. "The trajectory of his sales is steadily upward, and the span of potential readers is unusually broad for him, including readers of traditional crime fiction and literary fiction," said Michael Pietsch, executive vice president and publisher at Little, Brown. *The Night Gardener* sold 41,829 copies in hardcover, according to Little, Brown. (Nielsen BookScan, which claims to count about 70 percent of sales for a typical hardcover, counted 29,109.) Michael Connelly, who is also published by Little, Brown, routinely sells more than ten times as many in hardcover, and Pietsch believes that Pelecanos can get to that level with a breakout book connected to a successful movie adaptation. "There's still a lot of gunpowder lying around," said Pietsch, meaning that while *The Night Gardener* was a major step up in sales for Pelecanos, it didn't touch off the explosion of interest in him that, say, *Mystic River* did for Dennis Lehane. Little, Brown thinks it can turn Pelecanos into a brand that produces a best seller every time out.

Whether or not he achieves greater commercial success, Pelecanos said, "I've had a dream career, and at this point more money would be money stacked on top of the money there." Every writer wants more readers, of course, but Pelecanos realizes that he's been able to provide for his family while settling into a deeply satisfying life's work as an artist that would have been impossible to imagine when he was a young man.

He's very clear about what that work is. In an online chat session with readers in 2000, he wrote: "When I started out, I didn't feel as if Washington, DC, had been fully represented in literature. And by that I mean the real, living, working-class side of the city. The cliche is that Washington is a transient town of people who blow in and out every four years with the new administrations. But the reality is that people have lived in Washington for generations, and their lives are worth examining, I think. I didn't have a specific plan in the beginning, but the way it's worked out, I've pretty much covered the century in Washington, going back to the 1930s, and the societal changes that have occurred there."

In addition to imparting a lot of period-specific information about food, drink, shoes, bars, muscle cars, music, movies, sound equipment, tipping, sales work, and how and when to hotbox a cigarette, he has used the formulas of the crime genre to explore the city and its social order. Perhaps the biggest historical theme moving beneath the action is the long engagement of white ethnics and blacks, part marriage and part war, the crucial turning point of which was the riots of 1968. They loom so large in his historical imagination because they mark the fall of New Deal Washington and the hope for unity that shaped it. They mark, as well, the emergence of a harder and more desperate Washington where government—both federal and local—was widely understood to be part of the problem, not the principal guarantor of justice and equality of opportunity. Many whites, especially immigrants newly arrived in the middle class, abandoned this declining city in a suburbanizing age.

"We lived right up here when I was little," Pelecanos said as we cruised slowly through an alley in Mount Pleasant. "The National Zoo's right over there. You could hear the lions roaring at night." He pointed out the back of the house on Irving Street NW that his mother's parents owned back then. "This is where everybody was. Kids played out back, and there were sleeper porches. You slept out here when it was hot. We moved to Silver Spring when I started school."

We got out of the car on the corner of Klingle and Park roads to look at a historical marker, number 9 on the Mount Pleasant Heritage Trail. On one side of the marker is a photograph taken in 1977 of the residents of Blue Skies, which, a caption explains, was "a group house devoted to antiwar work and social justice." The neighborhood, in transition then, attracted "political activists, artists, and unconventional family groups." There are a couple dozen adults and children in the picture, an integrated countercultural household posing proudly in front of their home at 1910 Park Road. One of the small boys sitting on the stoop is Adrian Fenty, now mayor of Washington.

Despite his suspicion of institutional power, Pelecanos believes that Fenty has done a good job, finally beginning to right the damage done by decades of capital flight, resegregation, and misgovernment. He acknowledged that it might seem odd to hear such boosterish optimism from a writer whose collected works reinforce the city's image as a murder capital and decry fundamental inequities in American society. "But hey," he said, "we've had a couple of good mayors; the construction of the Metro is beginning to pay off; there are finally a few good signs out there." When we drove down H Street NE, he said, "This was black Washington's place to shop, ten long blocks, and it all burned down. Just now, 40 years later, it's coming around."

On the other face of the historical marker at Klingle and Park is a photograph of the family of another illustrious son of Mount Pleasant: the Pelecanos clan at the table on Thanksgiving Day, 1962. George's older sisters, Alice and Jeannie, and his mother, Ruby, wear Sunday-best dresses, jewelry, and makeup. George, who at 5 already has his distinctive sleepy-eyed look, appears to be counting the seconds until he can devour the turkey. His father, Peter, stands over the main course, carving tools at the ready, a hint of a hard little smile on his lips. Crew cut, clean-shaven, projecting banty male confidence in suit and tie, Peter Pelecanos looks like a Spartan variation on Glenn Ford in *The Big Heat*.

There's a story of Mount Pleasant in the juxtaposition of the two photographs on the marker, a fragment of a larger story of the city that Pelecanos has told in his novels, but there's also a meditation on the meaning of family. For Pelecanos, history and family coalesce in an interest, running deeply throughout his work, in how his male characters handle the pressures the changing world exerts on their sense of themselves. Michael Connelly, an early supporter of Pelecanos's career who became a friend, told me, "He's totally consumed with the idea of what makes a good man." For Pelecanos, as for a lot of men, any discussion of that topic begins with his father.

"My father never laid a hand on me," Pelecanos said. "He was a badass, and I knew that, and that was enough. He'd boxed, and he was an ex-Marine. He fought on Leyte, real island fighting. I knew he'd killed people with his hands, but he didn't talk about it. Those guys didn't talk about it much."

Andrew Walsh, a friend of Pelecanos since childhood who is now a professor of religion at Trinity College in Connecticut, explained the mythic power that grandfathers and fathers exerted over boys of their generation. "Our grandfathers had come over, alone, from tiny villages in Greece when they were fourteen or something, and made it. We knew at first hand the romance of immigrant success. George's grandfather and father worked like dogs, and together with other people like them climbed up from poverty to respectability. And then our fathers had fought in World War II. So we thought we led dull, average lives by comparison."

On his first try at college, Pelecanos had to drop out after one semester to run the family diner for a few months while his father recovered from a heart attack. "I got to do something a lot of boys never get to do until later," Pelecanos told me. "I proved to my dad that I was a man." It was 1975, and he was eighteen, hanging out with his friends and chasing girls. It took a sustained effort of will to submit to his father's working grind. "For a guy who liked to party, to get up at 4:30 and go [to work], it changed the way my mom and dad looked at me."

His novels are so full of diners that an attentive reader could get a pretty good education in how to operate one. If a customer asks for an old-fashioned item like liverwurst or buttermilk, go get it, and keep a little on hand to encourage return visits; keep the peace among employees by allowing each to choose the music on the radio for part of the day; cut off the cash register tape at 3 p.m. to exempt some of the day's profits from taxes.

The novels are full, as well, of scenes in which fathers and father figures try to teach younger men how to live. In *The Turnaround*, Alex Pappas, who has lost one son in Iraq, tries to pass on to his younger son both his diner and what he learned from his own father: "Work is what men did. Not gambling, or freeloading, or screwing off. Work." Meanwhile, Raymond Monroe, whose son is serving in Afghanistan, teaches his girlfriend's young son to walk like a man. "Chin up, and keep your shoulders square, like you're balancing a broom handle on there. Make eye contact, but not too long, hear? You don't want to be challenging anyone for no good reason. On the other hand, you don't want to look like a potential victim, either." Sometimes the father figures demonstrate that forgiveness requires more strength than does vengeance, but often the most dramatic lessons-by-example in masculinity come the hard way.

In his fiction, Pelecanos stages again and again an iconic showdown in which a small businessman emerges from behind his counter or walks tall off the sales floor to face off against gangsters. In *Hard Revolution*, a crew of bank robbers runs afoul of a fellow whom we know well as a type from other Pelecanos novels, a type for whom his father serves as the template: an immigrant who fought on Guadalcanal, operates a small diner in a rough neighborhood downtown, and carries a .38. This do-or-die striver has dropped by the bank to deposit the previous day's take, and he's not about to give up his hard-earned American money just because he's outgunned. A bloodbath ensues. Such scenes are, in a sense, valentines to men like Peter Pelecanos, investing hardworking dads with heroic qualities on a par with those of gangsters, private eyes, and cowboys.

"There's a line we've talked about in a western, *Ride the High Country*, that I think is really important to him," Connelly told me: "'All I want is to enter my house justified.' I think that's George's thing." But steeped though he may be in the seemingly timeless moral certitude of the western, Pelecanos traces the ways in which the definition of a good man, a man who at the end of the day or of his life can truly enter his own house justified, changes over time. His male characters negotiate tricky paths between the traditional manhood represented by his father and the options for masculinity that have opened up since the '60s. The older model may have been potent in its virtues, but it had significant flaws, not least of which was a general acceptance of racism as the natural way of things.

Pelecanos told me a story about a script meeting for *The Pacific*, HBO's companion piece to its World War II combat miniseries *Band of Brothers*. One reason he accepted the invitation to write for *The Pacific*, which is scheduled to air in 2009, was to honor his father's service to his country, but that didn't cause him to shy away from ugly complexity. "Somebody at this meeting brings up the fact that we don't have any black major characters, and then somebody else says that the military was still segregated, and blacks were often forced to do menial jobs instead of fighting. So, I said, how about a scene in which the guys are watching black soldiers clean up the bodies on a landing beach, and they say, 'Look at those niggers. They've got it so easy, they never have to fight'? These are the heroes, characters we care about, and yet they're saying these terrible things, because that's true to what it would have been like." It was too much, even for HBO. "There was this long pause," during which the rest of the creative team considered presenting the heroes of the Greatest Generation as bigots. "Nobody said a word, and after a while they just went on to something else like I'd never spoken."

We dropped by Cardozo Senior High School in Washington to visit Frazier O'Leary, who teaches AP English and coaches the baseball team. "My parents went here in the 1930s," said Pelecanos. "It's black and Hispanic now." Pelecanos first visited O'Leary's class five years ago under the auspices of a PEN/Faulkner Foundation program that brings writers into the schools. He has returned regularly.

As we looked out over the empty baseball field, O'Leary, a hale former athlete with a thick white mustache and a paunch, talked about his plans to raise money to renovate it and rename it in honor of the great shortstop Maury Wills, a Cardozo graduate. "I started playing on this field in a semipro league in 1967," O'Leary said. "I was the token white guy in the whole league."

He shares with Pelecanos a sense of the riots of 1968 as a turning point in his life, as well as in the city's history. At the time, O'Leary, who had done a tour of duty in Vietnam, was an Army lieutenant in military intelligence stationed outside the city. "They told me to put together a riot platoon," he recalled. Having assembled the soldiers, "I looked around, and I could see that these guys would have deserted the second we got out there. It was 1968. They didn't give a damn about the Army, and they sympathized with the rioters." He never had to lead the platoon into action. He left the Army later that year, got his degree at American University, and started teaching in 1971. He has been at Cardozo since 1977. Pelecanos said, "I like them to do *Hard Revolution*" when he visits O'Leary's AP English class "because a lot of his students don't know about the riots."

Continuing on the theme of violence and its lasting consequences, we fell to talking about Kermit Washington, a local basketball star at Coolidge High School and American University in the late '60s and early '70s who went on to the NBA. "Good player," said Pelecanos. "A strong guy." But all anybody remembers about Washington is that during an on-court altercation between the Los Angeles Lakers and the Houston Rockets in 1977 he hit Rudy Tomjanovich, who was rushing in from the blind side to break up the fight, with an infamous punch that shattered his face and nearly killed him. Tomjanovich, who is white, eventually recovered, played again, and went on to coach the Rockets to a championship. Branded as a thug, Washington, who is black, bounced from team to team for a few more seasons before retiring. Tomjanovich forgave Washington in latter years, saying, "He made a mistake, and everyone deserves a second chance."

Then O'Leary brought up a former student who had gone on to college and graduate school. "She's brilliant," he explained, "but her brothers are drug dealers. It's crazy at home; she can't study. She lives in one of the neighborhoods George writes about." Pelecanos asked what she needed. "Just a room someplace quiet," said O'Leary. Pelecanos considered for a moment and said, "Okay, if you do the legwork and get me a piece of paper so I can write it off, I'll finance it."

The two men looked out across the field, a little embarrassed. O'Leary appeared to be crossing a delicate job off a mental to-do list. A look of physical pain crossed Pelecanos's face as he considered the possibility that somebody reading this story might think that he was trying to act like a big shot. A pragmatist suspicious of grand social theories and official initiatives, he believes in "pulling kids through the keyhole one at a time," which requires judicious doses of money as well as sound mentoring.

On the way back to the car he said, "Frazier is one of my heroes, a guy who's really doing something good for kids in this city. You should be writing your story about him."

———

David Simon, cocreator of "The Wire," who recruited Pelecanos to help write and produce the show, described him to me as "a moralist." He meant that Pelecanos, "rooted in the immigrant tradition," is "rigorous about doing everything he said he was going to do and doing it well," but also that Pelecanos centers his writing on characters' struggles to do the right thing in a compromised, difficult world.

Pelecanos has fashioned a distinctive plot structure that allows him to explore those struggles while meeting the demands of the crime story. His novels typically feature a main plot in which a protagonist wrestles with multiple moral problems that offer no easy course of action—what to do about an implacable enemy, what to do about an incorrigible son, and so on. These problems are often related to family and to the life-changing consequences of acts of violence buried in the past, brewing in the near future, or both. Meanwhile, in an intertwined high-action subplot, one or more doom-seekers crashes heedlessly through the novel, headed for an apocalypse. The moral plots have grown richer and more dominant over time, so that the principal pleasures of reading Pelecanos lie more and more in his portraits of the inner lives of complex characters seen at home and at work, as well as in the evocation of place and time.

As Connelly put it, "George is past the backbone of the book being the investigation of a crime; the backbone will be family, or something like it. George is the ace when it comes to delivering mystery with a message." Pelecanos has worked hard to attain that status, and his peers have taken note.

"Here are the choices if you want to write more than one novel: get better, stay the same, or get worse," says Laura Lippmann, who writes mysteries set in Baltimore. "George chose to get better with every book." Lehane, another luminary in the tight circle of crime-writing friends that includes Pelecanos, Connelly, and Lippmann (who is married to David Simon), divides Pelecanos's novels into three phases. "His early books have a beautiful sense of character, but he's still getting his head around the mechanics of structure. In the middle period, you see rock-solid structure, and by now it's a perfect fusion of obsessive character studies and narrative. At this point, he's comparable to Dreiser, not Jim Thompson." He's a novelist, in other words, who happens to write crime stories.

"I learned to write on the job," says Pelecanos. "I really got out of the first person on *The Big Blowdown*," his fifth novel (1996), a period piece set in the 1930s, '40s, and '50s. "That's where I got to the generational view, getting into the heads of all kinds of characters, and that's when I started to say, Okay, now I'm a writer. From then on, you see more variety, more different kinds of characters. I started writing more social novels." From private eye stories, featuring his troubled alter ego Nick Stefanos and then Derek Strange, a black ex-cop with a deep sense of social responsibility, he ventured out across the crime subgenres—criminal noirs, pulps, procedurals, historical dramas, tales of average Joes pushed too far. He doesn't outline before he writes, but he does his homework. Relying more over time on research has obliged him to cultivate sources. "I do police ride-alongs, interviews; I go to trials just to listen to the language; and I've made a lot of contacts on the other side, too, people who've done bad things in their lives and are eager to talk."

He has also tried to change some bad habits. He pines for the novice energy of his first novels, he says, but he can't read them now because "I had been timid in those books about being honest about race, and I wanted to change that. I hadn't let the characters speak as they would speak. I was walling them around too much, idealizing the black characters too much. You have to not be afraid to be misinterpreted."

More fully inhabiting his black characters and letting them speak as they would speak has drawn some critics' ire. The author and activist Ishmael Reed has fulminated against Pelecanos, whose black characters, Reed has said, "speak like the cartoon crows in those old racist cartoons." Writing in the *Washington Post*, the novelist Guy Johnson accused Pelecanos of purveying broad ghetto stereotypes that create "doubt about whether he knows his subjects well enough to capture them."

"For me, it's not so much about black and white as it is about knowing Washington," said Pelecanos. "I get letters from black readers saying, 'Thank you, you got something right.' Like, after *Hard Revolution*, I heard from a few different people about the riots. Stokely Carmichael has always been blamed for inciting them, but he didn't, and I had to get that right. But, more often, they'll write to say

I caught something about how people talk, or they'll say, 'How did you know about that bar?'" You read Pelecanos for the way his characters experience a workplace moment, the rush of being out among people drinking where there's music, the rhythm of an unremarkable weekday evening in a lower-middle-class household—not for poetic language, intricate plotting, or gloriously inventive action tableaus. Going into people's heads is what he does. "If I shouldn't be allowed to go into a black character's head, then I shouldn't write women, or *The Pacific*, since those people aren't like me, either."

Pelecanos has pursued his character studies into a variety of fictional people: white and black, male and female, contemporary and historical. Putting them in motion through the plots of crime stories produces surprising results. Nick Stefanos, his first hero, progressively drinks his way out of a starring role and becomes a supporting character in later novels. Every instinct bred by crime stories and action movies encourages a reader to expect that Lorenzo Brown, the ex-con trying to keep his nose clean in *Drama City* (2005), is headed for a spectacular showdown with gangsters—but he steers around it. You never see the serial murderer in *The Night Gardener*, and the frustrated cops don't, either.

Pelecanos was a writer, story editor, and producer for *The Wire*. He wrote crucial scenes as different as the ex-junkie Bubbles' breakthrough at a twelve-step meeting and the western-style standoff in an alley between Omar Little, the street legend who robs drug dealers, and Brother Mouzone, the prim shootist from New York. Pelecanos also created Cutty, a character who turns away from the street life and opens a boxing gym, and gave *The Wire* its Greek gangsters, even providing the background voices shouting in Greek when the cops raided a warehouse. In story meetings, he refereed arguments between Simon and Ed Burns, the show's other cocreator.

"Ed and I are often butting heads in a way that somebody who doesn't know us might think is toxic," Simon told me. "George's essential role was to be the gravitas, to make the decision. We'd present our best arguments, and he'd sit and listen until he couldn't stand it any longer. He was the one with the storytelling chops to decide. He has a really strong ear for theme and idea. He writes books and scripts that are about something. When George says you won an argument, you feel good because it means the idea was good."

Expanding on his description of Pelecanos as a moralist, Simon said, "We didn't know we needed Cutty until George invented him.

It's not about plotting, it's about defining some aspect of human endeavor that wasn't covered by other characters. Institutionally, not much is redeemed in *The Wire*, yet all of us believe in the individual's ability to act. George said, 'We need a moral center.'"

Burns told me a story about scripting the death of Wallace, a likable corner boy gunned down by his pals. "It could have been just Bodie, who was pretty much a monster back then, who would just walk up and kill him. But that would have left nothing for Poot, and it would have sealed Bodie as a character. The way George wrote it, Bodie can't finish it, and Poot, who's a good friend of Wallace, has to step up and do it. That transcends genre; that's squeezing all the juice out of a scene." Bodie opens up as a character from that point, grappling with a dawning understanding that the large forces bearing down on him make it almost impossible for him to act honorably and survive. "That's why you hire writers like George," said Burns, "because they find what's inside a scene, what's inside the character."

The Wire, in return, left its mark on Pelecanos. It "changed the way I look at a lot of things," he said. "In the past, I would go down to a drug corner and go, 'Why doesn't the government do anything about this?' Now I see better that they're not gonna do something about it, and just throwing money at it won't work. The people who live there have to take things into their hands."

———

Driving up Georgia Avenue toward Maryland, following the historical route of the Pelecanos family and others who moved up into the suburban middle class, we passed through a redevelopment district. Banners hanging from streetlights announced that "Good Things Are Happening" on Georgia Avenue. Crossing into Silver Spring, we entered a classic post–World War II suburban landscape of detached houses, each set off by a lawn.

"This is where I grew up," said Pelecanos. "Whittington Terrace. It was Jewish, Italian, Greek—ethnic people buying their first house." We parked at Forest Knolls Elementary School and got out. From the schoolyard, we could see into the back yard of the house he grew up in. "I climbed the fence and went home every day for lunch," he said. "Same thing in high school. That's how I got in trouble."

He was referring to an accident with a gun when he was seventeen in which he nearly killed his pal Frank Carchedi. The boys, who had been tight since first grade, were fooling around with Pelecanos's father's unregistered .38, and it went off. "I blew the side of his face off," said Pelecanos. "He just looked at me and said, 'You shot me.'"

I asked if the moment resurfaces when he writes violent scenes. "Honestly, yes," he answered. "To shoot somebody at close range like that, you don't forget." He has written elements of the episode into more than one novel, including *Down by the River Where the Dead Men Go* (1995): "The right side of his jaw was exposed, skinless, with pink rapidly seeping into the pearl of the bone. You're okay, LaDuke, I thought. You turned your head at the last moment and Coley blew off the side of your face. You're going to be badly scarred and a little ugly, but you're going to be okay."

Pelecanos told me that his father had his arms full of groceries when he came home after Carchedi had been rushed to the hospital. "He was carrying these big bags, and he came in, and there was blood all over the walls. The wound had geysered. He just dropped the bags, they slid right out of his hands, and he turned white."

"The truth of it was, it wasn't a real sinister thing," Carchedi, now a successful area businessman, told me on the phone. "It was a couple of teenage kids being knuckleheads, playing around. But it was an important experience, in a way. It made us both stronger, and if anything it made us closer. It was a pretty lonely place out there when it happened." No criminal charges were filed; the men remain close. Pelecanos is Carchedi's daughter's godfather, and he named the mayor in *The Wire* after his friend.

Carchedi said, "It was more or less a flesh wound, which sounds funny to say, like Monty Python or something, considering how bad it looked and the surgery I had to have. But it was a bloody mess, and it changed us." One aftereffect of the episode he detects in his old friend's writing is a deep respect for the transformative power of violence, part of a larger skepticism about the fantasy figure of the action hero with a gun. "Reading his books, on the surface you think that the way to be is the characters who are the tough guys, fast and loose on the edge, alpha-male types. You feel like kind of a loser because these guys are out there drinking and playing, but they usually end up being losers. We're attracted to the fantasy of these guys, but as the book wraps up, it's the guy who gets up and goes to work in the morning who ends up really cool."

The shooting drew in the starkest terms the line between youthful hijinks and the kind of catastrophe that can end a life or warp it beyond redemption. Carchedi said, "It was a turbulent time. Things were different in the '60s and '70s, and every kid wasn't tethered by a cell phone, but that was as far out there as we ever got. We were basically good kids. We did well in school; we listened to our parents. We'd get out on the edge. We took risks, and we'd do crazy things that parents now, who are so on their kids, would be horrified by, but one of our bonds was that we knew we weren't gonna go over that edge. A lot of that was the strength of our families—blue-collar, ethnic. That was behind us, and kept us accountable." The shooting was the two boys' big mistake, and they still wonder at the sheer dumb luck that allowed them to recover from it.

Carchedi feels that dwelling on the incident can lead to a romantic misreading of Pelecanos that confuses a dutiful, responsible family man with one of his own characters. "If you look at the stories written about George, they focus on the macho side, the tough side—and he does have that side. He was on the streets; he was that kind of kid and young adult. But he's mellowed, and he's quicker to talk about family than about this other stuff. George is really focused on family, in his books and in his life. He's taken a path that a lot of guys in his position would not have taken. I know for a fact that he's turned stuff down because he wanted to stay here with his family. He's flown high, but he could have flown even higher."

———

"My worldview changed because we had children," Pelecanos said. We were sitting in the den in his house, not far from the house in which he grew up. Books with his name on their spines lined two shelves. His wife, Emily, 50, and their kids—Nick, seventeen; Peter, fifteen; and Rose, eleven—came and went, attending to weekday evening business.

Pelecanos was talking about crime writers with kids and those without, and how you can tell the difference—for instance, in their appreciation of the life-altering consequences of violence. He takes a shot in passing at Quentin Tarantino in *The Turnaround*: a therapist who works with wounded soldiers at Walter Reed Hospital talks bitterly about audiences laughing and clapping through the episode in *Grindhouse* in which a woman mows down enemies with a machine gun grafted onto the stump of a severed leg.

Pelecanos described a turning point in his life, his experience in Brazil in 1993, when he and Emily went there to adopt Peter. (Nick and Peter are adopted from Brazil; Rose from Guatemala.) They had document problems and ended up spending the whole fall there. They were struck by the nakedness of the poverty and despair they saw. "You couldn't walk around at night; there were fences with nails in them around the houses, kids with murder in their eyes. Here it's more hidden. It radicalized me a little bit, and it made me want to reach a bit higher, like Steinbeck."

Thinking about the changes in his writing encouraged by fatherhood, he said, "The answer to 'What makes a good man?' has changed. Some of the men stop themselves. They're more in control of their impulses. And if they cross the line, they know they'll have to give up what they are."

Fights

Boxing Stories

IF YOU READ THE sports section, James Fallows once observed, then nothing in the newspaper seems fresher to you when it's hot off the presses, and nothing goes stale as quickly. He's right. A day-old sports section is much staler than a day-old front page, and infinitely staler than a day-old comics page, which remains entirely fresh even if you read the next day's comics before you get to it. Who won or lost, who's two games out of first place in the division, who averaged 3.6 yards a carry . . . it all seems urgent the morning after it happens, and then suddenly and completely irrelevant a day or two after that.

If you read the sports section, you know this. But chances are that you're not familiar with the one exception to the rule. Boxing stories don't get stale. I'll explain why in a minute, but first we have to confront a hard truth: you don't know about this exception because you skip the boxing stories. Admit it. You skip them. Admit that you'd rather read about a sort-of-ebullient cleanup hitter's contract negotiations (short version: he's going to be making a lot of money for a long time) or the micro-minutiae of a basketball star's stunningly dull existence (ball, video games, money, call mom; repeat).

Not that there are so many boxing stories to skip. Boxing wedges its way into the margins of daily papers' sports sections only occasionally, usually for one of three reasons: 1) a big fight catches the attention of the general sports press, in recent years often because it featured either Mike Tyson, who managed to mock-convince one

Original publication: *Epicenters*, May 2007.

winking sportswriter after another that this time he could be serious, this time he might really have changed, or Oscar De La Hoya, who was cute and famous, no matter how overrated he may have been as a fighter; 2) a local fighter on the rise is about to challenge for a title; or 3) something very bad happens to a fighter, in or out of the ring.

Most general-assignment sportswriters don't know much about boxing, but they do seem to enjoy writing about it, perhaps because the fight world's built-in quality of anachronism (it's always 1926 at the fights) inspires them to indulge fantasies of being wisecracking, typewriter-pounding guys in snap-brim fedoras who crank up a two-piece phone and shout, "Honey, get me Rewrite!" For that reason, and because stylish delivery of the story often has to make up for both writer's and reader's disinterest in boxing for its own sake, writing about boxing in the daily paper tends to be extra-purple. Play a drinking game with your friends in which everybody has to drain a beer every time the word "gritty" or "grimy" appears in a #3-type story, the kind about something very bad happening to a fighter. Also, everybody has to drink when there's a punchy short sentence—put the over-under at, say, five words. Also, keep an eye out for purple paragraphing.

Know what I mean?

Purple.

And punchy.

Everybody has to drink when that happens, too. You'll all be retching in no time.

Now, let me explain why boxing stories, in violent contrast to other sports-section stories, don't go stale.

It will help to have an example in front of us. I have one on my desk now, in the sports section of yesterday's *New York Times*. Most of that section's contents have already acquired the desolately superseded feel of abandoned homesteads overgrown by prairie grass. The Patriots came from behind to beat the Dolphins. The Redskins came from ahead to lose to the Buccaneers. Somebody returned a missed field goal 108 yards for a touchdown, the longest play in NFL history. The Los Angeles Kings blew out the Columbus Blue Jackets, and the Los Angeles Galaxy (part of the trend toward ambiguously singular-plural team names, like the San Jose Liquidity or the Boston Crabbiness) won the MLS Cup. It all may have seemed exciting at the time, and it retained some interest on Monday morning when I read it as fresh news around a bowl of cereal, but by Tuesday it was a sere wasteland.

Then there's the boxing story, a good example of the #3-type, by Geoffrey Gray. James Butler, a once-promising super-middleweight (which means he has to weigh no more than 168 pounds for a fight, which means that he could lay out any 350-pound football blimp or slap-happy basketball bad boy in about eleven seconds), has been charged with the murder of Sam Kellerman, who wrote and acted a little and dabbled in boxing and was the younger brother of Max Kellerman, a fairly well-known television commentator on boxing.

Gray deftly juxtaposes their stories. Butler came up the hard way, in the projects. His father wasn't around; his mother alternately went off partying and harshly disciplined her sons. Butler had talent, and he could hit, but he never mastered his power or himself. He made it as far as a title shot, but lost. He's known as a headcase, most famous for an incident in which he coldcocked a victorious opponent in the ring after the decision had been rendered and the gloves were off. Butler spent four months in jail for that assault, not his first visit to the joint. He was also diagnosed with bipolar disorder, but the medication made him sluggish and heavy, and therefore unable to fight, so he didn't take it.

Sam Kellerman, the son of a prominent psychoanalyst and an artist, attended Stuyvesant High School and Columbia University, and tried his hand at theater, television, and music. He also indulged a romance with boxing that brought him to the Kingsway Gym in Manhattan. Alexander Newbold, who trained both Butler and Kellerman there, made a policy of encouraging his fighters to get to know each other, and the two young men from different backgrounds became friends. Butler was staying with Kellerman in his apartment in Los Angeles when Kellerman was killed—bludgeoned to death from behind while sitting at his computer.

Butler turned himself in three days after Kellerman's body was discovered. His alibi sounds flimsy, and of course he can't make bail. If convicted, he's looking at 25 years to life. Unless the public defender assigned to Butler's case can prove he's mentally incompetent, they're going to put him *under* the jail, as my high-school social studies teacher used to say.

The story's not even recent news. Kellerman was murdered in October of 2004; Butler has been in jail for the past year. Jury selection in the case begins next week. That's the occasion for the long, well-written story in the *Times*. (Yes, "grimy" shows up in the opening sentence, so that's one beer you have to chug right there, but you're going to be disappointed if you're counting on this story to get you and your friends drunk.) And yet the story's not at all stale; in fact, if I reread it in six weeks or six months or six years it will still be fresher than the previous day's nonboxing sports news.

Why? Certainly not because of the story's novelty. It's a familiar #3-type story: hard-knocks guy trying to find his way to a better life meets well-insulated guy attracted to lowlife, hard knocks lead to harder knocks, things end badly. Of course, Butler's not typical, since most fighters don't suffer from psychiatric disorders, or kill people. Most of them just have an appetite for hitting, and that appetite finds expression even if they are raised by middle-class sweethearts far from the street life. The lurid freakishness of stories like Butler's helps attract the attention of editors and reporters, but it's a mistake to regard that freakishness as pervading the fight world. Nor is freakishness the secret ingredient that keeps a boxing story fresh. To the contrary, the freakish aspect of a boxing story can go stale, just as Mike Tyson's volatility or Oscar De La Hoya's cuteness can go stale. Tyson and De La Hoya are boxers (I use the term loosely in Tyson's case, at this point) so famous that, as commentators like to say, they "transcend boxing," which means that they're sort of like other famous athletes: news about them seems very fresh, then not so fresh, and the change happens fast.

No, what's eternally fresh about the story of James Butler lies in the nakedness of its encounter with ultimacy, with what religious people sometimes call "first things." Here's Butler's mother, for instance, talking about raising him: "Maybe I was too strict with him, too stern, I don't know. I wanted my sons to be strong because the world is cruel, it is chaos. If you are weak, you fall. I believe James fell." She sees right through the muscles, the toughness, the punching power, to the cracks in her son's foundation. The brutal penetration of her insight seems all the more potent because it comes from the guy's mother, for God's sake, and not from, say, an opponent's trainer. This kind of thing happens all the time in boxing stories. They're going along describing who did what, and then suddenly somebody's mom is explaining the underlying cruelty of creation, the chaos at the heart of the world.

And Butler's mother does not shirk her own responsibility for his fate. She allows that maybe she was too rough on him, and she knows she hurt him by often choosing nightlife over motherhood. "Ma was hanging out, know what I mean? I don't think James liked that, Ma out partying." Alexander Newbold, the trainer who tried to build camaraderie among his stable of fighters by getting them together outside the gym, also accepts blame. "This is my fault. If it wasn't for me, James would have never met Sam and all of this never would have happened." He's not taking responsibility for a blown defensive assignment or something like that, as upstanding characters in the sports section will occasionally do; he's taking responsibility for life and death.

Compare all this to what's going on in the rest of the sports section. For instance: "Guillermo Ramirez, a reserve player for the Los Angeles Galaxy, entered the M.L.S. cup on Sunday fresh off the most inaccurate shooting season in league history. But with the championship on the line, he did what no one else on the field could do—score." That's sort of dramatic, and there may in fact be a lesson about the subtle clockwork order of the universe hiding in there somewhere, but that lesson isn't in play in the story. The lesson remains so latent that it may not be there at all. Or, to turn from a news story to a profile, here's the father of professional football star Carson Palmer and college football star Jordan Palmer talking about how well things have turned out for Jordan at the University of Texas–El Paso. "Oh my God, my wife and I talk about that all the time. This isn't a place Carson would have wanted to come, but we're so thrilled for Jordan. It was the right place, time, and circumstance." This story might potentially offer a mirror image of the story of James Butler, a fatherless man who was in the wrong place and circumstance at the wrong time, but who cares? Happy quarterbacks, like unhappy receivers, are all the same.

Fight people, a tribe of heroic talkers, are not all the same, but they share a willingness to touch and articulate the ultimacy in their stories in ways that other sports figures usually can't. Reporters expect no less of fight people, and they put those lines in the story. It could be that Guillermo Ramirez sat around the locker room after the MLS championship game talking about his theory of cosmic retribution and karmic balance, but nobody thought it belonged in a story about the Galaxy's victory. But a reporter writing a boxing story, especially a #3-type, would regard as essential a quote from a fighter's mother arguing for the fundamental chaos and cruelty of the universe. So it's not just that fight people can touch the ultimacy in their own stories; the genre demands that they do.

Boxing stories can make every other kind of sports story begin to seem like a mayfly in comparison—insubstantial, weak, and short-lived. Here's Don Turner, a boxing trainer, doing an Alexander Hamilton turn: "I know there's a lot of bad people in boxing. Boxing is like society, and the American public is basically bad people." When was the last time you heard a football coach say anything like that? Turner goes on: "When I was a kid growing up, I never dreamed that this society would come to what it has today. I know that there's always people out there who will try to steal Mike from me"—Michael Grant, an impressive physical specimen who eventually failed to pan out as a heavyweight prospect—"and try to steal from both of us when we stay together. And those people should know what kind of person I am. I live an honorable life. When I'm wrong, I admit it and apologize for what I did. But I'll get in your face if I think you're wrong. And I'll come at you with a baseball bat if you try to take what's mine."

Okay, Turner's speech appeared in a magazine, not a newspaper's sports section, but the point is: that speech will never go stale. I've had it tacked to a bulletin board over my desk for years. Every once in a while I reread it and am reminded that boxing stories, perhaps alone among sports stories, are built to last.

In March 2006, James Butler pleaded guilty to voluntary manslaughter and arson in the death of Sam Kellerman. He was sentenced to twenty-nine years and four months in prison.

Mirror, Mirror

LARRY HOLMES, UNRETIRED ONCE more, had returned to the gym in earnest. Word that he was sparring again went around Easton, Pennsylvania, his hometown and headquarters. He was preparing to fight Brian Nielsen in Denmark for the near-meaningless IBO title; after that, perhaps Holmes and George Foreman would finally settle things between them in the ring. It was October 1996; Holmes, who had been heavyweight champion from 1978 to 1985, would soon be 47 years old.

The watchers were back in the gym, too. Holmes had a crew of paid cornermen and helpers, but a looser circle of informal observers hung around the Larry Holmes Training Center just to see what he was up to. They—we—had been on hiatus during his most recent retirement, but now it was time for the watchers to reconvene.

Cliff, a thick-built, patient man who served as one of Holmes's seconds, was sitting on one of the folding chairs at ringside, waiting for the boss to come out of his locker room. Alan, who dropped in from time to time to videotape sparring sessions for his private collection, was also sitting in a ringside chair, waiting for Holmes. Seemingly engrossed in fiddling with his video camera, Alan said to nobody in particular, "I wonder if this Nielsen is the stiff everybody says he is." After a pause, Cliff looked over at him and said, "Well, he's big, and even if he is European, he *is* undefeated." Having enticed Cliff into a conversation, Alan put down his camera, turned to face him, and

Original publication: *Shadow Boxers*, Stone Creek Publications, 2005.

covetously complimented him on his ball cap, which bore a Larry Holmes logo. Cliff looked over at me, jerked his head at Alan, and said, "If he wants something you got. . . ." Cliff broke off, shaking his head, but he placated Alan by promising to see if he could get him a cap, then explained how to keep it clean: "You just put your caps in the dishwasher, on top with the glasses? Come out beautiful."

Alan and Cliff fell to commiserating about how hard it was to make a living. Alan had to drive all over the state to assemble bagel ovens for ten dollars an hour. Holmes would not provide make-work day jobs for his crew, so Cliff hired out to other fighters, too. Cliff needed to make some extra money to hire a lawyer for a young man in his family who had gotten into trouble. "It was self-defense and all," Cliff said. "He took a boxcutter away from the other guy, one of those big ones, took it away and hurt him. I mean really hurt him." Alan murmured, "Good, good," not getting the point. Cliff gave him a flat, disgusted look. Their conversation petered out.

They turned to watch two gloved-up middleweights, a novice named Russell and a more experienced southpaw, who had climbed into the ring and were walking about with studied aimlessness, waiting for the bell. When it chimed, they began sparring. Russell, a student at a nearby college, poked out his left as a sort of pro forma gesture to set up a heavy straight right, his best punch. His opponent, the southpaw, moved with greater purpose and snapped his jab more decisively than Russell's. They quickly fell into a pattern of sparring: Russell took a jab or two in the face as he came in to throw his one-two, then they fought in close for a while, during which time he forced the southpaw to retreat but took another shot or two for his trouble. Infighting, Russell had a beginner's tendency to duck his head and throw his punches blind. Effort, punishment, and mounting frustration turned Russell's pale face a dark, uneven red.

In the second round, warming to the encounter, they whacked each other more forcefully. A bright worm of blood crawled out of Russell's nose and into his mouth. He followed the southpaw as before, bored in to throw the pawing jab and the hard right as before, took his lumps as before. At one point, wishing to employ his superior strength but unable to land enough punches, Russell jammed both of his forearms in the southpaw's face and drove with his legs, just pushing. The southpaw, his head bent back sharply over the top strand of the ropes, made a high snort of surprise and pain. After that, they traded with increasing wildness, oversize gloves and headgear accentuating the sound of the blows. The third round offered more of the same, with Russell taking three punches to give one. He looked mad, blood smeared over the middle of his face. The southpaw looked mad, too, and embarrassed to have made that odd sound when Russell forced his head back over the top strand.

Just as the bell sounded to end the third round, Holmes and his cornermen came out of his locker room and moved toward the ring. One of them, Charlie, a bald man with broad forearms, made a shooing-away gesture with both hands and called out, "That's enough." The middleweights climbed out through the ropes on the other side. They had wanted to go another round, although there probably would not have been much value in it. They were not really sparring anymore; they were just fighting.

Cliff got up and went over to work the corner of Holmes's sparring partner. Alan got up to film the proceedings. Holmes, hands wrapped, wearing blue sweats and a blue T-shirt with the sleeves cut off to give his thick arms and shoulders room to work, was putting cotton balls in his ears and smearing his face with petroleum jelly. One of his cornermen approached with the gloves. Time to get down to business.

The watchers, too, got down to business. Charlie settled himself outside one corner of the raised ring, Cliff outside another. Saoul Mamby, Holmes's chief second and trainer of record, a resourceful little guy who had held the WBC super lightweight title back when Holmes was heavyweight champion, took a third corner. A dapper fellow named Ben, whose official job title was "driver" and whose duties included playing an endless checkers tournament with Holmes during downtime, took the fourth. They all struck intent poses—arms crossed and frowning, or one foot up on the ring steps, elbow on raised knee, chin on palm—as their boss circled in the ring, jabbing from time to time and smothering his sparring partner's hooks. The cornermen had spent cumulative weeks, months of their lives watching Holmes hit and not get hit; they were as good at watching him do it as he was at doing it.

———

Wherever fighters train, watchers gather, observing in silence the familiar, repetitive routines of the gym. Some just hang out on their own time, like dissolute railbirds in a pool hall, but watching in the gym is also an important element of what cornermen, matchmakers, gamblers, and reporters *do*. It can be a profession, not just a form of idling.

Holmes, famously thrifty, only needed his cornermen for a couple of hours a day, so he did not pay them a living wage. But he did pay them something for their time, and there was not much for them to do other than watch. Their gym duties were minimal: wrap his hands, give him water or Vaseline or the bucket when he needed it, hold the mitts while he banged them, rub down his shoulders and arms to keep him loose. It made Holmes feel good, of course, to have attendants, competent men alert to his welfare and demands, an articulate living shell that smoothed his passage through the world and reminded him of his importance. But he did not need much encouragement—an occasional "That's it, champ" or "Be first!" would do—and he certainly did not need their advice on how to box. He had been fighting for most of his life, often against the most potent big men in the world, and his style was not going to change. No matter who the other guy was, Holmes would jab and throw looping rights off the jab, blocking and slipping return punches or scuttling them with well-timed jabs. He did not need anybody to remind him to stick and move and entangle incoming punches in his long arms, banging his opponent's biceps with his elbows when he did.

It had been a long time since Holmes heeded the independent opinion of a cornerman. When he fought Gerry Cooney, for instance, on a hot June night in Las Vegas back in 1982, he had made it clear to his distinguished corner that all he wanted was basic service. "Just keep me cool," he told Eddie Futch and Ray Arcel, two of the wisest and most respected trainers around. Holmes was 32 then, and he already had a long fighting history: scrapping informally in his teens until he learned the fundamentals of boxing from a gentle retired fighter; absorbing more advanced lessons in craft while serving as sparring partner for Muhammad Ali, Joe Frazier, and Earnie Shavers; fighting up through an especially deep and dangerous division during the heavyweight golden age of the 1970s; beating Shavers, Ken Norton, Ali, and everybody else in his way; defending his title eleven times. When he fought Cooney, in a bout that stirred popular passions and was then the most lucrative of all time, he ignored Futch's tactical advice between rounds. When Arcel tried to give him smelling salts, Holmes ordered Futch to keep that crazy old man away from him. What Holmes wanted from the pair of sages in his corner—who between them had 152 years of exquisitely tempered experience on this violent planet—was ice, water, damage control (although Holmes rarely suffered cuts), and to stay the hell out of his way while he fought his fight.

That's all he wanted from his corner now. At 46 and counting, Holmes had grown old in ring-time. Having saved and invested his purses, he was financially independent of any promoter or backer, and he saw no reason to shell out for a big-name trainer. He had Saoul Mamby, but, tricky as Mamby had been as a boxer, he was no professional trainer. Holmes had Cliff and Charlie, too, and Ben, but in essence he trained himself. Mostly, they watched him do it. What, besides an employee's expression of fealty to his employer, was that good for? What practical utility was there in Holmes's cornermen watching him train?

The answer, I think, is that they served as projections of Holmes, whose classical boxing style and sheer working drive suffused the gym and anybody who spent time in it. Watching him day after day over the years, his intimates had absorbed his moves, his priorities, his instincts; they had learned to know boxing as he knew it, to see it as he saw it. So if Cliff or Charlie told the boss that he was spending too much time with his back to the ropes in a sparring session, the cornerman served as the vehicle by which Holmes, in effect, reminded himself to stay in the middle of the ring to take best advantage of his long jab and elegant footwork. The cornerman was not really offering his own opinion—rather, his eyes were Holmes's, extended from the fighter's body on invisible stalks so that Holmes could observe himself, comparing his own performance on any given day to a composite ideal he had assembled over the years by watching himself train and fight through his cornermen's eyes. As instruments of Holmes's vigilant attention to himself, the cornermen were, in that sense, like the mirrors that line one wall of Holmes's gym, reflecting back to him not only his technical acumen but also the more intangible qualities of will and resolve that add up to a fighting self. In addition to running, hitting the bags, and sparring, Holmes readied himself for a fight by looking in the mirror provided by his corner.

Even the gym's greenest novices, to the extent they absorbed and reflected back Holmesian principles, could help the master prepare himself. Once, at the end of an afternoon training session, as the last fighters packed up and left, Russell found himself standing next to Holmes, who turned to him and said, "How's my jab look to you? Still strong? I still got it?" The short answer was *Yes*. The long answer was *Yes, your form is still perfect and it's still an all-time great jab, but you don't throw it with the speed you once had, and you throw it many fewer times per round than you used to, and sometimes you don't react in time to an opportunity to throw it.* Russell gave him the short answer.

If Holmes did not think Futch and Arcel had anything to teach him back when he was 32—and since then he had accumulated a decade and a half of additional experience—then he could not expect a college boy with exactly one amateur fight to his credit to offer a useful critique of his jab. So what was Holmes saying? Maybe it was *I know I'm old, but I think I have enough left to win one more title. You've been around the gym, you've seen me train, you know my style and you've seen the top heavyweights out there. You know I can do it if things break my way.* Or maybe Holmes was saying *Are you paying attention and learning anything while you're here? This is the best jab you'll ever be this close to. Study it.* Or maybe he was just saying *Mirror, mirror. . . .*

———

Mirror, mirror . . . works the other way, too: a gym's most celebrated fighter also serves as its most polished reflecting surface. The lesser fighters who trained next to and against Holmes, keeping an eye on him even when they jumped rope or ran on the treadmill, made him a mirror in which they could see their ideal selves in action. They looked to his example, the best available embodiment of fistic virtue, when they wanted to imagine themselves mastering technique, achieving more perfect discipline, moving more confidently in a world of hurt. *When I'm better at that,* the lesser fighter could say to himself, *I'll be more like Larry, but I'll still be the same me I see in the mirror every day.*

Sometimes the pressure of a fight can force this mostly unconscious internal monologue into plain view. Take, for instance, the matter of Holmes's jump jab, an esoteric move that turns up tellingly in the repertoires of other boxers who train at his gym. Throwing a jump jab, Holmes leaves his feet entirely, in profile to his opponent, legs together and torso bent toward the target as he snaps a hard punch from the shoulder. There is no leg drive, so it is not a crushing blow, and it is riskier than throwing a regular jab, since he takes longer to return to defensive posture, but the very confidence of the move tends to dishearten the other guy. The jump jab says *I'm flying, my arm is a thunderbolt, here I come from the sky.* Holmes only uses it when he is deep in the rhythm of a round, usually in a training session, occasionally in an actual fight, and he rarely uses it in more than one round. Its appearance indicates that he feels himself to have established command, that he can land a punch whenever he wants. Suddenly it seems to the opponent that no matter what he tries to do, he finds himself walking into yet another perfectly timed and aimed blow. Holmes does not give in to exuberance and overuse the jump jab; having thrown two or three to show he is in charge, he puts the move away in his toolbox and gets back to throwing regular jabs and one-twos.

The sense of command implicit in Holmes's jump jab is so strong that it rubs off on other fighters, who take it with them when they leave the gym. Once I saw Richie Lovell, the son of Holmes's business manager at the time, land a series of recognizably Holmesian jump jabs in the second round of a four-round bout with a squat, hirsute guy named Eduardo Rolon. Lovell had been emulating Holmes in fine style, nullifying Rolon's uncomplicated attack with footwork and parries, jabbing, crossing off the jab, circling and moving. Holmes, the master and model himself, yelled instructions from his ringside seat.

Lovell threw the jump jabs in the second round, as if to celebrate the fact that he was boxing so well and to place a stylistic bow atop his imminent victory, but then, curiously, all the fight seemed to drain out of him. He began acting as if, having already won the bout, he would be satisfied to just get through the mere formality of the rest of it. He spent the third and fourth rounds moving more and fighting less, eventually abandoning offense altogether and just bouncing off the ropes to clinch. Rolon, fighting in his hometown, kept moving forward and punching, and the judges awarded him a victory by split decision. Lovell deserved no worse than a draw, but he could not complain: he had made possible the bad decision by fighting so poorly in the last two rounds.

Lovell forgot, or never learned, that the jump jab and the mastery associated with it are two separate things that only appeared to be inseparable when he watched Holmes throw the punch. Holmes concludes that he is in command when he sees that his opponent has been worn down by an accrued beating—outboxed and frustrated, yes, but also tired, addled, and hurt, and therefore unlikely to produce a late-round surge. Lovell had not *beaten* his man—he had just boxed better—so Rolon still had the wherewithal to exhibit just enough sustained aggression to give two judges an excuse to award him the fight.

Now, Art Baylis, one of Holmes's sparring partners, had watched Holmes throw jump jabs at other men, as Lovell had, but Baylis had also been hit by Holmes with enough jump jabs in the gym over the years to inscribe the move's import on his very flesh and bones. Once I saw Baylis throw a couple of jump jabs of his own in a fight, seemingly out of sheer joy, just at the moment when it became plain to all that he was going to win. Baylis, a small heavyweight who also fought as a cruiserweight, appeared to swell with power when he threw the jump jabs, as if expanding to conform to the ideal embodied by his boss. His opponent seemed to shrivel up, acquiescing. Holmes, watching from ringside, nodded and smiled, like a man pleased with what he sees in the mirror.

The Prospect

ON THE EVENING OF June 10, 2006, an hour and a half before making his debut as a professional heavyweight, a ruggedly built young man named Tom Zbikowski sat on a reversed folding chair in a dressing room in Madison Square Garden, having his hands wrapped. Sam Colonna, who had trained the 21-year-old Zbikowski since he was thirteen, sat on another folding chair facing him, doing the job with unhurried care. The gauze bandage, the tape, the pad over the fingers but not the knuckles, more tape over and under and around, a standardized and regulated routine that every practitioner does just a bit differently. Two blue-blazered officials from the New York State Athletic Commission stood over Colonna, watching him work with the theatrically intent look of boxing officials everywhere.

Like most of the fight world's habits, hand wrapping is both practical and ritual. Done properly, it protects the hands from damage without giving a fighter an unfair advantage. Like boxing gloves or a football helmet, wrapping functions as both armor and sword, a protective measure that allows you to hit harder and more frequently than you could without it. One of the officials murmured, "That's beautiful." Colonna said "Thank you" without looking up from his work.

Boxers all over the world wait out the last anxious stretch before a fight in rooms like this: pale green cinder block walls, gray floor, a drop ceiling with fluorescent lights, some folding chairs and a folding table. Through a metal door there was a cramped bathroom with a shower that nobody ever used and a toilet that altogether too many people had used.

Men, most of them large, crowded the dressing room. In addition to Zbikowski, Colonna, and the officials, there was Zbikowski's other longtime trainer, Danny Nieves, and his flexibility trainer, his lawyer, his father, his brother, his neighbor, his roommate, a half-dozen middle-aged tough guys with various connections to his family, and Angelo Dundee, a grand old man of 82 best known for having trained Muhammad Ali. Dundee lent his largely decorative presence to Zbikowski's corner to mark him as a young fighter worth watching.

Zbikowski was making his debut on pay-per-view TV and in the Garden, rather than in the ballroom of a chain hotel somewhere, because he played football for Notre Dame. He was a captain and star of the team, a playmaking safety who specialized in getting his hands on the ball one way or another—intercepting a pass, mugging an opposing ball carrier, delivering a teeth-loosening third-down hit that forced the other team to punt (he also returned punts)—and then taking it back the other way, shedding the tacklers he didn't outrun. He had just completed his junior year, in which he was named a third-team All-America, and fans and expert observers alike expected big things of him and the Fighting Irish in the fall, after which they expected to see him drafted sometime in the first three rounds by an NFL team. He was not the biggest or the fastest safety in the nation, but knowing that he could beat the hell out of everybody else on the field gave him a quality of sheer physical command that mere players of ball games can rarely match.

Novelty acts have on occasion fleetingly crossed over from football to boxing, some football players incorporate boxing routines into their fitness regimens, and a couple of NFL players have had actual boxing careers after retiring from football, but this was different. Zbikowski, a boxer who played football, had his first official amateur fight when he was nine years old, weighing in at eighty pounds, and he ran up an amateur record of 68–13. Boxing had made him better at football, but football had kept him from devoting himself fully to boxing. Now the NCAA had cleared him to fight professionally, with certain restrictions on publicity, while retaining his eligibility as an amateur. He had a three-fight deal with Bob Arum, a leading promoter, and he hoped to fight again in February—ideally, about six weeks after he ran back a punt to win the national championship game.

It would be most unfortunate, then, for him to get knocked on his ass in his debut that night.

The referee, Arthur Mercante Jr. came in to give prefight instructions. He said, "Your first pro fight, right? Things are a little different up here." Zbikowski nodded. Amateur boxing may be a lot rougher than other sports, including football, but compared to pro boxing it's a full-contact form of tag, like fencing in comparison to a real swordfight. Pros have more opportunity to take their encounter to its logical conclusion. They fight more and longer rounds, referees let more damage accrue before stepping in, fair judges reward punches that hurt rather than those that merely land, and pros do not wear the amateur's protective headgear. Less padding, literal and figurative, shields a pro from life-changing doses of elemental force. Then there's the primacy of money—purses, promoters' self-interest, TV profits. Money can protect a fighter, but it can also deposit a near-naked man in the path of serious harm.

After Zbikowski peed in a cup and handed it to the official who watched him do it, his flexibility trainer fastened a white belt around Zbikowski's middle, just above the hips. Wires connected the belt to a car-stereo-sized machine that sent electrical impulses deep into the fighter's thick torso. He was carrying a lot of football muscle, which looks impressive but can get in the way of efficient fighting, so he had to take extra care to stay flexible, a cardinal boxing virtue. The trainer stood behind Zbikowski, put his hands on his shoulders, and pushed to twist his trunk, gently but firmly, much farther around than you'd expect a serious weight lifter to be able to go.

Zbikowski resembled a tight-wound mechanism receiving the final increments of tension. The winding-up had gone on for the better part of eight weeks, ever since the end of spring football practices. Zbikowski had sparred 150 rounds during an intensive stretch of training, some of it in Florida under Dundee's supervision, more appropriate for a title fight than a four-round debut. The final week, in New York, had been a grind of open workouts, press conferences, photo ops, medical tests, and waiting around, all the while making sure to eat right and get plenty of rest. Zbikowski was not a big talker and not happy to sit around doing nothing, and he had to put up with altogether too much of both. It would be a relief to get in the ring and do something to somebody.

———

Eight weeks before fight night, on a bright, warm Saturday in April, over 41,000 people, many of them wearing jerseys bearing Tom Zbikowski's number 9, showed up to watch Notre Dame's football team play its annual spring scrimmage, the Blue and Gold Game.

Notre Dame's football prospects appeared to be on the rise again after a long stretch of disappointment that had been hard on its fans, who only pretend to accept that the Fighting Irish can't win every game and that other teams may actually be better than theirs. Other teams might *play* better on a given day, but they're not, you know, *better*. After all, as Jerome Bettis and other distinguished returning alumni would say at the postgame press conference, Notre Dame football is *special*.

Up in the stands, Eddie and Sue Zbikowski watched the youngest of their three children play ball. Eddie, a barrel-chested extrovert with close-cropped white hair, squinted into the sun and talked about "all this," by which he meant not just Tom's nimbus of heroic promise but also the glow of good fortune and accomplishment that came with having a son at Notre Dame and, more generally, with having achieved a suburban middle-class life, "with the bermuda shorts, the barbecues, the whole thing." *All this* seemed like a kind of Valhalla to Eddie, who played with relish the role of an old scrapper from Chicago's West Side. "Where I grew up," he said in the clipped accent of white-ethnic Chicago, "usually when we'd say our friends were in college we didn't mean they were at Notre Dame." They were in the joint, he meant. He spun tales of Outfit guys he grew up with, of beatings, shootings, a bloody-knuckled regular-guy golden age receding into myth. Sue, a petite woman in an oversize white number 9 jersey, leaned over to say, "Don't encourage him. He'll go on like this all day. I call him the Embellisher."

Tom's passion for boxing, said Eddie, took them from the suburbs to the West Side in search of good trainers and opponents in Chicago Park District gyms and on the Catholic Youth Organization circuit. These were surviving remnants of the neighborhood network in which young men of Eddie's and previous generations learned the manly art. Eddie said, "I said, 'Tommy, please, don't make me go back to the city,' but Tommy learned a lot from the other kids—their problems, their toughness. It made him a man fast. He learned not to be a bully, not like these rich kids in the suburbs who think they're tough and don't know what it is."

On the field, Tom patrolled the middle, looking to hit somebody, but the offense seemed to be avoiding him, denying him a chance to make a big play. A waterbug of a running back juked past him; a few plays later, Tom found him near the sideline and squashed him.

After the game, after Tom had said suitably captain-ish things for the reporters who collected around him, and after he had smiled and signed his way through the mob of kids waiting outside the stadium's gates, he put on a Chicago Police ball cap and crossed the emptying parking lots to a stretch of grass near the stadium where the players' families were having a cookout. A couple of hundred people—current and former players, awed-looking high school recruits, parents, siblings—milled around in the late afternoon sun, drinking beer and pop, eating burgers and the extra-tender Italian beef hauled down from Chicago by the Zbikowskis.

In the air here, in addition to the smell of burning meat, was the specialness of Notre Dame and its football tradition, the jacks-or-better sense of sitting pretty. The well-established middle-class families take *all this* as their due, and those from working-class backgrounds can feel the upward trajectory delivering them to the good life. Tucked within the multiple cushions of middle-classness, Notre Dame, and the sports elite, they can't help but feel secure, and they let it show. At Ivy League schools, you're supposed to act like it's no big deal to be there, but Notre Dame families don't affect to hide their satisfaction at having made it to South Bend, and that goes double for football.

Mike Joyce, the lawyer from Chicago who handled Tom's boxing business, stood off to one side with a beer in his hand, a raven at the picnic. He was telling a typical boxing story about a promoter stealing purse money from a fighter on the eve of a major bout. The promoter had a reputation in the fight world as a pretty good guy, not a monster, but hey, he saw an opening and he took it. Promoters, officials, managers—almost everybody in the fight world except the fighters—go around with stingers on the ends of their tails, and every once in a while they just have to sting somebody; not because they're evil, but because that's what they do.

Joyce, who also ran political campaigns, had to do business with such people to launch Tom's boxing career, while also protecting his charge and taking care not to interfere with his football career. So far, so good: Tom would make $25,000 for a four-round bout, slotted in a choice spot just before the main event, Cotto-Malignaggi, on a pay-per-view card. "If Tommy wasn't making his debut on TV," said Joyce, "I'd put him in the sticks in Indiana somewhere, just to break his cherry, and put him in with a complete stiff. But you can't do that on TV, in the Garden. Everybody would say, 'Look at the pampered Notre Dame kid.'" Bob Arum's matchmaker needed to come up with an opponent who at least appeared to be able to fight a little, but without overmatching Tom. It was one more thing to worry about.

Anybody who genuinely cares about a fighter worries all the time.

Sure, other athletes can blow a bright future by performing poorly, and any athlete can get hurt; as Tom often pointed out, football offers many opportunities to get hurt, with so many highly motivated big men flying around on every play, slamming into each other's ankles and knees and hips. But in the fight world, they'll hurt you on purpose. Fighters do it in the ring to win fights, and fight people do it outside the ring for profit, or just because they've got that stinger and can't help noticing that your sleeping bag is unzipped.

Joyce believed, though, that he could shelter Tom from business as usual in boxing. "He's got good people around him, a rock-solid family, protection. And he's white, and there's the Notre Dame thing," which meant not only that alumni would support him but that casual sports fans and the major-sport media apparatus would be interested in him, making for more pay-per-view buys and bigger gates, all making him worth more to promoters, who would therefore protect their investment with greater care. "And if he's in the NFL first, too, that's more interest in him. The business will come to him. He can dictate terms to it. I'm already getting requests from big-name companies for endorsements," which of course NCAA rules precluded him from acting on. Maybe Tom was sufficiently insulated by race, by class, by football and the association with Notre Dame. Maybe he was just too special.

———

With less than an hour to go before his bout, Zbikowksi started shadowboxing at half speed in his dressing room. He was wearing white boxing shoes with no socks, shiny white shorts with a gold number 9 in a blue shamrock on one leg, and a T-shirt bearing a Polish eagle and the legend STO LAT, which means "a hundred years" and translates roughly as *Good luck*.

Lance Armstrong, who had been invited to visit, came in with his manager in tow. Zbikowski, emerging slightly from his darkening prefight mood, smiled with one corner of his mouth and interrupted his half-speed moving and feinting to say, "Hey, you're the guy from *Dodgeball*." After an exchange of pleasantries and an obligatory dukes-up photo op, he went back to work. One of the other fistic characters made an egregiously off-color remark about the availability of Sheryl Crow, Armstrong's former girlfriend. Armstrong took it all in stride. He seemed excited; he was the celebrity in the room, but he'd never been to the fights before.

Word came in from the hall that Kevin Kelley, an old favorite at the Garden who was in the deep twilight of his career, had just been KO'd with a liver shot. Only one more fight to go. A functionary came in with Zbikowski's boxing gloves, custom jobs in Notre Dame gold. Colonna and Nieves put them on their fighter under the scrutiny of the blue-blazered officials.

A hush fell over the dressing room. Time for Zbikowski to break his prefight sweat. The other men moved closer to the walls to give him more space to work. Danny Nieves put on padded mitts and Zbikowski started banging them. He threw a combination, slipped the counterpunches that Nieves sketched with the mitts, then stepped to the side and popped the mitts with another combination, a complicated, liquid sequence. Nieves said, "Put a hole in him." Zbikowski paced between bursts of punching.

The pacing brought him close to Armstrong, who extended his cupped bare hand palm-down in imitation of Nieves with the mitts and said, "Let's see it." Before the words were even out of his mouth, Zbikowski set his feet, pivoted, and whipped an uppercut into the hand with a loud gloved smack. See the target, hit the target, kill the target. It happened much faster than Armstrong expected. He made a big deal of shouting, "Wow!" and cradling the smacked hand, making everybody laugh, but something else moved beneath the comedy, as if he had dangled a hunk of meat into a tiger's cage and been startled by how murderously the big cat took it.

Zbikowski went back to banging the pads. Nieves said, soothingly, "Blind him and cut him with the jab." Pacing, Zbikowski took deep breaths, feeling himself growing tighter. Having played football on national TV, he'd had plenty of experience in trying to relax under pressure, but, as he had said earlier, "It's not the same thing. When it's just you, it's different. And it's not like a fight in a bar, when it happens all at once. Knowing the night before that you're going to fight. Waking up, knowing it. It's just you, and it's different."

Somebody said, "Got everything?" Nieves said, "I got the mouthpiece and the rosary. That's all we need."

Eddie Zbikowski said, "You don't need me, right?" Tom nodded. Eddie kissed his son on the cheek and left to find his seat. Other nonessential personnel followed. Soon only the cornermen—Colonna, Nieves, and Dundee—and the officials were left. One of the officials handed out clear latex gloves for the cornermen to wear during the fight.

Word came that the bout immediately before Zbikowski's had

ended, another knockout. The crowd noise filtered in through the cinder block walls, louder when somebody opened the door.

Colonna smeared petroleum jelly over Zbikowski's upper body and face, then Nieves put a shiny hooded white robe on him. The cornermen wore matching jackets. Angelo Dundee had a folded towel over one shoulder. How many hundreds, thousands of times had he done this? How many of his prospects had panned out? How many had disappeared into the half-world of marked-up guys who used to be pretty good with their hands?

Word came from the hallway that it was time for Zbikowski to make his ring walk. He went out the door into the narrow hallway, which was lined with a couple dozen of his clapping, shouting football teammates, who had come to New York to support him. He went out through the crowd to the ring, where the gospel singer Bebe Winans was singing a sly rendition of the Notre Dame fight song. In this setting, the rah-rah tune sounded precious, rather than inspiring. Zbikowski had argued for not using it as his ring walk music, but he had lost that argument to the promoter's marketing people, who saw it as an opportunity to brand a potential moneymaker.

———

Ideally, you insulate a promising fighter with sound training, good management, and people who care about him, and you bring him along by peeling back the insulation bit by bit in settings as controlled as you can make them, exposing him to a wider and deeper assortment of hard knocks. You gradually introduce him to better sparring partners and opponents, a broadening variety of fistic problems: booming punchers, tricky technicians, southpaws, tall guys, short guys, granite-headed hardcases. You start him out in four-rounders, and, if all goes well, work up to ten and then twelve rounds, the championship distance.

You want each new test to make him a little more capable, rather than doing harm to his body or his fighting spirit. If he's going to be confounded, you want it to happen in the gym. In a bout, with only the relatively thin cushion of the referee and the rules to protect him, anything can happen: a watershed beating, a blot on his record, a permanent crack in the foundation of his self-confidence. The possibilities for life-changing catastrophe seem nearly limitless. So, since you can't kidproof the world, you do your best to worldproof the kid.

"Angel Manfredy caught me with a body shot when I was thirteen or fourteen, the worst I ever felt," said Tom Zbikowski. "That was right around when he beat Gatti." One body shot from an accomplished professional, delivered in the gym under the right conditions, can teach a kid a great deal about boxing and about himself. The same shot in the ring could wreck him for good.

Zbikowski was talking about it while tucking into a plate of pasta and meat, drinking only water, in a restaurant in Fort Lauderdale. It was late May, two and a half weeks before fight night, and he was in town to train under Angelo Dundee. He wanted to keep his weight up around 215 for the fight, so he needed to eat at least 5,000 calories per day to keep from being whittled down to a stick figure by a daily triathlon of training. In the mornings, he sparred at a boxing gym; in the afternoons, he did speed workouts at a boutique gym, sets of jumps and lunges against resistance to build explosive quickness for football; at night, he worked out in a weight room, but not *every* night. After all, he didn't want to overdo it. During the leftover portions of his day, he made appearances at charity events, ate, and slept whenever possible.

Zbikowski was training for two careers, not just a four-round fight. But he only had one body, which at 5–11 was considered smallish for a pro safety and very small for a contemporary heavyweight boxer, and the two kinds of training had different objectives. Football requires bulk, agility, and strength expressed in furious all-out bursts lasting only a few seconds. For boxing, he should squeeze his power into the smallest possible package, emphasizing supple quickness and the endurance to sustain a high workrate for three-minute stretches. His prime fighting weight looked to be no more than 195, which would make him a cruiserweight (and he could possibly make 175 and fight as a light-heavy), but there was much more money to be made as a heavyweight, so the extra football beef wasn't entirely dead weight.

The difference between boxing and football goes much deeper than physical demands, of course. The fight world is a loosely regulated Hobbesian scramble for the money, each against all. Football, closely managed at every level by legitimate governing bodies, is almost Confucian in its systematized order. "With football, it's a process," said Zbikowski. "High school, college, pro, you get evaluated at each level and move up." They time you in the forty and fractions thereof, measure your body fat, grade your decision making, crunch your statistics, and out pops a rating. If it's high enough, you move up to the next level, like a civil service job. "There are still a lot of busts, a lot of things can happen, but there's more of a process. And if you're not in the NFL you can go to Europe or the Arena League." Nothing's ever 100 percent sure when anterior cruciate ligaments, teammates, and a bouncing oblate spheroid are involved, but football offers a much more certain future than boxing.

"I'll try the NFL first," he said. "If it doesn't work out, I'll box. I set myself up pretty good by getting an education, but I'm not saying, 'If I fail, here's my backup plan.' I got a lot of drive to box." It was unlikely that an NFL team would allow him to fight in the off-season, but he wanted to find one that would. Off-season boxing would keep him in terrific shape, he pointed out, and it's not as unhealthy as night-clubbing, riding a motorcycle, or playing football, for that matter. (Mike Joyce's preferred scenario went like this: "The average NFL career is, like, three years. Say he goes double that. If his team lets him fight a couple times a year"—a very big *if*—"I could have him maybe 12–0, 15–0, when he retires. He'll be twenty-eight, twenty-nine, in his prime; I could have him in line for a title in two or three fights.")

While Tom plowed through the calories, the two older men across the table, his father and a broken-nosed orthopedic surgeon named Hackie Reitman, tossed off drinks and animatedly discussed Tom's appointment with destiny. The Reitmans and Zbikowskis met at the Mayo Clinic many years before, when Hackie's daughter and Tom's older brother, E. J., underwent treatment for cancer. Both kids made it, and as the friendship between the families grew, Hackie's taste for boxing rubbed off on Tom, a little boy already looking to test himself. Hackie agreed with Eddie that Tom had been marked for greatness. They understood his talents to be a gift to the world, not just to Tom, and insisted that he make time for charity work no matter how busy he got.

The older men wouldn't settle for anything less than greatness on any score, including service to others. To that end, and because Eddie thought that Tom should have another layer of career insurance, Tom would be flying to Chicago the next day to take the firefighters exam. Eddie saw even this possible future in heroic terms. "If he pulls people from burning buildings, after being captain of the Notre Dame football team and fighting in the Garden, I'll be happy with that." Tom, a matter-of-fact fellow with an uncomplicated inner life who mostly just likes to do things that scratch his inbuilt itch for bruising, received this grand pronouncement without comment or change of expression. A few minutes later, though, when Eddie became distracted by a couple of swag-bellied gents from Chicago who stopped by the table to reminisce about Outfit guys and the old neighborhood,

Tom said, "I hear the test's not that hard. They say you need to bring a pencil, but not an eraser."

———————

When Tom Zbikowski got to the ring on fight night his opponent, Robert "The Disciple" Bell, was waiting for him. Taller and heavier than Zbikowski, but nowhere near as fit, Bell was a self-assured guy from Akron, Ohio, with a knockaround curriculum vitae—soldier, bouncer, bodyguard, martial arts, toughman competitions—but no particular gift for boxing. He was officially only 2–2 as a pro at the age of 32, and all his fights, losses as well as wins, had ended in knockouts. He could perhaps hit some, but he could be hit and hurt by someone who knew how. The matchmaker had done his job.

For $3,000 and a chance to fight in the Garden and on TV, Bell played the role of villain, even wearing an Ohio State jersey to stir up Notre Dame fans still smarting from the previous year's drubbing by the Buckeyes. "I'm in it to make money," he said a few days before the fight. "I may not ever get a world title from boxing, but I may get the titles to some nice cars. In the boxing game, if you're not a big prospect then you're pretty much on your own," and he thought he was doing all right for a guy on his own.

Bell understood his subordinate place in this drama, but the fight's outcome was not foreordained. It happens often enough that the knockaround guy with no future and nobody special in his corner gets the best of the prospect with the big-name trainer in his corner and the multi-fight deal with a major promoter. Plenty of bright futures have clouded over when the bell rings. In such cases, fight people say that the prospect was *exposed*, meaning not only that his flaws were revealed but also that his handlers miscalculated, exposing him to naked force in a quantity or from an angle that he was not ready to handle. It happens more frequently that the prospect wins, but looks bad doing it. Usually, he's overeager and botches the job by rushing in headlong, spoiling his own leverage and timing in his haste to impress. The judges award him the decision anyway, but he and his supporters go away relieved rather than satisifed.

This time, however, the prospect did everything exactly right; when the bell rang, the tightly wound mechanism unwound with startling force and precision. Zbikowski jarred Bell with his left jab, taking his measure. Bell, for his part, overloaded his leverage to favor his right hand, with which he had little chance of hitting Zbikowski.

Bell missed twice with ponderous rights, ate Zbikowski's jab in return, and then tried the same right again, one time too many.

Zbikowski countered swiftly and decisively with a left hook to the body and another to the chin that badly hurt Bell, who instantly assumed an oddly inappropriate look of raptness, as if he had suddenly become aware of a fugitive strain of music threaded under the surging crowd noise and had stopped fighting in order to attend to it. This happens, sometimes, in the pregnant moment after a punch hurts a fighter badly enough to render him defenseless. His opponent, now punching at will, seems to accelerate to triple-time as the fighter in trouble lapses into undersea slow-motion.

Zbikowski kept punching until Bell subsided to one knee. Bell shook his head to clear it and rose at the count of six. Zbikowski walked across the ring from the neutral corner with an air of suppressed impatience and hit Bell with a single straight right that spun him around and sent him to the ropes in a bent-forward posture of open submission. The referee leaped between them to stop the fight, which had lasted just 49 seconds.

Zbikowski raised his gloved fists high as his teammates at ringside gave a deep-voiced exultant shout. The other 14,000-plus in attendance made noise, too. Bell stood blearily by the ropes, one glove on the top strand to steady himself, looking as if he couldn't hear the secret music anymore and was waiting for the world to stop spinning so fast. Like a guy who's too drunk and has been too drunk before, he knew that, as awful as he felt right then, he would feel bad only for a while; eventually, he would feel almost entirely well again.

The prospect's debut had been a success. If the opponent did not pose much of a test, the occasion did, and Zbikowski had aced it. After he got through with the postfight press conference, collected his check, and enjoyed a rollicking victory party at a bar across the street from the Empire State Building, he would go home, rest up for a week, and switch to football. Boxing would recede to the margins of his life for at least the next seven months, but he hoped to squeeze in a fight or two between the end of the season and the predraft combines. He also had a college degree to finish up, with a double major in sociology and computer applications, and he was waiting to hear how he did on the firefighters exam. Possibilities extended around him in all directions, although he was only interested in those that led to hitting.

Something in him craved the shock of contact. He wanted to know what he could do, what he could take, *who* he could take. Football and the cushion of the middle-class life his parents had made for their kids might yet keep him from finding out how good a fighter he could be, or it might work the other way: if he went deep enough into the fights to realize his true potential, he risked foreclosing his other options. The fight world has ruined promising and well-protected young men before. But, if everything broke just right, he might yet have the chance to take both football and boxing to the end of the line, where his talent and preparation would come up against the limits imposed by nature and other men's ability. That was where he wanted to go.

He wouldn't go any farther that night. As soon as the bout ended, the ring filled up with cornermen, handlers, friends, family, officials, TV types, and others, a living buffer of bodies pressing around him, faces alive with passion, voices telling him how special he was. His cornermen were cutting off his gloves.

As of this writing, in December 2011, Tom Zbikowski was in his fourth year as a safety and special teams player with the Baltimore Ravens. His professional boxing record stayed at 1–0 until the NFL lockout in the spring of 2011, which gave him an opportunity to fight again. Leaner but rusty, he quickly recorded three victories. Two were first-round TKOs, but he struggled in a decision over Caleb Grummet, a journeyman and MMA fighter who could take a punch. "My biggest worry," Mike Joyce told me, "is he has to get back to boxing basics, fundamentals, everything off the jab, not slugging. Guys aren't gonna always go down." Trying to destroy Grummet with one shot, Zbikowski punched himself out and became so exhausted that he nearly failed to last to the end of the four-rounder. "The aggressiveness," said Joyce, "some of it is football. He's playing with guys who weigh 325 pounds, so a heavyweight who's only 225 seems like he's not that big." But good defensive football logic—get there as fast as you can and put everything you've got into one decisive shot—makes poor offensive ring logic. Boxers must pace themselves through three-minute rounds, not six-second plays, and there are plenty of fighters with mediocre records, professional opponents who will never be regarded as special by any fan or promoter but who have been exposed to all kinds of advanced punishment, who can take Zbikowski's best shots and still keep giving him that hard little smile that says, "Nice one, pal, but that took more out of you than it did out of me."

The Biggest Entertainer
in Entertainment

FLOYD MAYWEATHER JR., THE welterweight widely regarded as pound for pound the best boxer in the world, is about as rich and famous as a 147-pound fighter can get these days. People who don't know anything about boxing beyond Mike Tyson and Muhammad Ali recognize him on the street (*Who's that little guy with all the bodyguards?*), although sometimes it takes an extra second or two. (*It's that boxer who was on "Dancing with the Stars."*) Mayweather, who used to be known as "Pretty Boy" and now answers to "Money," is famous, but he's not *famous* famous. He won't settle for that. He wants to be bigger than boxing today can make him.

"Boxing is Floyd's platform, but it's not a mainstream sport anymore," says Leonard Ellerbe, his manager. "To get into the mainstream, you have to do mainstream things." Mayweather has "elevated the brand and expanded the fan base" and become "an A-lister," as Ellerbe puts it, not only by winning all of his professional fights and earning a fortune ($50 million in 2007 alone), but also by dancing with the stars, palling around with 50 Cent and Mark Cuban, starring in a reality show on HBO, rapping, venturing into music production, promoting concert tours by Beyoncé and Chris Brown, waving the green flag at the Indianapolis 500, and appearing on TV talk shows. Ellerbe promises that more such dabbling is on the way, including movie deals and a "stimulation beverage." It is all part of what Mayweather

Original publication: "And Now, the Biggest Entertainer in Entertainment," *Play: The New York Times Sports Magazine*, June 1, 2008.

and Ellerbe both refer to as Mayweather's "ultimate goal" of turning himself into "a Fortune 500 company" and becoming "the biggest entertainer in entertainment"—kind of like what the Joker has in mind in *Batman* when he says he wants his face on the dollar bill.

But Mayweather's notoriety and income still rest primarily on one increasingly esoteric talent: hitting and not being hit. Astonishingly fast, shrewd, and confident, he's a sophisticated defensive technician who throws precise combinations and seems immune to fatigue. His opponents rarely extend him, and he trumped his one controversial victory (a decision over José Luis Castillo) by convincingly winning the rematch. At the age of 31, he has a gleaming record: 39–0 with 25 knockouts; victories over champions and former champions; and world titles in five divisions, from super featherweight (130 pounds) to light middleweight (154). Title belts have lost value as they have proliferated in the age of multiple sanctioning bodies, but still, Mayweather has collected a lot of them.

Raised in a boxing family, schooled almost from birth in the mechanics of winning a fight, Mayweather seems to have been destined to become a great boxer. He's not shy about comparing himself favorably to the best of all time. "No disrespect to Sugar Ray Robinson," he told me, "but was he undefeated? Did he win six titles in five weight classes?" Well, no, but Robinson, the welterweight and middleweight of the 1940s and 1950s who is generally regarded as the pound-for-pound king, won 175 fights (against 19 losses and 6 draws) in an era when boxers fought much more often and there were fewer titles and the weight classes were deeper and fewer. It's almost impossible for today's stars, for all their gaudy belts, to build up a record comparable to those of Robinson and his golden-age peers.

But having fought to the pinnacle of his declining profession and taken control of his career, Mayweather appears to be pursuing mainstream fame and money à la Paris Hilton more strenuously than he's chasing Sugar Ray Robinson and all-time greatness as a boxer.

———

On the evening of March 30, Mayweather was lying on a bed in the back room of a trailer in a roped-off area outside Florida Citrus Bowl Stadium in Orlando. In the stadium, a crowd of nearly 75,000 roared as professional wrestlers staged titanic blows and falls amid laser shows, fireworks, and loud music. The occasion was Wrestle-

Mania XXIV, and World Wrestling Entertainment's cameras and microphones were transmitting every engorged muscle, dire rasping pronouncement, and stirring turn of fortune to more than a million pay-per-view subscribers.

In the trailer, the lights were down and an anticipatory hush prevailed. Recumbent, Mayweather talked about balancing boxing and extracurricular activities. "I'll be honest, boxing comes so easy to me I don't even think about it," he said. "I'm here to entertain. . . . Work is work. I'm gonna make a lot of money, but this is also a learning stage of my life. I'm learning different ways to promote." Pronouncing himself happy to be doing business with the hard-selling WWE, he smiled and stretched, affecting the manner of a cat who has just burped up a canary feather. Ellerbe, a chesty fellow with a shaved head, leaned in from the doorway to add, "Boxers have such a short window of opportunity to earn a living as boxers."

Tyson, Ali, Joe Louis, Jack Dempsey, and other heavyweight champions had some harmless profitable fun appearing in pro wrestling shows, so why begrudge Mayweather the chance to do the same? He might even recruit wrestling fans to boxing. Boxing and wrestling are blood brothers, after all, sharing a lineage that goes back to the bare-knuckle era, when matches typically combined punching and grappling. The two amateur sports still have much in common, but the professional versions have evolved as polar opposites. Boxing wraps a veneer of showbiz around the craft of fighting, while pro wrestling wraps a veneer of fighting around the craft of putting on a show.

There are good welterweight boxers to fight, and Mayweather the entertainer isn't fighting them. Even when he does deign to box, he has been taking big-money fights against relatively easy opponents like Oscar De La Hoya, who is popular and long past his prime, and the undersize, overmatched British scrapper Ricky Hatton. But "to be the best, you got to fight the best," as Shane Mosley, an elite welterweight, says. Mosley and other critics ask how Mayweather can call himself the best fighter, or even the best welterweight, when he has not fought even one of the current top men in his weight class. First among them is the no-nonsense Miguel Cotto, from Puerto Rico, who is unbeaten, too, but there's also Mosley, who's as quick and tricky and experienced as Mayweather, and there are others in what may be the sport's deepest division. Mayweather can require them to battle for the right to meet him, and Mosley concedes that "you don't knock him for trying to make a little extra money." But at some point his refusal to fight other top welterweights begins to undercut his claim to superlative greatness as a boxer, and the cachet of Mayweather's brand rests on that claim.

Mayweather, who made $25 million when he beat De La Hoya in 2007, had recently reached an agreement in principle to a rematch in September. De La Hoya, who tends to fade in the later rounds, does not have the speed or stamina to keep the pressure on Mayweather. Why fight Oscar again when Mayweather could prove he's the best by fighting the best?

Mayweather snorted in disgust and looked to Ellerbe, who stepped in close to me and said, "A fight has to make sense. The other guy has to bring something to the table." In other words, the opponent must prove that he can attract a pay-per-view audience. "We're the industry leaders," Ellerbe said. "People are going to take shots at us, but it's like if there's a crap game and Floyd has a million dollars and these guys have $200, why's he gonna play with them? How can Cotto say he has a fan base when he fights on pay-per-view and does 160,000 buys with Zab Judah at Madison Square Garden?" (HBO, which televised the fight, says that figure is low.) Mayweather sat up on the bed and said, "If Cotto's such a big guy, why doesn't he fight in Las Vegas?"

Our discussion of Cotto, who has already beaten Mosley, irritated Mayweather. Having abandoned his pose of smug feline ease, he remained sitting on the bed, reaching up to thump my chest with the back of his hand for emphasis as he refuted point by point the argument that he's an overrated media darling who avoids guys who can beat him. Ellerbe chimed in urgently, leaning in from the other side to poke my arm. They wanted me to see the situation properly.

Having bought himself out in 2006 from Top Rank, his longtime promoter, Mayweather promotes his own bouts and owns in full what he earns in the ring. The most celebrated fighters of the past could not say that. From Louis the national hero to Ali the antiestablishment icon to Tyson the bankable bogeyman, they turned over the greater part of their earnings to promoters, managers, and backers, took their lumps as directed, and made a nice living while it lasted. Louis died broke; Tyson is working on it; Ali has hung onto a mere fraction of the profits he generated.

"We've established the model on how a boxer conducts his business," said Ellerbe, who, along with the music promoter Al Haymon, helps Mayweather plot the course of his career. "Floyd is in control. He already paid his dues and fought who he had to fight. Now he can decide what he's going to do." De La Hoya, who not only promotes his fights but also owns *The Ring*, the venerable boxing magazine, has similar autonomy. When Mayweather and De La Hoya fought, it was the only matchup of true free-agent stars in the sport's history. "I can write my own ticket in boxing," Mayweather said. "Money Mayweather like to be outside the box."

His opponent at WrestleMania, in a match billed as a showdown between the Biggest and the Best, was Paul Wight, aka Big Show, a fleshy giant with a rumbling basso voice and a smooth skull like the dome of a statehouse. The WWE listed Big Show at 7 feet and 441 pounds, equivalent to exactly three welterweights. If he wasn't quite that big, he was still enormous. He entered to his fake-bluesy theme song, wearing a one-strap singlet that made him look like a caveman in the *B.C.* comic strip. Mayweather entered in character: swaggering, accompanied by black-clad bodyguards and Ellerbe, in a white suit.

The bout opened with a cat-and-mouse phase in which the boxer eluded the giant's lumbering rushes and countered with combinations. Even his mock punches looked shockingly crisp in contrast to the steer-killing blows the wrestlers had mimed all evening. Big Show finally caught Mayweather and worked him over at length, delivering a ringing slap to the chest, body-slamming him, mashing his exposed limbs and at times simply standing on him. Mayweather screamed pitifully while Ellerbe rushed around the ring apron, shouting, "He can't do that!" A couple of bodyguards jumped in to save their boss, but Big Show crushed them.

Just when all seemed lost, Mayweather seized a metal folding chair and beat Big Show to the canvas. Removing his right boxing glove with a flourish, Mayweather retrieved a gold-painted mock knuckleduster from where it hung around the neck of one of his KO'd goons and used it to finish off his conveniently kneeling opponent. Outraged boos rolled down from the broader fan base that Mayweather, who had obviously enjoyed playing David as a heel, was trying to reach.

———

Mayweather's boxing pedigree would have been fairly common back in 1926, say, but it is exceedingly rare now. Floyd Mayweather Sr. led his younger brothers Roger and Jeff to the gym in Grand Rapids, Michigan. "Floyd Sr. was, like, a troubled teen," Jeff says. "He was getting in fights, he beat up a teacher and got in trouble, and one day he went to the gym and fell in love with it. Roger followed him, then me. It became like a family business."

The three brothers acquitted themselves remarkably well in the ring. Sugar Ray Leonard, the great welterweight of the 1980s, who beat Floyd Sr. by technical knockout in 1978, describes him as "a very fast, smart, competent boxer who lacked power and had fragile hands. I remember the quickness and snap of his left jab." Roger, the best of the brothers, won a pair of world titles. Jeff won a minor super featherweight title. If they never did beat the very best, the Mayweathers mixed it up with some of the most accomplished fighters of their time. "They never backed down from anyone," Sugar Ray Leonard says. Now all three brothers work as professional trainers, passing on the craft to younger men.

Floyd Jr. grew up at the gym. His father says, "I used to take him down there when he was in the crib, and as soon as he was out of the crib, when he was in the baby chair, I had him putting his hands up. It was in the blood, shoulder rolls and all." The shoulder roll is a punch-shedding move integral to both father's and son's defenses.

The son "almost didn't have a choice," Jeff says. "It was the only thing he knew, and people were praising him for it." The boy took to boxing with a verve that promised greatness. Jeff says, "It was like watching a young Sammy Davis, a young Michael Jackson." Floyd Jr. tore through the amateur ranks, compiling a record of 84–6. After the 1996 Olympics in Atlanta, where he won a bronze medal after losing a disputed decision, he turned pro at the age of nineteen.

Roger permanently replaced Floyd Sr. as Floyd Jr.'s trainer in 2000. Floyd Jr. no longer speaks to his father. "He acts like he made me by himself," Floyd Jr. tells me. "He left when I was sixteen"—to go to prison on drug trafficking charges—"and came back when I was 21, and he thought everything I had was his." Floyd Jr. doesn't speak to his uncle Jeff, either. "Not since 1999," he says. "Put his hand in the cookie jar without me knowing. Then I found out." Jeff says he did a lot of unpaid work for his nephew and had to cover his expenses.

The family drama of estrangements, intrigues, and feuds will be at center stage in the run-up to Floyd Jr.'s rematch with De La Hoya in September. This time, De La Hoya is being trained by Floyd Sr., who promises that he has a strategy to beat his unbeaten son. Roger, training Floyd Jr., resents his older brother's claims to have taught Floyd Jr. everything he knows. The hard feelings are real, but everyone involved also understands his role in selling a fight. The promotion for the first Mayweather–De La Hoya bout centered on *De La Hoya/ Mayweather 24/7*, a reality show that aired on HBO on Sunday nights, after *The Sopranos* and *Entourage*. Mayweather played the boastful jerk; De La Hoya brought birthday cake to his wife. Together they sold a record 2.4 million pay-per-view buys of the fight and, with the gate receipts and other profit, generated a record gross of more than $150 million. But, as Jeff points out, "the fight itself was horrible"— mostly because Mayweather played it safe. "People thought it was close, but I wouldn't pay $60 to see that again. Your key to selling the rematch is the father. People are into that, and the media can build it up all over again."

Floyd Sr. agrees: "I know for a fact that fight ain't nothin' without me, Floyd Joy Mayweather." He accentuates every syllable of his name.

The Mayweathers play the showbiz game, but something harder and more darkly specialized moves beneath their mugging for the camera. They're craftsmen who have given and taken millions of blows in the ring, in the gym and beyond. Floyd Sr. and Roger have done prison time, and domestic violence has been a recurring theme in the family drama. Floyd Sr. was famously shot in the leg by another of Floyd Jr.'s uncles, his mother's brother, as he held the year-old Floyd Jr. in his arms. The accumulated effect of all those many doses of force has transformed these men. To watch Floyd Sr., who at 55 can still make the bags jump, is to become intensely aware of the resilient, much-pummeled skull beneath the leathery face, the lean frame and outlook singularly adapted to fighting. Roger has that same wolflike look. Jeff, who attended college and has more meat on him, does not seem quite so starved and ready, but he shares with his brothers a quality of having been annealed by violence.

––––––––

Floyd Jr., wearing shorts and a sleeveless T-shirt, was in a nail salon in Las Vegas with his bare feet immersed in a tub of blue water, softening them up for a pedicure. His personal assistant, a young woman known as Vegas, sat in the next chair. Four bodyguards lounged in the waiting area. Leonard Ellerbe was standing off to one side, reiterating that if they couldn't find a fight that made sense, then Floyd just wouldn't fight anymore, no matter what his enemies said. "To organize your livelihood, to be an entrepreneur, that's what it means to live in a free society," Ellerbe said. "Two years ago, the promoters weren't saying Floyd is scared, 'cause he was with the company. Now, suddenly, he's scared and won't fight nobody?"

Mayweather said, "Other fighters have to fight. I don't have to fight." He doesn't need the money, obviously, but what about other needs—the glory, the challenge, the love of craft? "I already went through that stage when I fought 90 fights for free," he said. "I already proved it to myself. Once you reach pound for pound, you already proved everything."

Ellerbe said, "That's why we're out there grinding, creating opportunities. Boxing is still his main source of income right now, but all the stuff we've been doing prepares for postboxing." Two weeks before, in his trailer at WrestleMania, I asked Mayweather if he might train other fighters when he stops boxing. "No," he said. "I see myself more behind a desk." Now, as a young woman bent over his feet with a paring device, I asked him what he would do behind that desk. "Call the shots," he said. "People come in and I say, 'Deal with that,' and they deal with it." Then he added, dreamily, "Be on the computer all day," which struck me as odd, considering how many people who sit in front of computers all day must fantasize about being star athletes. Ellerbe cut in to return our discussion of Mayweather's postboxing life to the party line: platform, mainstream, entertainment.

When Mayweather moved to the manicure table, limping from the sweet soreness in his calves left by the pedicurist's massaging fingers, the conversation turned to the subject of family. He is unmarried and has four children, who live with their mothers. "You punish your kids?" he asked. "I don't believe in whuppin' 'em. My dad beat me, and when it was time to talk to him about important things, I didn't want to. So I don't put my hands on my kids. I want them to be able to talk to me." This was a 24/7 intimacy, more brand management for the media, but it was also as honest as he gets in an interview. He really doesn't want to turn into his father.

Right then, though, I could see his father in him. Mayweather is remarkably unlined for a man of 31 who has been hit often, and when he smiles he looks literally half his age, but seen up close in profile, the lines of his skull seem to press against the skin as if Floyd Sr. were emerging from within. The small gap in his left eyebrow and other signs of scarring around the eyes remind me that he has been boxing since he could walk. It's as if he has been worn smooth by the blows. His supremely capable body, too, bears the marks of the nearly three decades of training and fighting that produced it. The shots, the sit-ups, the miles all accrue. He has the look.

After the nail salon, Mayweather, who lives in Las Vegas, visited a commercial property he was thinking of buying, and stopped by a jewelry store. He and his crew traveled in a caravan of SUVs, like elephants marching trunk to tail. By the time we got to the Fashion Show mall, he had changed into a colorful long-sleeved T-shirt and jeans with "PB" (for Pretty Boy) in silver on one back pocket and "$" on the other.

Mayweather spent the next few hours trying on clothes and accessories, examining himself minutely in store mirrors. When strangers asked for an autograph or a picture, he obliged. Two shapely young women he knew showed up along the way, each departing with a gift or two in a shopping bag. His entourage of eleven watched him, ate food-court junk, and carried his purchases. By evening, some of his bodyguards had three or four bags in each hand.

Mayweather and his crew went off to dinner and whatever came next. He likes to stay up late and go out, but he doesn't drink, so he can train whenever he wants. He'll run or drop by the gym at 3 a.m. if he feels like it. Sometimes he feels like it.

Afterward, I thought, So *that* is what Floyd Mayweather Jr. will do with his life and his millions if he can't find a matchup that "makes sense"? That's what he's going to do with a boxing talent that might, if he insists on fighting the best, still transcend the limitations of his era and produce a career of all-time significance? He's at the peak of his powers right now, and it won't last forever. When he retires, he'll have all the time in the world to shop, wrestle, and dance on TV. The boxing fan in me wants to tell Mayweather to get busy and fight Cotto. If it's close, fight him again—fight a trilogy. Fight Mosley and whichever young contender emerges next from the pack. If you clean out the welterweights, move up and try a bigger man. I want him to be true to his craft, to deliver in full on his talent and training. On the other hand, nobody got hurt during his circus turn at Wrestle-Mania or his marathon shopping session, and he owed me nothing more than the on-message patter he'd been feeding me. By what right did I wish more hard fights upon a man who has given and taken so many blows already?

———

Two weeks later, Mayweather and his crew, in formal attire, occupied a couple of big round tables in a banquet room at the Millennium Biltmore, the grand old hotel in downtown Los Angeles that decades ago used to host the Oscars. He was there to pick up the fighter of the year award from the Boxing Writers Association of America at its 83rd annual awards dinner. You could argue that other fighters deserved the honor more and that Mayweather really should share self-promoter of the year with De La Hoya, if such an award existed, but his fame and riches had dazzled the voters.

In addition to fighters, cornermen, matchmakers, and other guests, there were scores of boxing writers in attendance, but no more than a handful made a full-time living at it anymore. Even more than boxing itself, writing about boxing has receded into a niche market.

So the gathered writers, lacking mainstream clout, could not help make Mayweather *famous* famous. But their opinion still matters to him, in part because they play a role in determining his place in the sport's history. "There's only two reasons to fight," Ellerbe told me more than once. "Business and legacy." Business comes first, but legacy counts, too, if only because it affects the brand. Members of the BWAA will vote Mayweather into the International Boxing Hall of Fame on the first ballot when he's eligible, but they will also take the lead in debating whether and where he belongs in the unofficial rankings of the top fighters of all time in his weight class and the exclusive canon of pound-for-pound greats.

Sugar Ray Robinson tops both lists. To understand just how high a standard he set, consider that he fought the indestructible middleweight Jake LaMotta, a bigger and stronger man, six times. They met twice within three weeks in February 1943, and between those two bouts Robinson beat "California" Jackie Wilson, who was no slouch. That single month was tougher than any entire year Mayweather has had to date, and Robinson's all-time standing does not suffer from his having lost once to LaMotta by decision. Going 5–1 against LaMotta means infinitely more than beating Ricky Hatton or the faded De La Hoya once or twice.

I recently asked LaMotta what he thought of Mayweather. (Robinson died in 1989.) He said, "I fought thirteen years, 106 fights, and I made $750,000, total. Fighting all the time keeps you strong, makes you able to take a shot better, but I would have fought less if I made more money." He added that he would have wrestled, danced, whatever, if anybody had asked him to and paid him for it. The old-timers and all-timers I talked to were divided in their opinion of Mayweather. Some, like Sugar Ray Leonard, thought he would do well in imaginary matchups against the best of previous eras. Others, like LaMotta and Carmen Basilio, who are both now in their 80s, thought he didn't have enough experience against strong competition. "He would have been in a lot of trouble," Basilio told me.

When the fighter of the year award was announced, Mayweather mounted the stage. He had shed his tuxedo jacket. His white shirt and boyish smile were brilliant. Flashbulbs went off. All the attention in the big room flowed to him. He seemed bigger than the event, stooping down to it from somewhere higher up the celebrity food chain.

The writers, sentimentalists who think they're cynics, oozed gratitude. A significant minority of them believed that Cotto is the best welterweight and that the Filipino super featherweight Manny Pacquiao is pound for pound the best fighter in the world today, but they loved Mayweather for his outsize persona and the reminder it carries of the sport's past glories.

When he got to the podium, Mayweather thanked everyone imaginable, even his dad, and noted that he had made $100 million in the ring, which he termed "a blessing." It was the usual song and dance, but there was a gentleness to his manner that I hadn't seen before. He was like a movie star at his high school reunion, muting his arrogance and trying to be a regular guy for old times' sake. He seemed to genuinely appreciate the honor.

He and his entourage hung around for a while, then moved on. There was a big world out there, a fan base to expand and a brand to elevate, and the night was still young.

Shannon vs. the Russians

"THE RUSSIAN DOMINATION OF the heavyweight title is finis, over and done," Shannon Briggs declared in an open letter last fall. Briggs, who referred to himself as "the Black Hope, the American Hope," had recently won the WBO's championship belt by knocking Sergei Liakhovich entirely out of the ring in the closing seconds of the bout. Now Briggs was calling out the champions recognized by the other three major sanctioning bodies: Wladimir Klitschko, a Ukrainian, and Oleg Maskaev and Nikolay Valuev, both Russians. "I am made in Brooklyn, USA," he announced, "and I am definitely in the heavyweight-title house."

In his next fight, Briggs will defend his belt in Atlantic City on June 2 against Sultan Ibragimov, a southpaw from Dagestan, in the northern Caucasus. As Briggs says, "It does seem like Shannon versus the Russians, doesn't it?"

Tradition holds that the heavyweight boxing champion is the baddest man on the planet. For most of the twentieth century, that man was an American. From 1937 on, he was usually black. The honor roll includes Jack Johnson, Joe Louis, Sonny Liston, Muhammad Ali, Joe Frazier, George Foreman, Larry Holmes, and Mike Tyson. Even though rival organizations have turned one title into several, and even though boxers in the lower weight classes are almost always more skillful than the big guys, ruling the heavyweights has been a

Original publication: "Shannon Briggs Says Nyet," *New York Times Magazine*, April 15, 2007.

special point of pride for Americans in general and African Americans in particular.

But in 2006, for the first time, the world's baddest man was in effect an Eastern European, a composite of the four principal titleholders. Briggs reclaimed one share last November by beating Liakhovich, a Belarussian based in Arizona, but American heavyweight primacy had clearly slipped away. It went first to Lennox Lewis, born in London to Jamaican parents, and when Lewis retired in 2004, it passed to the rising cohort from the former Soviet Union known as the Russians (even though they're not all Russian and Maskaev is, in fact, a naturalized American citizen).

The eclipse of the American heavyweight echoes the recent string of American failures in international basketball and baseball competitions and the continuing influx of athletes from around the world into these and other sports here at home. Formerly American-ruled games seem to be becoming like hockey and soccer, in which the United States is just one competitor among many, no more fearsome than Sweden or Spain. Jingoistic fans should worry that soon the only sport that homegrown Americans can count on dominating will be football, which almost nobody else plays. And those who believe that certain aspects of sport qualify as Black Things—like basketball or the heavyweight title—might even suspect a conspiracy.

Briggs played on these anxieties when he called himself the Black Hope, the American Hope. Joe Louis became such a contradictory hero, simultaneously representing African Americans and a nation that did not treat them as equal citizens, when he fought his rematch with the German champion Max Schmeling. That was in 1938, during the buildup to World War II. How did we get to the point where we need a Black Hope now?

———

"I think we're a little spoiled," Hasim Rahman said last August. "We make too much money too quick. We lose sight of the grand prize." Rahman, who preceded Briggs as America's heavyweight Black Hope, had just surrendered his belt to Maskaev, who completed the Eastern European sweep of the four titles. The new champion, for his part, said, "This is a message to everyone: European fighters are tough." Or, as Vyacheslav Trunov, Maskaev's former manager, once put it, "We fight like it's Stalingrad in 1942. We never surrender, and take no prisoners."

You hear this kind of talk these days in the fight world and beyond. It's not really just about boxing; it's about what used to be called national character. Eastern Europeans, the story goes, are tougher than Americans, who, spoiled by money and comfort, have gone soft in their gated community of a nation. The former Soviet bloc, by contrast, is like a vast gray housing project, stretching from the Balkans to the Bering Strait, from which issue streams of do-or-die strivers: fighters, basketball players, musicians, dancers, writers, hustlers, beauties, entrepreneurs, gangsters, all flowing toward the big money in the decadent West. Both halves of this story, the American decline and the rise of the Russians, are more mythic parable than serious analysis, but they're widely repeated and accepted, even by American boxers.

Larry Holmes, for instance, calls the post-Soviet heavies "ordinary fighters" but rates them well ahead of their American counterparts. Our guys, he says, exhibit "no dedication, no sacrifice. They want to party, be a star, play all that in limousines. That's not only in boxing, but in other sports, in society, and that's what's happening to young athletes—to fighters, too."

Like most Jeremiahs, Holmes makes a moral crisis out of a structural problem. Football, basketball, and baseball (which has also become a big man's game) snap up the quick, strong, determined 200-plus-pounders in this country. The decline of boxing into a niche sport during the latter part of the 20th century coincided with the growing hegemony of the major team sports, with their high-profile professional leagues and school-based amateur networks. A big kid who likes to bang is likely to be shunted into peewee football, and from there he can work his way up through the sport's well-regulated layers without ever coming near a boxing gym.

Meanwhile, the American boxing network has continued to shrink since its heyday in the first half of the last century, when no prize in sports rivaled the heavyweight title. Industrial society honored men who were good with their hands, and almost every working-class neighborhood had at least one gym. But in postindustrial America, a would-be boxer has to go well out of his way to find one of the few remaining gyms. The underfinanced national amateur system regularly comes up short in international competitions and produces few prospects who live up to their signing bonuses.

Boxing offers a path of greater resistance for American big men. (It's different in the lower weight classes, where participants have fewer opportunities in team sports and where there are still some dominant American champions.) Only a handful of boxers make the kind of money that thousands of professional ballplayers do. Why get beat up for nothing?

In Eastern Europe, by contrast, there's no football to claim the hard-nosed big guys, no baseball, less basketball, a lot less money, and a superior institutional apparatus for turning big men into competent boxers.

The Soviets and their client states strove to excel in boxing, as they did in gymnastics or swimming, exploiting enthusiasm for physical culture to propagandize the virtues of Homo Sovieticus. They set up extensive state-sponsored networks of gyms, combing the schools for promising kids and patiently teaching them balance, footwork, and other fundamentals. "The athletes do what they're told," says Eric Bottjer, a veteran matchmaker. "They go to the gym like other people go to work. Americans don't always do that."

The fall of the USSR allowed Eastern European amateurs to take the professional opportunities that opened for them in the West. German promoters and managers set up a pipeline to connect the farm system in the East to the money in the West. "The Russians" are not particularly good or tough when compared with heavyweights of other eras, and (Trunov's Stalingrad bluster notwithstanding) they have demonstrated a tendency to play it safe in the ring, but they also tend to be big, dutiful, schooled in the rudiments, and around in large numbers, and that's enough to rule the division in the wake of the American collapse.

How did Shannon Briggs, at the age of 35, come to be the lone American standing in their way? Brooklyn, he says, and asthma.

He came up hard in Brownsville. His mother worked and sacrificed to put him through parochial schools, but she became a heroin addict, then got into crack. She was "in and out of institutions" until her death in 1996; his stepfather, Briggs says, "died in prison, but he made me who I am, in some ways. He was a tough guy. My first fight, he made me fight the kid." Briggs was often on his own, staying with relatives or friends, drifting, out on the street and in charge of himself. "I had a lot of fights. I was an only child, a hardcase kid, in a rough neighborhood. But I always fought my battles."

When he was fifteen, he found a copy of a boxing magazine in a Brooklyn subway station. He read it to tatters and went looking for a gym, where his chaotic life began to take on structure. Hopes were high for him when he turned pro in 1992.

Briggs's professional career, long and mostly victorious though it has been (48–4, with one draw), has not quite borne out his youthful promise. He's a big hitter with very fast hands, and a deceptively clever tactician, but he has a reputation for wavering in his commitment to training and winning. He acknowledged his critics in his open letter challenging the other champions: "Underachiever. Asthmatic. Excuse-maker and fistic faker. My opponents and some other haters have called me all of those things."

Asthma has dogged him all his life. "I missed a lot of school," he says. "I was always sick. I was in the hospital a lot. Asthma kicked my butt." But if it wasn't for asthma, he might not be a boxer at all. How did a strapping specimen like him escape being recruited for football? "I couldn't play, nothing aerobic. Nobody picked me."

So he was "saved," as he puts it, to become "the first asthmatic heavyweight champion." He has learned to control his condition with diet, training, and medication. When I went to see him in January at his house in a gated community outside Fort Lauderdale, he said, "They say I'm taking steroids," acknowledging another common accusation. "Let me show you something." He got up from his living-room couch and went to a cabinet in the kitchen, returning with an armful of meds, which he dumped on the wooden chest that serves as a coffee table. "Singulair. Advair. Servent. Albuterol." He had pills, inhalers, nebulizers, even Zaditor drops for itchy eyes. "Somebody told me these eyedrops can help, so I got some. You want to talk about steroids? I'm *taking* steroids"—by which he meant the kind not banned by boxing commissions. "If you want to become heavyweight champion of the world and you got asthma, you'll do whatever it takes. You'll go to Africa and suck a cow's dick if it would help. All these pills, I can't sleep, too hyped up. And depression, and you get hungry, eat too much."

On fight night, the tension, adrenaline, and anxiety about having an asthma attack often bring on a crisis. The resulting chronic shortness of wind, made worse by spotty training, has shaped his fighting style. He comes out bombing, looking to overwhelm his opponent early. "My mother said, 'You gotta knock him out first, 'cause you gonna get tired,' and that's been my motto since Day 1." By the third or fourth round, he slows down, picking his spots, sometimes visibly laboring to fill his lungs. An opponent can win rounds by simply outworking him but still has to guard against the ever-present threat of a sudden knockout—as Liakhovich, who was ahead on points in the final round when Briggs launched him through the ropes and left him swooning on the ringside scorer's table, can attest.

Briggs, who stands 6-foot-4 and weighs up to 270 pounds for a fight, has become addicted to his own power. He admits that he breathes more easily and moves better when he weighs 255 pounds, but he says, "I'm breaking *bones* in the ring at 270." Carrying the extra bulk makes him look and feel more potent, but combined with his asthma, it also makes him more beatable, which helps explain why Liakhovich's handlers let their man risk his title against him. Briggs can thank asthma for that too.

"I haven't been the fighter I could have been," Briggs admits. "I didn't have enough confidence, enough amateur experience. I never had the right coaching until now. The asthma was always on my mind. If I didn't have asthma, I'd probably be one of the greatest fighters of all time."

———————

It was late. The lights were dim in Briggs's living room. He sat on the couch, an open laptop in front of him on the wooden chest. His asthma meds were still in a heap next to the laptop, where he had dumped them earlier.

At this reflective hour, he talked of retiring. "It'll soon be time for me to find happiness in my life, but I need to be financially stable enough to walk away from the game." He's "allergic to broke," he said, and he has a family (two kids), a mortgage. Defending his title will bring paydays, and he's under pressure too to carry the standard of the Black Hope.

"Oh, I definitely feel it," he said. "I'm the only guy with the punch and skill level." During our conversations he sometimes dismissed his Black Hope talk as "marketing," but at other times, like this one, he took seriously the notion of reclaiming an honor that belonged by rights to the line of Louis and Ali.

He wasn't the only one thinking about tribal honor. On his laptop, he took me on a tour of intemperate online boxing talk. I could practically hear Avar folk tunes swelling in the background when I read one post predicting that Sultan Ibragimov will be "way, way too tough for Briggs. . . . The kids from the Caucasus mountains grow up playing with guns, seeing their friends and family members murdered over minor insults. These kids are tough, mean, natural fighters. . . . So called 'tough guys' from underprivileged American backgrounds—the so-called 'inner city ghettos'—are like helpless babies compared to the people of the Caucasus. . . . You can see it in the glint of the eye in these Caucasians. It's scary, and it's the reason why boxing dominance is leaving the U.S.A. for the East."

Briggs said, "I don't get caught up in the race thing," but he told me more than once that promoters and cable networks favor the Russian heavies because they're white. He also enjoyed retelling the story of how he'd spread the false rumor that Liakhovich, known as the White Wolf, had called him a nigger. Briggs had been playing a pre-fight head game, trying to put his opponent on the defensive. At their postfight press conference, Liakhovich, plainly upset and still dazed, earnestly assured Briggs that he had never called him any such thing. "I smiled," Briggs said, "and I said, 'I know. I made it up.' He was, like, 'Whuuuh?'"

Briggs doubted a similar move would work on Ibragimov. "This guy I'm fighting now, he's more of a hard guy, or a wannabe. But I don't care. I don't care about that Russian mafia. Talk about, he's had street fights, in Russia. Me, too. Bring it." But a certain caution moved within Briggs's bluster. He sensed that he couldn't work Ibragimov, a fair-haired Muslim from a far-distant mountain land, like a regular white guy. The cultural reflexes, the leverage, felt different.

———

The next afternoon, I visited Ibragimov during a training session at his gym, Seminole Warriors, in Hollywood, Florida, only a few miles away from Briggs's house. At 6-foot-2 and 225 pounds, he's a small heavyweight by today's standards. His unpumped, uncut body has an old-school smoothness. Ibragimov is undefeated at the age of 32, but he has had only 21 pro fights, none of them against anybody particularly good.

His manager, Boris Grinberg, who in his tropical shirt and shorts resembled Ernest Borgnine on vacation, said, "All his tribe, his people, from the mountains near Chechnya. He real Caucasian." Dagestan is known for its freestyle wrestlers, but Ibragimov found his way to a government-run boxing gym at seventeen when he moved to Rostov. "Sultan has good pedigree," Grinberg said. "He's from basic Soviet school, but he's more like American fighter, or black fighter with white skin. So fast, so powerful, always attack." Ibragimov closes with an opponent rather than standing back at arm's length in the traditional Eastern European defensive style. "Russian fighters take distance, stand up," said Ibragimov, who's taking lessons to improve his English. "American fighters go to *fight*"—he mimed bobbing and crowding. "I like."

Ibragimov, who won a silver medal in the 2000 Olympics, moved to Florida in 2002. He showed up at the gym on his first day in America, having flown in late the previous night. "They want him to spar," Grinberg said. "First day. There was big black motherfucker"—he reached up toward the ceiling to indicate the man's impressive size— "and Sultan smaller, with white skin, not so muscles. But Sultan knock him out, in first round."

They had something similar in mind for Shannon Briggs. Ibragimov said, "All the heavyweights so tall now. I like fight tall guys. I aim for body, head, everything."

The bout, originally scheduled for March but postponed to June 2 when Briggs came down with pneumonia complicated by his asthma, is shaping up as a good test for both fighters, whose strengths and weaknesses seem likely to mesh in volatile ways. The winner gets the belt and at least one more good payday; the loser falls back into the pack of contenders, where also-rans, used-to-bes, and could-have-beens mix with up-and-comers.

The two men's different paths to the ring, their converging histories, make for a good story, too. Narrative is crucial to boxing because the significance of any given bout, even a heavyweight title bout, is never built in. As opposed to the Super Bowl, which means just about the same no matter who plays in it, each fight has to be individually packaged for sale. What's the story of Briggs-Ibragimov? Take your pick. The Black Hope versus the hard man from Dagestan; Brooklyn's own versus rising immigrant; old head versus young lion; Shannon versus the Russians, asthma, and the decline of the American heavyweight.

Briggs weighed 273 pounds when he fought Ibragimov, who outmaneuvered and outworked him on the way to an easy win by decision. Briggs retired after the defeat, then unretired and secured a title fight in Hamburg in 2010 with Vitali Klitschko, Wladimir's brother. Briggs was badly beaten, ending up in the hospital with multiple facial fractures and a concussion. But his willingness to take punishment for the full twelve rounds, combined with his imposing muscular bulk, put him in line for more paydays as a trial horse for Eastern European heavyweights.

After the Gloves Came Off

THERE WAS BOXING AT the Castle, the converted armory on Arlington Street, on a warm night in mid-July. Perhaps 500 people filled the building's main hall, filing into the rows of folding chairs set up around the ring or hanging around in the back drinking beer. Norm Stone stood near the pizza table, receiving. A boxer he manages, Joe McCreedy, a 22-year-old light-heavyweight from Lowell with a 5–1 record, was scheduled to fight later that evening.

Everybody came by to say hello to Stone—reporters, cops, boxers, managers, trainers, fans. Men shook his hand, slapped him on the shoulder, introduced the family. Some unconsciously broadened their own Massachusetts accents to match his, which is of weapons grade. Women he'd never met before kissed his cheek, some diffidently, as if leaning into a cage to kiss a grizzly, and some boldly, as if they knew he was really a teddy bear.

A solid fellow with a paunch and a shock of white hair, Stone cultivates a down-curving piratical mustache that makes him look like Hulk Hogan's smaller, smarter, dirtier-fighting brother. His epic bugouts have made him a celebrity in the fight world. Boxing fans have grown used to seeing Stone in a red-faced choking passion, trading punches and grappling with the opponent's cornermen, restrained by security guards, screaming curses (*You cuocksackah!*) that non–New Englanders require subtitles to comprehend. Over the past two de-

Original publication: *Boston*, November 2007.

cades he has turned getting mad on his fighter's behalf into an art form.

From 1988 to 2005, that fighter was John Ruiz, a heavyweight from Chelsea with a dogged, mauling style. With Stone in his corner as manager, cut man, head cheerleader, sometime trainer, and full-time fount of contagious aggression, Ruiz rose from obscure Boston-area scraps to the world stage and a heavyweight title. Fans and the fight press and the TV networks all complained that Ruiz was boring in the ring and out, but he overachieved heroically, outworking and out-lasting an impressive roster of opponents as he ran up a record that, as of this writing, stands at 41–7 with one draw. As much as for his unpretty fights, Ruiz became known for his and Stone's rare mutual loyalty. Don King, the virtuosic maker and breaker of alliances who has promoted most of Ruiz's bouts since 1998, told me, "They were like the Corsican Brothers. If you cut one, the other bleeds. When you got a person like Stone in your corner, the support is unparalleled and unprecedented." But the fight world's reptilian ethos acts as a solvent on any warm-blooded relationship, no matter how close. Even Stone and Ruiz didn't stay together for good.

For Stone, this Wednesday night at the Castle was a long way from championship fights in Las Vegas and seven-figure purses. The pro-moter running the show had agreed to put McCreedy on the under-card and pay him $800 only after the fighter committed to selling 75 tickets to his supporters. Still, ESPN2 was covering the main event, and McCreedy's four-round bout had a chance to make it onto the broadcast, which would be a nice break for the kid. The cameras rep-resented the attention of the wider world, a reminder that what hap-pened here could matter to an audience that extended far beyond the handfuls of rooters from Dorchester or Haverhill who'd come out to cheer on their own. Stone himself was living proof of the connec-tion between local and global. A son of Kensington Avenue in East Somerville, he had gone out with Ruiz into the great beyond, con-quered it, and returned to his people. Today, the toughest guy in the neighborhood; tomorrow, champion of the world. That, after all, is the story of Stone and Ruiz, regular guys who made it big together. King called them brothers; other fight people liken them to a father and son, or a married couple. Before they broke up, that is.

In 2005, not long after Ruiz lost his title by close and dubious deci-sion to a plodding seven-foot Russian named Nikolay Valuev, Stone announced he would no longer manage Ruiz. He said he was retiring to spend more time with his grandchildren. One could imagine, of course, that he must have a life beyond boxing, and he was indeed married and had a son and daughter and two young grandchildren, but it was difficult to accept that Stone would relinquish his livelihood at the age of 54 to spend his days dandling little darlings who couldn't walk or talk yet, let alone throw proper punches. Stone and Ruiz had come back from far more crushing setbacks than a controversial loss by split decision in Germany, where you have to decapitate a homestanding favorite and bury the head separate from the body in order to get the win. Ruiz was still a top-tier heavyweight, and he had lost and regained the title before. It seemed mysteriously out of character for Norm Stone to give up on him.

The highlight reel of Stone's raging meltdowns—and there have been many—includes the prefight brawl in 2003 with Roy Jones Jr.'s trainer over the selection of boxing gloves, and the drama at the Andrew Golota bout in 2004, during which Stone threatened to throttle the opposing trainer, cursed out the ref, and finally got himself ejected. On his way out he declared, on camera, "This is a fuckin' fixed fight." Then there's his swan song, the Valuev fight in Berlin. After the decision was rendered, Stone ripped the belt away from the hulking new champ and raised it in mock triumph. I like to revisit online a photograph of the ensuing melee in which Stone appears wonderfully intent on delivering a claw-handed shot to the face of some foreign SOB. In the image, Stone pulsates with anger, and yet he also seems strangely relaxed, even fulfilled.

Theatrical calculation went into these episodes, which Stone employed to protect his fighter's interests, pump him up, and reinforce the bond between them (*See how far I'm willing to go for you?*). "If they're on me," Stone told me more than once, "they're off him." But the tantrums also brought Stone a great deal of attention. Once they became his signature, he seemed to feel obliged to satisfy the audience's expectations.

While Stone provided the histrionics and zingers, Ruiz, dubbed "The Quiet Man," played it strong and silent and ground out the wins. The arrangement seemed to suit them. When at a press affair an opponent would say he was going to kick Ruiz's ass and everybody turned to Ruiz for a retort, slow-mounting ire would flicker around the corners of his mouth and eyes, but, after a well-timed beat, it was Stone who responded. Ruiz would nod along, receding in on himself, the drummer keeping time behind the horn player.

Whether managing Ruiz's fighting career or conducting his own, more informal one in his roistering youth, Stone has never been an x's-and-o's man. He knows more about feeling than technique. I once asked him what attributes he values in a boxer, and he promptly answered, "First, the heart. Really, the balls." Of "Irish, English, and French Canadian" descent, he grew up in Somerville, then left from 1967 to 1971 to serve in the Army in Germany and Vietnam. He had dabbled in boxing since first visiting a gym at the age of seven, but he was really a self-taught brawler. "I fought in the service," he told me. When I asked what kind of fighter he was, he said, "I was a drunk fighter." When I asked whether he was more of a tactical boxer or a free-swinging puncher, he said, "Depends what I was drinking. When I went into a bar, I expected to get in a fight. I didn't always win, but I always fought."

After he got back home, Stone drove buses for the MBTA. In the early 1980s, he started hanging around with his friend Gabe LaMarca at the Somerville Boxing Club, where he first encountered Ruiz, then a reedy, close-mouthed teenager. "I was sober a while by then. I seen this kid was riding his bike from Chelsea to the gym. To ride by Charlestown when you're Puerto Rican, that's something. We became friendly. I talked to some people, set up a salary for him."

Trained by LaMarca and managed by Stone, Ruiz started moving up and getting better. But even as he grew into a heavyweight to be reckoned with, he showed why he would always be difficult to sell as an attraction. "We'd drive six and a half hours to the fight and six and a half hours back, and not a word," recalls Stone. "I knew what he was about. He wasn't comfortable with people, and it was uncomfortable for everybody else. They complained about it. Made him a hard fighter to raise money for. But I knew he was gonna be good. He had it."

By 1996, Ruiz had put together a string of grueling victories that made it impossible to ignore him. He got his big break, a fight on HBO. The opponent was David Tua, a booming puncher well on his way to stardom. Beating Tua would set Ruiz on the path to a title shot. But Tua blasted him out in just nineteen seconds, still the only time Ruiz has ever been knocked out. "A lot of people lost confidence in him," says Stone. "Nobody wanted him on TV. HBO hated him. I couldn't sell him to a fuckin' glue factory."

Humiliated, Ruiz sank into deep despair. He didn't want to show his face at his own gym. Stone set to work on his fighter, convincing him that Tua had caught him with a lucky punch because Ruiz hadn't warmed up enough before the fight. Stone promised he would never let that happen again. "I had to get him back into the gym to face his peers," Stone says. "Took a couple of weeks. We sat down. We talked a lot. He didn't do anything without me, I didn't do anything without him. Finally, Johnny said, 'Get me the toughest guy out there. Let me see what I got.'" Stone started him out with easy matchups, working him back up the competitive ladder. "I had to do the right thing. Build him up. Protect him, and my investment." The loss to Tua had seemed like the end, but as Stone says now, "that's the one that made us."

Ruiz, his confidence painstakingly rebuilt, went on another impressive streak after the Tua fight, winning eleven in a row over the next three years, ten by knockout, taking out several prospects and the fading former champ Tony Tucker. That earned him a title fight in 2000 with Evander Holyfield, a future hall-of-famer best known for defeating Mike Tyson. Ruiz lost on a debatable close decision, then beat Holyfield convincingly in a rematch, then fought him to a draw in a third bout. Ruiz emerged from this brutal trilogy with the WBA's belt in hand, lost it, got it back, and defended it with honor, beating another series of talented big men—among them Kirk Johnson, Hasim Rahman, Andrew Golota, and Fres Oquendo—many of whom had been favored over him.

Stone handled Ruiz's business with comparable bulldog valor. "Stoney was always on me," Don King told me. "Always on me. In the morning, Stoney. In the afternoon, Stoney. I couldn't breathe. 'Jawny! You gotta think of Jawny! Do this for Jawny!' Tylenol made a million dollars off me with Stoney." King laughed his Old Scratch laugh. "Stoney was always fighting for Johnny. He just wants his man to win. That's why he gets thrown out of fights. That's why he yells and screams. He became more of an attraction than Ruiz. It made him look bad, but no one can deny the fervent passion and love for Johnny Ruiz. Even to his own detriment." A note of wonder had crept into King's voice. He couldn't fathom loyalty powerful enough to trump self-interest, but he admired it. "They say of lawyers that they're supposed to fall on their sword for their clients. He must have daggers all *through* his ass."

Promoters and TV networks complained that Ruiz was a bad draw, but he still managed to earn some good paydays. With Stone at his side, he brought in more than $5 million in purses for the Holyfield trilogy, $1.5 million to wear out Johnson, another $1.1 million to soldier through a twelve-round boxing lesson from the incomparable tactician James Toney. It wasn't Tyson money, but it added up. "If you look back over the history of the heavyweights," says Eric Bottjer, a respected matchmaker who worked for King during Ruiz's championship run, "there are a lot of guys with John Ruiz's abilities who didn't make a tenth of what he made."

———————

I met Ruiz for breakfast one summer morning in Copley Square in Boston. Watching him approach across the crowded plaza, what stood out most about him was how little he stood out. He was a former world champion, after all. Lennox Lewis, the last generally recognized preeminent heavyweight, had given up a belt to avoid fighting him. And yet Ruiz wasn't particularly imposing; he somehow seemed smaller than 6-foot-2 and 245 pounds. He was out of training at the time, his face a bit pouchy under heavy stubble. In polo shirt, cargo shorts, and flip-flops, he projected no special aura of power or physical pride.

Over a spilled drink or some other typical provocation, your average weightlifter might well take a quick look at Ruiz and miss the mashed nose and air of bland competence and decide that it would be all right to confront him. Obliged to choose between facing down Ruiz or Norm Stone in a rage, such a guy might even choose Ruiz as the lesser problem. This would be a hideous mistake, but an understandable one. The current popular ideal of a heavyweight boxer, exemplified by Tyson, is a pop-muscled cartoon of menace. It would have been news to almost everybody who passed Ruiz on the plaza that at no time in the past decade would Tyson's handlers have dared let him anywhere near this vaguely put-upon-looking guy with a fade haircut a little rucked up on one side from bed. Ruiz would have made Tyson cry and quit.

To understand why, you have to understand Ruiz's fighting style, which minimizes his opponent's advantages and maximizes Ruiz's own advantages in conditioning and strength of body and will. Ruiz specializes in being nine miles of bad road, beating men who are bigger, quicker, and graced with more radiant athleticism by dragging them into a contest of wills. He can hit, but he also clinches and mauls, putting his body on the other man to wear him down rather than exchanging clean, crowd-pleasing punches.

"The best way I can put it," Ruiz said over pancakes and fruit, "this guy I beat, Jerry Ballard, in the [postfight] press conference he said, 'Hey, man, you looked so skinny. I felt your jabs in the first round and I thought, *No problem*. But by the third round they were like cement blocks.'" The cunning application of brawn, the shoving and hauling, wearies a fighter to the point that he's vulnerable to punches that didn't hurt early on. "That's what breaks them down."

People who fetishize pumped physiques might not appreciate that the smooth-bodied Ruiz is the stronger and better-conditioned man in almost every fight. "He is strong," agreed Holyfield, who is so stacked with defined muscle that he resembles an anatomical doll. "He would hold, push, mess up my game." Just talking about it on the phone made Holyfield tired. "If I had to choose to fight a guy, I wouldn't choose to fight John Ruiz."

After holding on for a while at the top, Ruiz appeared to begin a gradual decline from his prime as he entered his thirties. As he did, the symbiotic balance between fighter and manager went seriously off-kilter. Gabe LaMarca had quit in 2003, Ruiz says, after falling out with Stone over money, and Stone, who took on the trainer's duties, was growing ever more operatic, as if trying to compensate for Ruiz's waning aggression. All his grandest bug-outs date from this stretch. Ruiz, who had always relied on being in better shape than his opponent, began cutting corners in training. "Johnny would never miss a day's work, but he started missing days," Stone said. "Johnny lost it. It just wasn't there." By "it" he meant the essential will to fight. "Me, as close as I was to him, I tried pressing him and pressing him. But everything became an excuse, and Johnny wasn't a guy to have excuses."

Ruiz acknowledges that he slipped. "Since I won the championship, it's been nothing but a downslide for me as the team came apart. It affected me mentally and physically. It affected my training." The problem, he believes, was Stone, who was never a good enough businessman to exploit Ruiz's status as the first Hispanic heavyweight champion and didn't have the boxing mind to help him adjust to top-flight competition as Ruiz entered fistic middle age. Telegenic emoting didn't make up for these deficiencies.

Ruiz traces the beginning of the end all the way back to 1998. "Things started getting a little more crazy when we signed up with Don King. For Stoney, it was like the world was his oyster. The more he talked, the more he wanted to talk. The more he got on television, the more he wanted to be on television. In my mind he did too much, in his mind he didn't do enough. The weird part is he actually felt he was the fighter and the trainer, the manager, the promoter. I was like a phantom that came in the ring and left; that was one thing that felt kind of awkward." Ruiz can talk when he wants to, obviously. I asked if his Quiet Man persona had been exaggerated by Stone's tendency to suck up all the available air. Ruiz smiled thinly and said, "I wanted him to get publicity, set me up with reporters, and they were calling Stoney and he wasn't even telling me."

Ruiz came to regard Stone's dramatics as not just distracting and embarrassing but also dangerous. While Stone describes his ejection from the Golota fight as akin to a baseball manager getting himself thrown out to inspire his team—and Ruiz did win enough late rounds to squeeze out a decision—Ruiz told me, "Hey, he took the cut stuff," the coagulants and other treatments that a corner uses to keep cuts and swelling from becoming so grave that the ring doctor stops the fight. "I asked him, 'What would have happened if I got cut?' There was no cut stuff. I would've lost the fight because he acted up."

They also came to disagree about Ruiz's fighting style. "In the gym, he never done that shit, grabbing and holding," Stone told me. "He was flawless. But on fight night you get the fuckin' grapplah. That style was safe for him, so he kept doing it. Half of the things you tell a fighter, it goes in one ear and out the other. If he had done in the ring what he done in the gym, he'd have been making 25 million a fight." Ruiz, for his part, now says Stone and LaMarca made him one-dimensional. "When I was a kid, my stepfather taught me all kinds of boxing styles," he said. "He would watch a fight on TV, then we'd try to do whatever he'd seen. I was knocking more guys out when I was younger." It was Stone, he said, who pushed him to clinch more and punch less, turning a fight into an endurance test. "My stepfather stopped coming around the gym," Ruiz said, "and I wondered about that. Later I found out that Stone told him to stay away. He wanted control."

The breakup of Ruiz and Stone has produced the bizarre situation in which each now blames the other for the very tactics that allowed Ruiz to knock off so many gifted opponents and become champion. Eric Bottjer, the matchmaker, told me that the former partners can't yet fully appreciate what they accomplished together. "When a marriage ends, things are said, things you regret, but then later you let that anger go. Right now they're mad, but when these guys are older and they sit back, they'll see how much they did for each other."

Stone and Ruiz disagree, of course, about who broke up with whom. When, over lunch at an Italian restaurant in Wilmington, Massachusetts, I asked Stone for his version of what happened, he turned to his lawyer, who sat silently across from us in the booth, and asked, "Can I say I didn't retire?" The lawyer considered, then nodded. Stone turned back to me and said, "I didn't retire. Tony Cardinale fired me." He was referring to Ruiz's longtime lawyer and adviser. Stone said he asked Ruiz why he had been fired. "Johnny said, 'You got a little crazy.'" Then, according to Stone, Ruiz told him to "soften the blow" by saying that he was retiring, rather than that he'd been let go. Stone says he ended up going along with the sham as one last sacrifice for his fighter.

"I never fired Stoney," Ruiz told me, "and Tony didn't fire him, either. I did tell him, 'I want you to be part of the team—we stick together from the beginning to the end—but I want you to be more in the background.'" Stone couldn't handle that, Ruiz says. "Look, if he could've been around the fight and said everything and not got paid, he would rather have that than get paid and be in the background."

Stone's exile was a fifteen-month nightmare of seething tedium. "I just sat home and didn't do anything. Got up, had a coffee and a muffin, that was my day." He knocked around the house, aimless, gagging on anger and shame. "John was like my son. I gave everything for that kid. I had a bad taste in my mouth." Throwing himself so completely into the partnership now felt like a sucker's mistake. "I made an asshole of myself and then I'm looking for the train and they're on it and it's gone. Him and the lawyer are riding the train, and I'm still at the station. John made a lot of money. I didn't get paid for the work I done. That's the bottom line." The manager got his contracted cut over the years, but, as he sees it, Ruiz has at least a couple of million additional dollars that Stone should be passing on to his own grandchildren. "Johnny Ruiz was part of my family. I robbed Peter and gave to Paul, and Paul to give to John. I took out three mortgages on my house. I could have gotten a full pension from the T. I could be on easy street. How could he be so ungrateful? But people start whispering in his ear. When that happens, the guy closest to you is the first to go."

Fight people sue each other all the time. It's how they get paid, get even, register strong feeling, or demand respect. The breakup of Stone and Ruiz will end up in court, where money provides the means to keep emotional score. Whatever the outcome of the case, each man will need to go on with his life. Stone, who is 56, says people call all the time asking him to manage this fighter or that one. Ruiz is 35, "old for a fighter," as he says, but the younger heavyweights at the top of the division strike him as eminently beatable. He's going to make one more run at a title.

———————

Manny Siaca's gym is under the bleachers by a running track in Toa Baja, Puerto Rico, outside San Juan. Its concrete ceiling rises overhead in stairstep fashion; in the cavelike gloom below, heavy bags, sit-up benches, a speed bag, a rickety weight bench, and other tools of the trade are crammed into the margins around a single ring with unpadded ropes that burn a fighter's back when he sags against them. Worn, stained mats and sheets of plywood cover the concrete floor. Mosquitos abound. The walls sweat in the wet heat. On one of them is painted a list of the world champions Siaca has trained.

On a Saturday afternoon in mid-September, Ruiz was the only fighter on the premises. He looked good—bulkier than ever in the chest and shoulders, and already close to his prime fighting weight of 235 pounds. Stripped to the waist, slicked with sweat, he toiled through a two-hour workout: shadowboxing, jumping rope, hitting pads held by his trainer, hitting the heavy bag and speed bag. Ruiz, who lived briefly in Puerto Rico as a child, had gone back to basics there: weights in the morning, boxing in the afternoon, roadwork at night; eat heartily and sleep well; repeat. He seemed pleased with the simplicity of the daily life he woke up to. Living in a rented condo in Old San Juan with his second wife and newly christened baby, he worked hard every day, honing himself. "I feel rejuvenated here, training, going into a fight prepared," he said as he stretched, rotating his body at the hips and bending from side to side. It was a relief to be with a veteran trainer. Without Stone on hand to egg him on, he was taking a quieter, almost contemplative approach. Concentrating on refining his technique had rekindled his love of craft.

There was something different about the way Ruiz carried himself in the punching drills. Siaca had altered his balance, resetting it so that Ruiz stayed back on his feet a bit more and was less inclined to dive forward at an opponent when he threw a punch. He also turned his hips and shoulders more than before, improving the leverage of his blows. Siaca, lumpy and bespectacled, said, "You see? The punches, the power? Shorter, more chop." It was a subtle shift, but potentially an important one, as it could well denature the headlong style Ruiz and Stone had developed together. He would hit more crisply, but it's far from certain that a more conventional Ruiz, standing back to throw more punches that might well win over more fans, could still break a man down. "We have seen Ruiz with Norm Stone," as Don King put it. "Now we will see him without."

Ruiz would fight somebody soon, but he didn't know who, where, or when. Maybe King would line up a marquee bout for him with a highly ranked contender, the short path to another title shot. Or he might meet a make-work opponent or two first, while Cardinale angled for a bigger fight. All he could do was train hard and try to be ready.

A former champion who fights past his prime runs the risk of hanging on too long and becoming reliably beatable. Then he becomes a trial horse, a name that younger contenders can put on their résumé to establish their bona fides on the way to their own title shot. Such men in decline typically say they feel great. They always believe they've still got it, even as they absorb too much late-career damage. Ruiz would have to fight in order to find out which he was: a rejuvenated craftsman or a bereft singleton Corsican Brother who couldn't beat the best without his foaming soul mate.

Ruiz finished his workout at the speed bag. Its familiar clatter rose and filled the gym. He rocked from one foot to the other, alternating wrapped hands, in his rhythm, entirely consumed in doing it properly.

———

After the split with Ruiz, Stone was sure he could never work with another fighter. "I was depressed, missing the gym. It was my life. I was in a bad state. But I didn't realize alls I had to do was get off my ass and go to an AA meeting. It was 'Poor me.' Luckily, a friend of mine got out of jail and said, 'C'mon, let's go to a meeting,' and bingo, I'm back in the life, at the gym. Guy called me, told me to take a look at Joe McCreedy. He needs a lot of work on his defense, but he's a good kid, hard-workin' kid. Doesn't drink, no drugs." Still, it was only after a great deal of hesitation that he agreed to manage the young boxer. "I wasn't sold on it," he said. "It's here," he said, pointing at his chest. "Gettin' over Johnny." Eventually, he talked himself into one more fling. "I'll give it all I have, but I don't know how much I do have. It's been a long road."

McCreedy's mid-July bout at the Castle was supposed to help Stone figure out what his fighter had. In McCreedy's last fight, in October 2006, his jaw had been broken on both sides. They had to find out if the repaired bones would hold up in the ring, and also whether disaster could inspire McCreedy to discover a deeper toughness and desire in himself, as Ruiz did after being knocked out by Tua. That was the plan, anyway, until the state boxing commission informed Stone shortly before the evening's first bouts that McCreedy's had been canceled. The opponent, a bearded guy from Maine with the bright-eyed, questioning look of a psycho, hadn't gotten the required signatures on his medical paperwork.

Suddenly Stone and a tall black man from the commission were exchanging looks, stiffening, going into head-tilted pre-beef attitudes. "He threw me out of two fights," Stone muttered to me, still holding the prospective opponent's gaze with an infuriating come-and-get-it smile. "I don't know what his fuckin' problem is." Suits and uniforms intervened, and Stone let himself be steered away from trouble, but he and his nemesis continued to exchange yearning gazes.

The moment passed, though, and Stone just as swiftly regained his good humor when a two-year-old boy with a gorgeous head of tumbling dark golden ringlets ran up to him. Stone scooped him up in his arms, where he settled with regal familiarity. This was one of those grandchildren he had supposedly retired to spend time with. After a while Stone put the boy down, took him by the hand, and said, "Let's go tell Joey he can't fight." To me, he said, "Joey's gonna be bullshit."

Fighters and their cornermen were getting ready in the basement, a dingy, cluttered space broken up by crumbling once-white brick columns. The crews were scattered around folding tables strewn with jars of Vaseline and rolls of white athletic tape. Satiny robes on hangers dangled from exposed pipes.

Stone found McCreedy, took him aside, and broke the bad news. The young man stared at the floor, miserable. "Things happen for a reason," Stone said. "We don't always know what the reason is. You got all your people here, you go up and see them. And you get your money. You get paid." Stone put his arm around McCreedy's sweat-suited shoulder and gave him a bucking-up squeeze. "Thank God nothin' happened," he went on, gently insistent. "We didn't lose the fight. I'll make some calls, see if we can get you a fight quick. Okay? That's why I hate this sport, but I love it, too. It's bullshit, but it's the greatest sport there is. You're runnin' down the field with the ball in your hands and somebody comes out of the stands and tackles you. But then another time you run down the field and nobody tackles you and you get all the glory. So be a man. Go on up." The grandson took it all in, wide-eyed.

This could be a bitterly wasted night for McCreedy, or it could turn out to be a small but telling moment for him—and for Stone, who forged his bond with Ruiz out of shared disappointment as well as hard work. The bond, more than anything else, is what brought him back. "What I'm lookin' for now," Stone told me, "is someone that's gonna work hard, be at their own level, and not change."

The Greatest

RECENTLY (AS THESE THINGS are measured), and after almost three millennia of not imitating Muhammad Ali, a Greek boxer named Epeus started saying, "I am the greatest."

Epeus is a character in Homer's *Iliad*; he makes a brief appearance toward the poem's end, in book 23, during the funeral games for Patroclus. His moment at center stage begins when the bereaved Achilles proposes a boxing match, offering a prize mule to the winner and a two-handled cup to the loser. Epeus stands up to lay his hand on the mule, telling the assembled host that somebody else will have to settle for the cup. He freely admits he's not much of a soldier, but he claims to be the best boxer around, predicts extravagant suffering for his opponent—"I'll open his face and crack his ribs," in one translation—and suggests that the opponent's seconds stay close by to carry out the loser.

"Huge but compact, clever with his fists," Epeus so effectively radiates competence that the rest of the Greek army, including many of the *Iliad*'s most illustrious god-descended heroes, stand around scuffing the dirt in discouraged silence until a minor hero named Euryalos takes them off the hook by accepting the challenge. Naive, dumb, or brave, Euryalos gamely mixes it up with Epeus, who knocks his block off. Although the various translations disagree about the exact nature of the knockout punch—some call it an uppercut and others a hook, while most are content to say in less precise language that

Original publication: *Book*, October/November 1998.

Epeus smote the hell out of him—they all agree that Epeus sees an opening in the other man's guard and ends the fight in a hurry. In my favorite rendering, Euryalos goes down "the way a leaping fish / falls backward in the offshore sea when north wind / ruffles it down a beach littered with seawrack: / black waves hide him." It is the *Iliad*, after all, so he can't just fall over.

In two recent translations of the *Iliad*—Martin Hammond's excellent prose version of 1987 and Robert Fagles's celebrated "modern English Homer" version of 1990—Epeus in his prefight boast says, "I am the greatest." Neither translator has him add "of all time," as Ali usually did, but "I am the greatest" has since the 1960s been one of Ali's trademarked bits of the English language. (Another is that catamaran of a simile, "Float like a butterfly, sting like a bee," which Homer would have appreciated.) Because Ali repeated his poetic formulas with such Homeric regularity, anyone who has heard Ali say "I am the greatest" often enough—and there was a time when most of the English-speaking world fell into that category—will hear his mildly hysterical but still Kentucky-soft voice coming from the mouth of Epeus.

It may be startling to notice that Homer has been made to execute a flawless Ali Shuffle in the midst of his own poetic footwork, but bear in mind that the original footwork resembles Ali's in the first place. Fagles described it as an "ideal coincidence of popular usage and Homer's language." He told me, "I wouldn't have done it if I had to drag the phrase in by the hind legs, but 'I am the greatest' comes so close to the Greek." The effect, he concluded, was only to add resonance and depth to the original.

"I am the greatest" does not turn up in translations of the *Iliad* done prior to the rise of Ali in the 1960s. In George Chapman's seventeenth-century translation, Epeus delivers a lilting "at cuffes I bost me best." Alexander Pope's eighteenth-century version has Epeus saying, "th' undoubted victor I." In William Cullen Bryant's American *Iliad* of the nineteenth century, Epeus is matter-of-fact: "In combat with the cestus . . . I claim to be the best man here." Robert Fitzgerald's often colloquial translation of 1974, done well into the age of Ali, does not use the phrase either—his folksy Epeus weighs in with "I'm best, I don't mind saying"—so we must conclude that Ali's effect on Homer has been uneven at best.

It is an uneven effect but a measurable one, so that we are obliged to ask what it might mean that Epeus—a character in a book—has fallen under Ali's influence in recent years. When we call the *Iliad* a classic, we mean, among other things, that it is living literature constantly given new resonances by the succession of historical moments in which it is read. It makes sense that Ali, who rose to worldwide prominence as television sports and news came into their own, has inflected our retelling of Homer's boxing match. And the next line of Epeus's speech—"I am the greatest . . . So what if I'm not a world-class man of war?"—now raises echoes of Ali's famous refusal to be drafted during the Vietnam War.

An expert punch, like a well-turned phrase, can take on a life of its own. Ali has given us plenty of both: punches like the near-invisible "anchor punch" that ended the second Liston fight so abruptly, or the series of punches that started Foreman on his long trip to the canvas in Kinshasa, his armor clashing around him; phrases like "I am the greatest," "Float like a butterfly . . . ," and "I got no quarrel with them Viet Cong." They come down the years to us and with us, kept fresh in popular memory, on videotape, in common speech and the talk of aficionados, and, strangely enough, in book 23 of the *Iliad*. The punches and phrases will outlive their author; they already have outlived his youth and vigor. As Muhammad Ali's mouth and hands, once so insistently eloquent, slow down and eventually fall silent in the public forum, we are left to conjure with his handiwork and his words. They, and therefore Ali himself, enjoy the second life in popular memory that the Greek heroes held so dear.

Champion at Twilight

THE MAIN EVENT HAD gone the distance. Afterward, there was a press conference at which the loser had half-graciously accepted defeat and the winner had managed to half-insult the loser every time he tried to say something nice about him. The combatants and their supporters then repaired to a nearby nightclub for the postfight party.

Upstairs at the club, big, once-famous middle-aged men in suits gathered at a table. Earlier they had been lined up at ringside like decommissioned battleships in port: the former heavyweight champions Joe Frazier and Leon Spinks; Earnie Shavers and Gerry Cooney, booming punchers who had both challenged for the title and lost; the former Dallas Cowboys lineman Ed "Too Tall" Jones, who had dabbled in pugilism; and Darryl Dawkins, the former Philadelphia 76er, who never boxed but who once dunked a basketball so hard that he shattered the backboard and (he half-believes) the life of the man he dunked on, who later killed himself.

These dreadnoughts of the 1970s and 1980s were appropriate semi-celebrities for a nontitle bout with mostly nostalgic and novelty appeal. There had been no currently hot stars at ringside, no big-time rappers or supermodels, no Sopranos. But the bruisers in suits were an accomplished and physically impressive crew, all the more so for their advanced ages and filled-out frames. They had all been famous for beating other good big men—for pushing around and knocking down guys who were used to pushing around and knocking down other people.

Original publication: *Washington Post Magazine*, November 17, 2002.

When Larry Holmes, the former heavyweight champion, appeared at their table in casual street clothes and with a long-neck beer bottle in hand, he instantly became the center of attention. The other big men called out his name, gestured for his attention, and raised their drinks to toast him. He had beaten Spinks, Cooney, and Shavers (twice). He had held his own as a novice when he sparred with Frazier in his prime, and he had destroyed Frazier's son Marvis in less than one round in 1983. Holmes had never had the chance to beat up Jones and Dawkins, both of whom were much bigger than he, but next to him the two giants looked harmless. Holmes looked eminently capable of doing harm, as always. Hardhanded, resilient, solid through the body but light on his feet, he looked good for a 52-year-old man with 75 professional fights to his credit—even better when one considered that he had fought the 75th that very evening, the ten-round main event that went the distance.

The other veterans had retired long ago. Shavers, who had moved to England, worked the after-dinner speaking circuit. Cooney hawked memorabilia and was trying to start up a fund for former boxers on the skids. Spinks, who never recovered from winning the heavyweight title in his eighth professional bout and losing it in his ninth, had spent most of the evening cadging drinks. Frazier, who was there because his 40-year-old daughter had fought on the undercard, had politely asked the fellow next to him at ringside what town he was in. They were all done. It could be that Holmes, too, was finally done now.

Holmes's opponent, a strong fat man named Eric "Butterbean" Esch, never made it upstairs at the club. He was waylaid near the foot of the stairs by an excited, good-looking, overweight couple who repeatedly assured him that he was the man. While they were talking, more flushed, soft-bodied people collected around them, drinks in hand, until Butterbean stood with his broad back to the wall at the center of a crowd. There were fresh cuts and livid red marks around his left eye. Women kept trying to hug him, and everybody kept telling him how great he was. He was one of them, a regular guy with outsize dreams, and they were proud of him. That was not some bum he had just fought; that was Larry Holmes.

———

A week or so earlier, during the last phases of the buildup to the fight, Holmes and Butterbean were busy expressing personal dislike for each other in interviews. The promoter's tagline for the event was

"Respect: One will give it, one will get it," and he hoped to present their encounter as a grudge match, rather than, say, a fight between an old guy and a fat guy. On the phone with me from his office in Easton, Pennsylvania, Holmes tried to do his part to keep up prefight appearances. "He wants to be the man," he said of Butterbean. "He wants to run the show, and make out like I'm the punk kid. I'm a long way from being a punk kid. I beat guys he can't even dream of getting to know, let alone fight."

Holmes had been the best heavyweight in the world in his prime. He had come up through the ranks as a sparring partner for Frazier, Shavers, and Muhammad Ali, then he had beaten most of his former employers and a whole generation of promising contenders. Having held the title for seven years (1978–1985) and twenty successful defenses, a reign second only to that of Joe Louis, Holmes ranked high on all-time lists of heavyweight champions. He kept company in these rankings with Rocky Marciano, Jack Dempsey, Jack Johnson—the big boys. His exact place depended on the subjective judgment of the list maker, but only Ali and Louis were unfailingly rated above him.

Butterbean was a novelty act. At 35, he stood 5-foot-11 and usually weighed between 310 and 350 pale, hairless, near-neckless, jiggle-breasted, spherically distributed pounds. He once weighed in at 373 pounds for a fight. He came up in the early 1990s via Toughman competitions, messy affairs resembling reality TV as much as boxing, in which brawlers off the street exchange roundhouses like drunks in an alley. Butterbean eventually graduated to real boxing, although of a bottom-feeding variety. For most of the past decade, he campaigned as the King of the Four-Rounders, beating butchers, stiffs, and outright patsies in brief dust-ups. The appeal of these spectacles resided mostly in Butterbean's girth and potency. People enjoyed watching him club down an opponent with crude blows after walking unhurt through the other man's punches, like a monster in an old movie advancing upon a disbelieving victim who fires until his gun is empty, looks wildly at the useless weapon, and then throws it at the monster in a final act of desperation before being devoured.

One principal mission of the buildup to the Holmes-Butterbean bout was to present the combatants as evenly matched, a grand old man against a young lion. On the phone, Holmes tried to say the right things about his opponent—"Never take anybody lightly," and "They say he's tough and he hits so hard"—but his heart wasn't in it. "Look, I won't lie to you," he said, interrupting this train of promotional sweet nothings. "He ain't somebody I should be afraid of. I can't see that man getting inside on me. Maybe he lands a lucky punch, but I don't believe in luck. Not that kind." Now that Holmes was speaking his mind, a passionate note entered his voice. "Look, man, he cain't fight and I'm a kick his ass." So much for marketing double talk.

When I called Butterbean at his prefight hideaway, a casino on the Gulf Coast of Mississippi, he pushed the personal grievance line with greater conviction. "I don't like the man," he said of Holmes in his high, energetic, Alabama-accented voice. "He runs his mouth." This was in part a reaction to a crack Holmes made in his autobiography to the effect that Butterbean was a "circus attraction" and "a fat slob impersonating a fighter." Holmes claimed that his collaborator, a sportswriter, had put the words in his mouth, but he wasn't taking them back, either.

Asked to explain why he was fighting Holmes, Butterbean said, "One, I don't like him, and two, it's the fights after this one, after I beat Holmes, that matter. There's not a lot of money in a Holmes fight"—although Butterbean would make about $100,000, his biggest payday ever—"but people are already calling about the next one." He saw Holmes as a gatekeeper blocking his path not only to big-money fights, but also to legitimacy. Hidden somewhere in the breast of every good-natured buffoon is an aspiration to be taken seriously, and Butterbean, having reached his midthirties, was no longer satisfied to be a novelty act.

As a novelty act, though, Butterbean was gradually attaining the kind of celebrity for which most legitimate boxers, even distinguished champions, can only wish. He had already had a triumphant cameo in a WrestleMania broadcast, and an adept agent should have no trouble working him into the TV mainstream with appearances on talk shows, reality shows, advertisements, perhaps an animated Saturday morning show. Butterbean vs. Mr. T? It could happen. He's a natural for sitcoms, too. The King of the Four-Rounders clocks the King of Queens—ha ha. An overprotective dad meets his daughter's new boyfriend, and it's Butterbean—hee hee. Butterbean might spend many years in that kind of limelight, and he was already well on his way to entering it, but now he wanted to be accepted by fight people as a real boxer, too. He could begin to win their acceptance by flattening Holmes.

———

The fight was held on July 27 in Norfolk, a Navy town that has seen more prosperous days and hopes to see them again in the near future.

Some elements of a downtown revitalization are already in place. The USS *Wisconsin*, a decommissioned battleship, has been converted into a museum. There's a semi-high-end mall named for Douglas MacArthur at the lower end of Granby Street, the old central shopping artery. Farther up Granby, the desolate serenity of a supplanted downtown is relieved by the presence of a couple of places to eat and drink and dance. The Scope, the arena where the fight would take place, is just off Granby, closer to the bus station than to MacArthur Center.

Larry Holmes's locker room in the Scope was big and stark: white tile floor, white cinder-block walls, buzzing fluorescent lights set into the low off-white ceiling, a row of mirrors framed by naked incandescent bulbs. Holmes, big and stark himself in white boxer-briefs and a red polo shirt, sat in a folding chair an hour before fight time. A half-dozen seconds and close associates were in the room with him, most of them wearing matching red-and-white athletic suits of a stiff synthetic fabric that whisked and crackled whenever they moved.

The state boxing commission's doctor came in to take Holmes's blood pressure and to ask ritual questions while Holmes put on socks and laced up and tied his white boots. Any cuts or knockdowns suffered in the gym? No. Any recent operations? No. Any eye operations, in particular? No. There was an ugly mouse under Holmes's right eye, which has given him serious trouble for years, but he didn't intend to let Butterbean hit him in the eye anyway. The doctor chose not to press the matter. On his way out, the doctor passed the referee coming in to go over the rules. Holmes, who has been boxing since the late 1960s, knows the rules.

When the referee left, Cliff Ransom from Holmes's corner started working on his boss's right hand. First he rubbed it thoroughly, working it into suppleness, then he wrapped it in gauze and fitted cotton pads over the punching surface of the knuckles. Next came the bandage-like wrap, over and around and over and around, then a cocoon of tape. Holmes helped him by flexing the hand and making a fist, testing the job at each stage. When Ransom was finished, Holmes smacked the newly wrapped hand into his left palm a few times to test it. One of his cornermen called out, "Big Jack!"—an old nickname for Holmes—"Knock 'em out so they don't come back."

Ransom started on the left hand, which required special attention because Holmes lands ten times as many punches with it as he does with the right. While Ransom worked, Holmes said, "He said he takes a good punch. We'll find out how good." When it was all done, Holmes didn't like the way it felt, so Ransom cut the entire wrap job off with scissors and started from scratch. The second time felt better. Holmes held his hands out to a representative from Butterbean's corner who had come in to observe the wrapping, as mandated by the rules of boxing. The representative nodded, then a neutral party, a fellow who worked for the arena, signed both wrap jobs with a black marker. Holmes got up and began stretching and shadowboxing. After a while, he sat down again and watched the undercard fights on a muted television monitor. He sang snatches of songs, lustily if not well. First, "Thin Line Between Love and Hate," then "Stand by Me," then "You Send Me," to which he improvised a new set of bawdy lyrics.

All this time, his cornermen were mostly standing around and watching him. This is what cornermen do, an ancient routine enacted under buzzing fluorescents in cinder-block rooms all over the world. They have duties to perform during training, and there are times during a fight when they must perform decisively under pressure to close a cut, propose a tactical adjustment, or save their fighter from serious harm, but mostly they watch and wait and offer their warm, breathing presence. An old pro like Holmes no longer needs or asks for much advice, so his cornermen didn't even get to take pleasure in passing on their hard-won experience. There was an easy, sprung rhythm to their routine. At any given moment, most of them would be still, but one or two would be in motion—pacing, or triple-checking a detail like the supply of bottled water and Vaseline. When one stopped, another would start. Every once in a while, somebody would call out something encouraging—"Undisputed champion of the world!" "Seven years!" "Big Jack!"—and the others would nod and murmur. Then the round of movement and stillness would start up again.

"Old" and "fat" are not the disqualifying absolutes for professional athletes that they might seem to be. Watching a cleanly contested tank-town bout between an old guy and a fat guy can turn out to be a lot more interesting than watching two muscleheads clinch and roll around in a marquee title fight. And by any reasonable standard, both Holmes and Butterbean were in good shape, despite the failure of their bodies to conform with the ripped-and-cut conventions currently in vogue. Holmes was nowhere near as quick as he had been in his prime, but he was still very quick for a big man, and he made up in experience some of what he had lost in reflexes. Speed is power, as fight people say, and knowing from long practice when to throw a punch or block one is a form of speed. For his part, Butterbean was not fast but he was strong. Most of that strength was locked up inside him in raw form, inexpressible because he did not have the technical ability to put it to work as leverage, but he was still hard to move, hard to hurt, hard to stop.

Still, sports commentators and editorialists, when they noticed the upcoming Holmes-Butterbean bout at all, generally took the position that it was meaningless, or worse: a farce, a joke, meaningful only to the extent it proved that people will pay to see any freak show. These pious responses made me all the more curious about what the fight might actually mean to Holmes, who appeared to have relatively little to gain and much more to lose.

In the days before the bout, he was still trying to talk himself into believing that whupping Butterbean would matter to him and to others. When I asked him, on the phone, why he was fighting Butterbean, he said, "A carpenter don't have to retire when he's 52. Why do I?" A good question, but not a satisfying answer to mine. He was sitting in his office in the L&D Holmes Plaza, a pair of brick-and-glass office buildings with a fine view of the riverfront, on Larry Holmes Drive in Easton. He was rich and comfortable and accomplished enough to suit almost any son of the working class made good. Why, really, was he fighting Butterbean, and why was he fighting at all at his age?

To begin with, Holmes stood in line for government cheese as a boy, which means that he always finds it hard to pass up a payday, even when he doesn't really need the money. And, while earning a quarter-million dollars for an hour's work, he wanted to show people that he was still good at his job. He had been having trouble finding anybody to fight, though. Titleholders, contenders, and those with even an outside chance of becoming contenders would no longer have anything to do with him, since he could only make them look bad. Holmes could still find an opponent's flaws, and getting beaten by a 52-year-old would ruin a career. A good fighter could probably defeat him just by staying busy in every round, but there would be little glory in it for the victor. That left one potential big-money opponent: George Foreman, a contemporary who—like Holmes—had fought on into middle age. Foreman had made a fortune and—unlike Holmes—achieved ubiquity on television as a boxing commentator and a pitchman for cooking implements, car repairs, and fast food. Holmes had been trying for years to coax him into the ring, but it appeared that Foreman had grown too rich and fallen too far out of shape to take the risk. If Foreman wouldn't fight, Holmes would settle for Butterbean.

Finding a notable opponent was part of Holmes's continuing effort to extract his due from a public that, he feels, has never offered it in full. His comparing himself to a carpenter, a steady working man, was telling. He has always been a businesslike worker, rather than a crowd-pleasing showman, in the ring. His pragmatic boxing style, founded on the left jab and good defense and the timeless premise of hitting without being hit, never made much concession to popular tastes. Posterity unfairly tends to reduce him, perhaps the finest technical boxer on the short list of heavyweight all-timers, to the champion who, in one writer's words, "made boxing seem strictly an act of commerce." Bracketed in history by the two premier celebrity boxers of the television age—Ali, who made boxing seem like political theater, and Tyson, who makes boxing seem like nonconsensual sex—Holmes has been partially eclipsed.

For Holmes, a respectable payday for an easy fight and a chance to show his skill at center stage in front of 7,000 fans in a packed arena and a pay-per-view television audience were reasons enough to take the fight, but he offered yet one more. While I was asking him about how much money he would make, he blurted out a seeming non sequitur: "Let me ask you this: Who do you think is the greatest of all time?" I asked if he seriously thought that fighting on into his fifties against increasingly unimpressive opponents would eventually place him above Muhammad Ali and Joe Louis on all-time lists. Holmes said, wonderingly, "I didn't even know I was going to say that. It just came out."

But he did have a point, sort of. He has held up much better than Ali and Louis, both of whom faded badly in the twilight phase of their careers. Ali, at the age of 38, was barely able to defend himself when Holmes put him out to pasture in 1980; Louis, comebacking at 37, was knocked through the ropes and into retirement by Marciano in 1951. Since turning 40, by contrast, Holmes had won twenty fights and lost only three. In 1992, at the age of 42, he fought consecutive twelve-rounders in which he first scored a prodigious victory over Ray Mercer, who was at the time the most feared heavyweight contender, and then lost a closely contested title fight by decision to Evander Holyfield. In the latter fight, Holmes wore a contact lens to protect his right eye, on which he had recently had surgery for a detached retina. Always confident of his defensive ability, he had the gall to be genuinely exasperated—like a guy on a big date—when it popped out in the third round.

Butterbean would indeed gain some credibility as a boxer if he beat Holmes, but he had almost no chance of winning. For Holmes's part, beating Butterbean was certainly not going to leapfrog him past Ali and Louis in the all-time rankings, and it wouldn't remove him from the media shadow of Ali and Tyson. Holmes enjoyed unimpeachable legitimacy; Butterbean enjoyed growing celebrity. Each craved what the other had, and each saw beating the other as a way to get it. In that sense, both were probably fighting in vain.

The gloves, red Everlasts, arrived in Holmes's locker room. Holmes said, mostly to himself, "Better get myself together." He stood up, stepped into his foul protector, and stripped off the red polo shirt. He had weighed in at 254 pounds, 30 to 40 pounds above his fighting weight during his reign as undisputed champion. Even in his prime, Holmes always had a can-do working man's build, not an ultradeveloped anatomical model of a body like Holyfield's or Ken Norton's. Now, well into middle age, his chest and stomach sagged and there was a broad layer of suet around his middle, but his comparatively slender legs were still strong, and he still had the labor-thickened shoulders and arms of a plasterer. The muscles, big but not cut, moved smoothly beneath the skin.

Holmes, still standing, put on his white trunks. Ransom applied Vaseline to his torso and then his face. One of his cornermen was intoning a mantra: "Take control. Take control. In the ring. Take control." Even if Butterbean was not a real boxer, Holmes had a fight to win in front of an audience.

Somebody opened the locker room door for a moment to call out, "Five minutes." Time to put on the gloves—left first, then right, with white tape at the wrists to cover the laces and secure the fit. The neutral party signed the tape. Ransom put on a pair of practice mitts and Holmes banged them for a while, getting the gloves properly settled onto his hands, then went into a familiar shadowboxing sequence: left jab, left jab, right cross, more lefts, grunting and circling first one way and then the other as he threw punches. He looked so utterly competent, sagging middle and all, that it was hard not to sympathize at least a little with his complaint that he could still fight and nobody worthwhile would fight him.

In the ring, a woman was singing the national anthem with the requisite soulful flourishes and quavers. Strains of it echoed down the backstage hallways and filtered through the closed door of Holmes's locker room. Inside, Holmes's crew collected near the door, readying themselves for the ring walk. Holmes, still warming up, did a tricky crabwise shuffle and threw a combination. He reached down with a glove to adjust his protective cup. "Got to protect my future," he said, grinning. "Oh, I forgot. I don't got no future."

The national anthem was over, and Butterbean's ring-walk music, "Sweet Home Alabama," was playing. The door opened, and word came from the hallway that Butterbean had made his entrance. Holmes left off warming up, slipped into the red-and-white robe that someone held for him, and went through the doorway without breaking stride, his crew stepping aside to admit him into their midst and then gathering around him in motion. In a tight mass, the group went down the hall to the heavy black curtains that masked the entrance to the arena proper. They paused here, waiting in the backstage twilight, eager to enter the loud brightness on the other side. Smoke from a special-effects machine drifted in thick skeins, catching stray bars of light that stabbed through small gaps where the curtains did not meet flush.

Now Holmes's familiar ring-walk music began: "Ain't No Stopping Us Now," the old Philadelphia soul anthem. Everybody in the crew stood up a little straighter. Functionaries pulled aside the curtains, and Holmes and his people went through into the light and the roar of acclamation that greeted his appearance. This might be the last time.

After the usual prefatory huffing and puffing, the bell rang and the combatants got down to it.

In the opening minutes of a fight, Holmes looks as if he is in trouble. He backs away from an advancing opponent, stiff-legged and blinking, arms extended in what seems like a desperate attempt to save himself from incoming blows. Far from denoting a steely determination to prevail, his manner seems to say, "Hey! Watch it with those fists!" A naive spectator would think that Holmes, realizing he can't cope with his opponent, has panicked. Actually, Holmes is taking measurements of the other man's style, using his long arms as calipers to calculate the distance between them at which he can hit without being hit in return. The more straightforward the opponent's style, the sooner Holmes gets inside it and figures it out. Then he settles down to the grind of winning rounds.

It took Holmes less than one round to parse Butterbean. That done, he ceased retreating and set himself up at medium-long range, jabbing and making small, well-timed changes in the space between the fighters to maintain his advantage in leverage. He began landing punches with the straight-and-true authority of a master carpenter driving nails. His arm-extended defense now revealed itself as a form of command rather than submission. He does not wait for punches to be thrown before he blocks them, preferring to reach into his opponent's space and smother punches before they take final form. When he had found his defensive rhythm against Butterbean—when he had figured out and entered Butterbean's rhythm—he stymied developing punches like a parent taking food out of the hands of an enormous baby who is rearing back to throw it.

Butterbean, by contrast, comes out for a first round as if he could punch a hole in the universe. His size and fierce demeanor can briefly distract a spectator from recognizing that he takes forever to load up leverage for a punch and then bring it around his keg-shaped torso in a wide arc, that he has a rudimentary understanding of footwork and feinting and self-defense, and that he doesn't know much about how to hit somebody who knows how to defend himself. In the first round he charged Holmes a few times, stamping and throwing out-size blows, a couple of which landed, but not flush. Holmes shook them off.

By the second round, the two men had tacitly worked out the terms under which they would contest the rest of the bout. The pace was steady, if slow, and there was very little clinching. Holmes stood in the middle of the ring in his characteristic fighting posture, head cocked, frowning intently, like a dog catcher extricating a foaming stray from under a porch. Butterbean tried to get at him, but not with the sustained free-swinging gusto he typically displays in four-rounders. Feeling the pressure of having to go ten rounds for the first time, facing a skilled boxer who would make him pay for his mistakes, he tried to pace himself and grew overcareful. He threw left hooks, but Holmes smothered them or swayed out of their path. Butterbean had trouble getting into position to throw a right, and when he did manage to throw one, it fell short. Holmes, seeing it coming, had already stepped away. While Butterbean was thinking of what to do next, Holmes would step in and jab him a couple of times, perhaps following up with a right. Sometimes, Holmes would throw the right hand all by itself, a crisp shot that jarred Butterbean's big head back against the roll of flesh that padded his squat neck.

Butterbean, frustrated, did not land many punches. He hurt Holmes only once, by accident, when the fighters clashed heads near the end of the fifth round. Butterbean's head, which resembles a marble dome, makes an ideal instrument for butting. When the bell rang to end the round, Holmes, in a daze, mistakenly visited a neutral corner and was headed for Butterbean's when he finally located his own. It took him most of the minute between rounds to recover, but he came out clearheaded for the sixth.

By then, both men already knew how the fight would turn out. Butterbean's left eye, the one closer to Holmes when they were in boxing position, had been reddening and swelling as Holmes pounded it with jabs, and in the middle rounds a cut opened in the eyelid and began to bleed. The blood on Butterbean's face seemed to be satisfying to both men: Holmes was outboxing a man seventeen years his junior; Butterbean was taking his medicine, going the distance against the odds.

Murray Sutherland, Butterbean's cut man, yelled at his fighter to keep his left hand up and punch to the body—to protect the eye and take away Holmes's legs—but Butterbean, who flinched whenever Holmes feinted a left jab, wouldn't or couldn't do what he was told. Expecting Butterbean to suffer a terrible beating, Sutherland had brought along an extra-large supply of cut solution, topical thrombin in a 1/1000 mixture, to control the bleeding. Sutherland, who was a light heavyweight contender in the 1980s and who now supervises Toughman competitions, understood the difference between the combatants.

Holmes, with a good sweat going and the fight well in hand, made in-the-rhythm whooping noises when he punched—*Yoop! Hughgh! La-yoop!*—and let his gloves drop down out of defensive position. He was now dismissing Butterbean's punches with slight head movements and nuances of footwork. This was disheartening for the younger man because it seemed that Holmes no longer needed to bother blocking his punches or even to think about them. Butterbean's best shots were minor distractions from the more engrossing task of punching Butterbean in the eye.

Before the tenth and last round, Butterbean's seconds told him—as they had been telling him all evening—that he had to turn the boxing match into a brawl. "Three minutes," said one. "You stay right on his case. You're gonna get hit, but . . ." There was no other way to get inside Holmes's long arms.

Butterbean rediscovered his abandon and did what he could to make the fight messy, hoping to create a chance to land a lucky knockout punch. He had no success until, in the round's waning seconds, he threw a left hook that glanced off the outside of Holmes's right shoulder. It looked like nothing, a missed blow, but Holmes stumbled backward and sort of sat on the lower strands of the ropes for a moment before getting up. The referee called it a knockdown. Holmes stood, looking disgusted, while the referee counted to eight.

The final bell sounded a few seconds later. Functionaries and cornermen climbed through the ropes and filled the ring as Holmes grimaced into a ringside camera to indicate his displeasure with the referee. Butterbean went around with his right glove raised high to the crowd until Sutherland corralled him. Sutherland smiled as he tended to Butterbean's mangled left eye. His boy had gone the distance with Larry Holmes, and the record would show for posterity that he had scored a knockdown. That was something.

The judges all scored the fight in Holmes's favor by a wide margin, and most people in the crowd saw it the same way, but there were exceptions. A young couple in ringside seats repeated the usual two-syllable protest in unison, giving it their shouting, red-faced best, as if they were only two among thousands of enraged chanting partisans. A curiously archaic-looking fellow—dark suit, slicked-back hair, pencil mustache—wandered along press row saying, "*Holmes* won that fight? He just walked *around*." Somebody else yelled, "You da man, Butterbean," but the sentiment hung awkwardly in the air. Butterbean was clearly not the man that night.

———

When I called Butterbean three days after the bout, he still didn't understand exactly what Holmes had done to him. He hesitated and second-guessed himself on the phone just as he had in the ring. "If we done it over," he said, "I'd go all-out in the middle rounds, just go at him and keep going at him like I used to do." Then, as if disagreeing with something somebody else had just said, he added, "Yeah, but maybe if I'd gone out in my old way, I'd a got knocked out."

He was certain, though, that fighting Holmes had been a mistake. "I took the wrong guy for my first ten-round fight. He's too slick." Butterbean wanted to fight another real boxer, but he wanted to fight one who wasn't so slick, a brawler who would consent to stand directly in front of him and trade punches.

Why had Butterbean made the unwise leap directly from four rounds to ten, and against a great technical boxer? Because, he said, he had been in a hurry to prove that he was a real heavyweight. "I wanted to prove the critics wrong. I wanna be taken serious. There's always that little bit in me that says, 'I'll show you.' That's the move I'm making now. It's the path that'll quiet a lot of the people who say I'm not a real boxer."

I asked if perhaps the most insistent voice Butterbean was trying to silence was in his own head. "Yeah," he conceded, "it might be that I want to prove it to myself. It may not be nothin' to prove but to myself." There was a pause in which I could hear him breathing into his phone, then his marketing instincts returned to him in the way that a fighter's senses return to him after a hard shot scatters them. "Hey, when I write my book, it'll make a good chapter."

"Everybody's calling, saying they're surprised Larry looked so good at 52," said Jay Newman, Holmes's publicist, when I called him in Easton after the fight. I asked if that response was giving Holmes any crazy ideas about continuing his latest comeback. "It gives *me* crazy ideas," admitted Newman, but he didn't really expect Holmes to fight again. "Not unless there was a million dollars in it for him," and that seemed unlikely. "It makes no sense to fight again for less."

After a pause, Newman added, "And even if Larry's not feeling like he's done, the guys in his corner have been with him a long time. They're starting to get tired." Holmes's crew had lived significant portions of their lives vicariously through the body of their boss, watching him stretch and work out and shadowbox and spar; worrying about his meals and digestion, his bad eye and breakable right hand; making the ring walk at his side and dutifully urging him on from ringside as his weigh-in figures went up and his punch count went down. That was a heavy burden of lives and aspirations for one body to carry—too heavy, perhaps, for a 52-year-old body, even one that had retained a large measure of its competence and force. There were other, easier ways to make money.

Newman said, "The niche market for us right now is grand openings. A Champs, a Circuit City, they fly Larry in, he signs some autographs, gets his fee, and that's it." A former champion of Holmes's stature can work this circuit in perpetuity—not just in-store appearances, but also conventions, corporate functions, after-dinner speaking, motivational gigs. He moves through a landscape of hotel ballrooms, airport concourses, parking lots with grand-opening banners and knots of balloons fluttering in the breeze. He tells stories about forcing a way against adversity, about taking care of your assets. He laughs, he gets laughs; because he's a boxer, it's often okay if he tells an off-color anecdote or cusses a little. When he appears at ringside as a distinguished retiree, he's announced to the crowd, which gives him a respectful hand. And if he's Larry Holmes, he's sizing up the young men in the ring and telling himself, with pride and regret, that he could still whup them.

Bedtime Story

I WAS IN A CITY far from home, working on a magazine story. I spent the day and evening going around asking questions, watching people do what they do, filling up a couple of pocket notebooks. Among other places, I visited the dog pound, a place of grimness even though—or because—the people who worked there seemed gentle and well-intentioned. All those pit bulls, muscled up with nowhere to go, flexing as we walked past on the other side of the bars. They were desperate and accommodating, and they knew that something was wrong. They could smell all the dogs that came before them. Where had they gone?

Around midnight I retired to the dingy motel where I'd been put by the magazine that sent me out to do the story. In an effort to cut down on expenses, its travel office had found me a place where if you wanted to line up some crack or a prostitute all you had to do was hang out for a while in the parking lot. It had been a long day and evening, with drinking at the end of it. The pit bulls were on my mind. I don't have much use for dogs but I kept coming back to the sight of the animals lined up in their cages, going all rigid and alert and eager to please when visitors came by. They had thought something was going to happen, even if they didn't know what it might be, but it didn't happen. Life would go on like that for a while until, I guessed, some were adopted and some were taken out and killed, and then other dogs would take their place, and soon it would be the new dogs' turn to win the lottery or die.

One thing to do in a dingy motel is to watch dingy TV. There was lots of it—tedious sports shows and talk shows, unfunny comedies, dumbass celebrity updates, bad movies of the '80s, a charnel house of shitty writing and stale ideas. I ran aground for a while on an off-brand show or movie about the crew of a rocket ship who go around fighting space vampires. The heroes dashed from here to there shouting fakey jargon and toting futuristic weapons that looked like the weapons we have now with nonfunctional molded-plastic appendages glued to them. The vampires glowered, hissed, and suppurated. It kind of ruins the space-opera magic to wonder what the actors' parents think when they see them on the screen, but that's what I usually wonder about. The talented darling who starred in school plays and expectant local fantasies back in Elk Grove Village or Mamaroneck or wherever is now wearing fangs and slathered in gory makeup and being blown unconvincingly in half by a plasmoid megablaster. I picture the parents thinking, "Well, at least he *is* on TV."

The lameness of it all caught me just right—in that end-of-day, far-from-home, buzzed-from-work mood—and laid me low. Deep gloom descended.

I went through the channels a few more times, only growing more despondent, until I happened upon round one of the middleweight title fight between Marvin Hagler and John Mugabi—held 22 years before, almost to the day. Hagler had his hands full, but he knew what to do about it. He was settling in to cope with Mugabi's strength and power by taking him deep into the fight, wearing him out over the long haul and finishing him late. Mugabi, a blowout artist, had gone ten rounds just once and six only twice in his twenty-five fights, all wins. The turning point would come in the sixth round, when Hagler, having blunted the force of Mugabi's early-round assault, would take over the fight by giving his man a spine-jellying pounding, then settle in to finish him inside the distance, KO'ing him in the eleventh.

All of a sudden I felt a lot better. I turned down the sound and put out the light. On the screen, Goody Petronelli, Hagler's trainer, radiated calm and ease as he talked to his fighter between rounds. Everything was going to be fine; Petronelli's every gesture said as much. His main task was to create a recurring pocket of serenity to which Hagler could retreat between hard-fought rounds for rest and reflection. Demonstrating a for-example combination he wanted Hagler to throw, Petronelli moved his own hands as if arranging flowers. Let's just fix a couple of little mechanical things, he was saying, and it's your fight. Doesn't matter how strong the other guy is. Doesn't matter what he's done before this or who he's done it to. We know how to beat him. We know how to beat everybody. Hagler wasn't exactly looking at his trainer and he didn't exactly nod, but he heard him.

I took off my glasses and put them on the cigarette-stained bedside table, put my head down on the pillow, and was dreamlessly asleep before either fighter struck a blow in the next round.

Cities

Ghosts

MY DAUGHTER LING-LI, WHO is eight, has lately been menaced by ghosts. They begin gathering at bedtime, preparing to invade her dreams. Deep in the night, awakened by a particularly vivid nightmare after a string of lesser ones, she pads down the hall to my room and comes around to my side of the bed. "I'm having Bad Thoughts," she says in the dark, her voice low. "Bring everything." I am the resident expert on bad dreams, having had them all my life: half-seen, slavering beasts surging through doors that won't lock and windows too small to fit the frame; a long walk down the corridors of hell with a baseball bat on my shoulder; the same unspeakably hideous movie on every channel and the TV won't turn off and then, somehow, I'm in the movie. Technique is an antidote to fear, I've learned, so I taught Ling-li when she was very small that an ally can enter your dreams to bring you specialized equipment you can use to repel various menaces, and that eventually, as your powers as a dreamer grow, you can dispense with the ally's intervention and train your sleeping mind to produce the equipment when you need it.

Over the years, she and I have assembled an arsenal for her that includes a net for catching monsters; a fire extinguisher, added during her fire-fearing period; a flying castle, and a winged horse to get there; and the Slippery Suit, to foil the bad guys who forever yearn to grab her and spirit her away to their extravagantly unhappy lairs. We've recently added a small, smooth stone you keep in your pocket.

Original publication: *My Town: Writers on American Cities*, US State Department, 2010.

When ghosts appear, you put your hand around the stone, which causes a strong wind to blow up, sending those diaphanous sons of bitches scudding away, howling in frustration. But I may have made the case for my own expertise a little too well; instead of training her own sleeping self to carry these items, she still prefers to wake me up and instruct me to bring them to her, as if I were her ectoplasmic gun bearer or attorney.

Ling-li's worries about ghosts date from a recent family outing to Georges Island, in Boston Harbor. We spent a few hours there exploring Fort Warren, in which Confederate prisoners were kept during the Civil War. No doubt some of them died there. In lightless galleries deep within the fort we held hands and shuffled blindly, feeling with our feet for irregularities in the naked stone floor, straining to make out even a faint shape in the blackness, immoderately relieved when up ahead another visitor's cell phone cast a brief, greenish glow. On the return ride on the ferry, Ling-li and her little sister, Yuan (who is not afraid of ghosts), joined the crowd of kids hanging on the rail at the bow in the watery September sunlight, screaming happily into the wind as the boat sawed through the wakes of other craft. Back on the mainland, we walked past the offices of a company that conducts haunted house tours of Boston. Ling-li approached the guy in a top hat who was drumming up business at a lectern out front. Affecting an archaic accent and a dastardly manner, he at first refused to confirm or deny that ghosts were real, but eventually, upon further interrogation, told her that he himself was a ghost. She absorbed this news without comment, and we went on our way. The encounter with the mock-Victorian tour tout and the spookiness of the fort, reacting together, initiated the current ghost cycle in her dream life.

When people ask me what I like about Boston I usually say that it's old (for a New World city) and you can go almost everywhere on foot. Neither quality is typical of American city life. I grew up in Chicago, a city that now feels to me like an experiment, a cyclopean model train set scattered just the other day across the prairie. All the pyramids and cathedrals of my childhood rose and fell within living memory—the high-rise housing projects marching away along the verge of the expressway, the monumental ruins of steel mills and factories tumbling in slow motion into the high prairie grass that eventually reclaims a deserted lot in Chicago. And Chicago stretches across the flat Midwestern landscape on such an inhuman scale that on a windy February night it feels as if a destination eight blocks distant lies just over the curve of the earth.

To a Chicago-trained sensibility, Boston feels jammed-in, as if long ago someone had gathered up a great deal of urban material—triple-deckers, college quadrangles, bridges of stone and steel, the golden dome of the State House, lawn chairs and trash cans placed in parking spaces to reserve them for whoever shoveled the snow out of them—and packed it all tightly into an oddly shaped location at the edge of the ocean. I live in Brookline, a separate town tucked into a concave depression in the boundaries of Boston proper; my neighborhood, my adopted landscape of home, is a collection of familiar wrinkles in the city's scrunched-up fabric. The street I live on, a double row of duplex houses set nearly cheek to cheek, lies between higher ground on one side and train tracks on the other. At night from my windows I can watch the Green Line trains, lit up like excursion boats, passing behind the houses across the street. On winter nights, when I build a fire in the fireplace, the approaching and receding sound of trains comes down the chimney. Bracketed by two fingers of the Green Line track network's handlike spread, the swelling contours of Aspinwall Hill and Fisher Hill, and the main thoroughfares of Beacon Street and Boylston Street, we're holed up here like mice in a niche in an old stone wall.

But coziness requires its own antidote: I like to run at night, after the girls have been put to bed with stories and stuffed bears and night lights. Starting off down the block, I leave the house behind me with the porch light on and another light up in the office window where my wife sits at her desk. I cross Beacon Street and enter Brighton, part of Boston proper, passing houses and then apartment buildings with windows blue-lit by TV. Warmed up and letting out my stride, I cross Washington Street on the diagonal by the police station, the presence of which does not entirely deter the city's famously incompetent and irate drivers from running red lights right in front of it. I follow the gentle downslope of Market Street toward the river. The sidewalks are nearly empty and traffic is light.

The river, lined on both banks with paved paths, is one of Boston's longest, deepest wrinkles—an intimate natural alley, partially screened by trees and brush, that funnels you semisecretly through the city, intersecting with streets only where it comes to a bridge. I pick up speed on the riverside path, falling into long-haul rhythm, seized by a growing feeling of insubstantiality as I pass from a stretch of gloom through a better-lit patch and back into gloom again. The occasional rat darts across the path almost underfoot. Sentinel ducks and geese standing watch at the edges of sleeping flotillas of their kind sound an alarm at my approach and then the all-clear when they determine that it's only me. A pale heron rises up with a start from the shallows and with a couple of sullen wingbeats glides away over the water. Once, as I went by a thicket of tall reeds that always stirs whisperingly at my passing, a coyote came out ahead of me into a bar of moonlight, looking back over its hunched shoulder as it crossed the empty road, and paced me for a while before disappearing into a dark wedge of marshy ground on the other side.

I pass the occasional fellow runner or late dog-walker; in good weather, courting couples sit on benches overlooking the water. But the living are outnumbered along the river by relics of the dead: Richie Forte, killed in Vietnam, for whom a park in the Nonantum section of Newton is named; David Berray, who died in the World Trade Center on September 11, 2001, and is remembered on a plaque next to a playground in Cambridge; Longfellow and Eliot and Weeks and Weld and all the other harrumphing old-timers who gave their names to bridges and boathouses; the legions of long-dead authors whose books gather dust in the stacks of the libraries of the universities that front on the water—Harvard, the Massachusetts Institute of Technology, Boston University. Not far from the memorial to David Berray there's an authoritative-looking granite marker inscribed with a fantastically untrue claim: "On this spot in the year 1000 Leif Erikson built his house in Vineland." Ebenezer Norton Horsford, a nineteenth-century baking-powder entrepreneur with a passion for amateur archaeology of the most poetic sort, is responsible for the marker. He also had a fanciful Viking tower erected farther west on the river, and led the effort to commission the statue of Leif Erikson that peers out at ramp traffic, palm shading brow, from the grassy median of Commonwealth Avenue at the edge of Back Bay. Perhaps Horsford's labors finally calmed the unquiet Viking ghosts that gathered at his bedside, although we'll never know, because Horsford's long dead, too, of course.

Sometimes I try to explain to Ling-li my urge to be out at night, unencumbered, moving fast, fitting myself into the landscape's seams and the cycle of its rhythms. She plainly thinks it foolhardy to choose to be so exposed and alone in the dark, but I try to make her see that the night run is a technique of belonging, of inscribing yourself into a place and the place into yourself. Repeating and varying your routes, you stitch yourself into the texture of your home ground so that you can't be easily pulled from it—not by your enemies, and not even by those who love you. It's true that when you run at night you feel the chill of the thinness of the world, the tenuous weakness of your connection to anyone or anything—especially in the cold and wet, and most especially on a Sunday night in the dead of winter—but she doesn't yet understand how you also strike a blow against this loneliness precisely by seeking it out. As the city's ghosts grow more familiar to you, by degrees you join their fellowship. For every half-seen figure at a second-floor window or in a passing car, for every phantom shape that flickers in your peripheral vision as you pass a stand of trees or a cemetery on a riverfront rise of ground, there are many more you don't see, many more who, rather, catch a glimpse of you: a strangely familiar shadow against the greater dark.

When I return home, I stretch and shower and put on sweats, then pad through the quiet house, turning off lights, checking the stove and the locks on the doors, making sure all is well. My wife has gone off to bed already. Before I join her, I stop in the girls' room to kiss them goodnight in their sleep. I often sit in their room for a minute, listening to their breathing, the house ticking over in the stillness, the muted rumble and whoosh of a late train. I'm the only spark of conscious life in the house, passing soundless and unseen among unheeding sleepers. Yuan once told me, "You're like a bad guy who likes me and protects me from the other bad guys." Sometimes I linger a little longer in the girls' room, waiting to return fully to my body so that I can lie down next to my wife and sleep.

The Elements of Providence

SUNSET ON AN OVERCAST late October evening, shortly before the year's final lighting of WaterFire. The tide is up, surging in from Narragansett Bay, temporarily reversing the direction in which the city's rivers flow. Fallen leaves drift upstream on the Providence River, which passes between manmade walls through the heart of the city. Where the waters divide, some of the leaves wander to the right into the canal-straight Moshassuck River, but most of them pass to the left into the larger Woonasquatucket River and on into the great circle of the river basin by Waterplace Park, in front of the Providence Place Mall.

Boat-borne volunteers, dressed all in black like Kabuki stagehands, have loaded logs and kindling into 100 braziers—steel-lattice containers shaped like three-foot-high martini glasses—that float, moored, in the three rivers. The reflected lights of the city, brightening in the deepening gloom, seem to rise up out of the depths to move just under the water's surface. On a riverside walkway, a young man in a ball cap carries a stepladder from bridge to bridge, mounting it to light the candles in ornate chandeliers that hang from the spans' undersides.

The recorded music begins with the chimes of a summoning bell, then droning strings and flute. More than half a mile of riverfront has been wired for sound, 60-plus speakers connected by UHF transmitters and receivers, time-delay circuits, and a couple of miles of heavy audio cable. The music, a contemplative mix that will range through-

Original publication: *Washington Post Magazine*, September 17, 2006.

out the night across classical, new age, the margins of pop, and ethnic and traditional styles from around the world, is loud enough to pervade the scene but does not force you to raise your voice to compete with it.

Water, fire, and music: public art at its most elemental. On about 20 evenings from late spring to late fall (the exact number of lightings depends on the eternal essentials: tides, weather, and corporate sponsors), WaterFire's orchestrated merger of simple, recombinant components draws large crowds of locals and visitors to Providence's revived downtown. Attendance has approached 100,000, equal to more than half the city's population, at some midsummer lightings. From modest beginnings as a small, one-time First Night event in 1994, WaterFire has grown into an important civic institution with a dozen year-round employees and a $1 million annual budget. An individual lighting involves 100 volunteers, additional subcontractors, and a 24-hour cycle of prep work and cleanup.

It seems as if everything in the city wants to fit itself into the order and rhythm of the event. A bus grinding uphill provides counterpoint to boats sliding silently through the water. A train whistle sounds in the pause between tunes. Buildings seem to attend, crowding down to the water's edge. People, too, of course. They arrive in couples, threes, larger collections of family or friends. They stroll along the banks or find a place to sit and look at the water, waiting for the fires.

A flotilla of six wood-tending boats enters the circular basin, the upstream end and ceremonial center of WaterFire. Black-clad volunteers lean out with torches from the boats to light the braziers. The fires brew up smartly, crackling and settling, throwing out sparks that sail on the breeze before extinguishing themselves in the water with a tiny hiss. The bittersweet, autumnal, deeply New England smell of burning wood spreads through the city.

I've been attending WaterFire lightings off and on for the past decade. Every time I come, I am taken by a rush of feeling that has two distinct parts. One is a sense of intimacy with Providence, an old city by American standards (it was founded in 1636) and an insular one, where I'm always acutely aware that veiled, closely held local meanings shadow the official history retailed at monuments and landmarks. The other part of my response is that at every lighting I find myself resolving to be a better person—to contribute more to the public good, to be more neighborly, more patient with my kids, more appreciative of my wife, to notice beauty. I suspect that the two reactions form the halves of a single whole, that to touch the city's soul means to be touched by it in turn. This time I'm going to try to figure out why WaterFire gets to me the way it does.

———————

WaterFire has turned Providence into an "event place," a city that employs a signature cultural asset to draw visitors. The usual roster of event places includes major American cities such as New Orleans (Mardi Gras), Chicago (Blues Festival), San Francisco (Chinese New Year), Philadelphia (the Mummers Parade), and Washington (the Smithsonian Folklife Festival, among others). Looking farther afield, to Europe, there's the Palio in Siena, Carnevale in Venice, the running of the bulls in Pamplona, Oktoberfest in Munich, and all manner of religious and folk observances with centuries-deep cultural roots.

Providence, which would seem to have more in common with, say, Youngstown, Ohio, than with those other cities, makes an unlikely addition to the list. Although Providence is architecturally distinguished and historically significant—as an ancestral home of religious freedom in America, among other things—it has been better known for generations as a depressed, corrupt, cartoonishly parochial Rust Belt city on the skids. It has also been overshadowed by Boston and New York, the cultural capitals to the north and south. Now, though, WaterFire draws culture-seeking travelers in surprisingly large numbers.

"The piece is designed to have very soft edges," says Barnaby Evans, the Providence-based artist who created WaterFire, meaning that it welcomes all types of wanderers-in, fitting itself to all kinds of agendas and schedules. I have arranged to run into him at the lighting. Salt-and-pepper-bearded, wearing a leather jacket, he greets passersby and stoops to pick up a plastic cup somebody dropped on the river walk. "It's the opposite of the theater model, where the shows all go off at eight, all the restaurants have to feed everybody before that, everything has to happen on schedule."

His model is the *passeggiata*, the Southern European habit of the evening stroll during which you take the air while participating in an informal street pageant that sustains community and connection to place. Because American life is so dominated by the car, the television, air conditioning, and other technologies that discourage casual but meaningful encounters in public space, Evans intended WaterFire to satisfy the resulting hunger to commune with fellow citizens and the city itself. The mall can't meet that need; neither can Google.

This passeggiata's neighborliness might not necessarily seem welcoming to outsiders, but, Evans argues, WaterFire appeals to visitors because it requires no special knowledge of the city. "As a completely new event, it doesn't have localized identity in the way that some older ones do," he says. "It's deliberately universal. Seeing it the first time, you have every right and opportunity to interpret it as authoritatively as somebody who's lived here." Tourists, often blamed for ruining event places by diluting their local character, actually help WaterFire succeed. "With tourists, you have that new energy, that discovery, going on. It's not the same as centuries-old religious and ethnic festivals with layers and layers of meaning and neighborhood-to-neighborhood rivalries you wouldn't hope to understand at all as a tourist."

I'm not a local, but I'm not exactly a stranger to Providence, either. I grew up in Chicago, where I first encountered an exquisitely gloomy, peak-roofed, demon-haunted Providence in the pulp fantasy stories of H. P. Lovecraft, the city's literary hero. There's a single phrase in Lovecraft's *The Dream-Quest of Unknown Kadath*, which I first read when I was ten years old, that hooked me on Providence for life: "There is Providence quaint and lordly on its seven hills over the blue harbor, with terraces of green leading up to steeples and citadels of living antiquity." I have lived in the Northeast more than half my life, and in Boston, only 45 minutes north of Providence, since 1997, and I know my way around the real Providence almost as well as I know my way around Lovecraft's city, but I will always remain an outsider. In Rhode Island, one of the most proudly local and unhomogenized places in America, people give directions by referring to buildings that were torn down long ago. If you don't know what they're talking about, you're out of luck. For a Chicagoan, too, Providence's greater age makes the place seem all the more inscrutable: smaller than my city, yes, but denser, tighter, more deeply layered with secret history. WaterFire raises the ghosts of Providence; I half-sense them, indistinct presences collecting along the riverfront, drawn by the light, warmth, and sound.

———

The lighting is now in full swing, a rhythm it will sustain until 1 a.m. The music rises and falls, as do the fires, replenished by the boats. Other craft decorously ply the waters: refurbished water taxis from Bangkok, long black gondolas, and a glamorous little boat fitted out with a canopy under which two couples sip wine at a wooden table by lantern light.

WaterFire's intimate yet grand scale adds to its potency. I could easily throw a cell phone across the Providence River, but it's still wide enough to seem like a significant body of water. WaterFire's half-mile-plus stretch of riverfront terrain feels rich but compact, complex but knowable. After an hour or two of strolling up and down its length, I find myself returning to and lingering at the junction of the three rivers, where the land narrows to a point like the prow of a ship thrust into the Providence River. Standing on that point, where the secondary line of braziers on the Moshassuck converges with the main line of braziers on the Woonasquatucket and the Providence, I feel for a moment as if I may have found WaterFire's heart. The moment will pass, though, as the music changes, the night deepens, and my own perspective shifts with each phase of rest or motion.

———

I walk to Pot Au Feu, a restaurant near the far downstream end of WaterFire, to see Bob Burke, its well-connected proprietor. Barnaby Evans and several others have told me to talk to Burke if I want to understand what WaterFire means for Providence. I find him at the downstairs bar in his restaurant. Like almost every other provider of food and drink located anywhere near the riverfront, he's doing excellent business tonight. Burke, whose swept-back silvered hair, good suit, and bow tie are offset by the crinkled mouth of a recovering class clown, takes me for a walking tour of his end of downtown. Water-Fire enlivens the blocks by the water, but when we turn inland the aroma of wood smoke follows us down darker, quieter streets.

As we walk, he tells me about the falcons that hunt squabs from a deco skyscraper known as the Superman Building (for its resemblance to the Daily Planet building in the comic books and the old TV show), and about the landing pad for zeppelins on its roof. He explains that there are people in town who brag about "the Big O in the Big O"—that is, having sex in the giant letters atop the Biltmore Hotel that spell out its name. He shows me the Arcade Building, claimed by some to be "the first indoor shopping mall in America," the two dissimilar classical facades of which preserve in stone a nearly two-centuries-old disagreement between its architects—the perfect Providence story in that it features antiquity, independent thinking, a beef, and a quirky result.

To understand WaterFire's importance, Burke says, you have to talk about downtown Providence's amazing comeback in the past couple of decades. First, there was a classic postindustrial decline, spanning the mid-twentieth century, that bled the life from the city. "Downtown was a graveyard with lights," he says. "In our minds, we were dead and buried. We all knew why we were in the Guinness Book of World Records." Extensive concrete decking covered the rivers, including a 1,147-foot-wide platform listed by Guinness as the widest bridge in the world. Atop it was an intersection known as Suicide Circle. Pedestrian-unfriendly streets, city-dividing highways, railroad tracks, parking lots, and other dead spaces dominated the cityscape. Reduced from a cultural and commercial hub to a desolate crossroads for cars on their way to other places, the once-lively downtown felt entombed, like its paved-over rivers. Most citizens, urbanites as well as suburbanites, shunned it.

But Providence was lucky, it turned out, to have been so depressed and passively led that it failed to wreck its elegant building stock with the sort of sweepingly misguided urban renewal projects that trashed other cities' downtowns in the 1950s and '60s. That made it easier, beginning in the 1980s, to refit downtown as a place where people want to go: to shop, to have fun, to encounter culture, to imbibe the city's history and character, and, when WaterFire's braziers are lit, to enjoy a passeggiata in the company of their fellow citizens. Since Burke bought Pot Au Feu in 1986, he says, Providence has added more than 12,000 restaurant seats, part of a downtown boom that has also brought stores, office space, and hotel rooms.

The most crucial step of the comeback was uncovering and rerouting the rivers to restore the city's connection to the water, giving it a new physical and ritual center. Burke says that this monumental project, completed in the early 1990s, "had a profound effect on the collective unconscious of Providence. When you began to tear those bridges apart and uncover the land, dig into the earth to move the rivers—and we all saw the unearthing—we were thereby psychically exhumed from our urban grave." In his account I hear echoes of Lovecraft, whose oeuvre features both live burial and reanimation.

Burke insists that restored infrastructure could not have, by itself, produced new life. "You still have to make the streetscape, the hardware, interesting to people," he says. "And for that you need software—like WaterFire, which is the great example. It brought people in the region back to the city, got them in the habit again." Visitors started coming, too, from Massachusetts, Connecticut, New

York, and beyond. It's no exaggeration, he says, to credit WaterFire with making downtown Providence a destination.

The numbers back him up. An economic impact study of Water-Fire in 2004 shows that it attracted at least 1.1 million visitors to Providence. More than half came from out of state, and most of these travelers cited WaterFire as the reason for their visit. The study estimated WaterFire's direct economic impact for the year at $33.2 million. "We were surprised by how big the numbers were," says Donald Keinz of Acadia Consulting Group, which conducted the study. "They make WaterFire a bigger draw than the Newport Folk Festival or the Newport Jazz Festival, a bigger draw than anything in the state except Newport itself."

With its resonance of both baptism and funeral Mass, WaterFire turns the process of urban redevelopment into something nearly sacred. "Remember, 60 percent of this state is Catholic," says Burke, whose full name is Robert Ignatius Loyola Burke. "We have this great outdoor sacrament. The ritual, the reverence, the holiness, the smoke like incense, the chants—all that resonates with Rhode Island Catholics in particular."

Before we part ways, I ask Burke if he thinks of a particular place as the heart of WaterFire. He replies, "I love to stand on what is now the Crawford Street Bridge, the new one," a graceful, modest span all the way at the downstream end of WaterFire, closest to Pot Au Feu. "One, it has the prettiest view, because the elevated braziers make a spectacular reflection in the water." The last fifteen braziers on that end do not float on the river; rather, they are mounted directly on the granite pediments of the old, Guinness-worthy Crawford Street Bridge, and rise a few feet above the water, all that remains of the decking that covered the river. "Two, symbolically, that's the spot. That's where the old bridge was, so that's where the city was reborn. And, three, if you turn and face south on the bridge, you get the smell of the bay, 25 miles away, from Newport. There's always a breeze there. That's the spot where the wind whips up the bay, and if you're a real Rhode Islander you can breathe in the ocean air and feel your roots."

I walk to the new bridge to see for myself. There's a little outward bulge in the middle of the downstream side that seems to enjoy its own permanent breeze bearing a taste of sea air. I stand there, savoring it, admiring the reflection in the water of the raised braziers. My subjective map of WaterFire keeps changing. I had thought of the circular basin at the upstream end as its center; or, if not the basin, then the point in the middle where the three rivers meet. But no, it turns out that WaterFire's secret center could be here, at the downstream end, which I had thought of as the place where the event peters out.

Of course, the next resonant spot I find may supplant these others. WaterFire's elements encourage you to conjure with them, to keep recombining them as you make the artwork your own. Barnaby Evans says that you don't need to know anything about Providence to come up with an authoritative understanding of his creation. Bob Burke says that only a true Rhode Islander who knows the lore of Providence can fully understand it. WaterFire leaves room for both to be right.

————

Walking back upstream, I find that the riverfront has become a vast open-air love zone. It's almost 10 p.m.; the fires burn hot and bright in the lovely dark. The crowd appears to consist mostly of couples now, thousands of them, young and old and in between, leaning together as they stroll, hunkering down by the water in jumbled pairs.

Evans has the greater community in mind when he says that he intends to bring people together, but his creation practically yanks couples into a clinch, too. The forgiving mysterioso lighting, mood music, pleasing smells in the air, and warm feelings pervading the crowd all frame your woo-object to best advantage. You feel the city around you come alive with possibility, elevated from the normal, and the same thing happens to the two of you. The moon, hanging between office buildings, can turn even the most prosaic steel-and-glass cubicle-hive into a romantic tower on a stage set for romance. There are just enough things to do and material to work with to shape the evening into a series of quiet pleasures without distracting you from each other. *Let's go up on that bridge and see what it looks like from there. Let's walk back down the river and stop for a drink. Let's sit by the water and watch the boats. Let's just listen. Let's . . .*

————

I'm on my way to work a shift on a wood-tending boat, something I've wanted to do ever since I attended my first lighting. I've worn black and brought gloves, as instructed. A supervisor at the dock speaks into her headset, and a few minutes later a boat swings in to pick me up.

Once aboard, I join a crew of six whose job it is to keep the fires stoked. The boat has run low on wood—about five cords of salvaged pine and cedar is burned per hour—so we stop to resupply at one of the half-dozen bridges that span the river along WaterFire's length. Snugged under the bridge, we reach up beneath its arches to grab logs stacked there, toss them behind us into the boat, then make off down the river to continue our rounds.

The job has a rhythm to it, part of the larger rhythm of WaterFire. You grab a log with each hand from the pile in the boat, then, ranged along the gunwale with other volunteers, you take your turn to place your logs into a brazier as the captain maneuvers the boat by it. Up close, the fires toast your face, and it takes a few attempts to get the hang of timing the boat's coasting approach and keeping stray embers from singeing your hair or eyebrows as you dump in the wood. It's all done without sudden movements or loud talk, with a stately smooth-ness encouraged by Evans as part of WaterFire's aesthetic. There's something at once restful and inspiring, like meditation, about the routine: being out on the water, doing your job among others, holding the logs ready as you pull up to the brazier, waiting your turn, reach-ing into the heat and light to put them in, feeling the fire rise up with new force as the boat pulls away and moves to the next one.

Why have I grown so attached to WaterFire? Not just because it satisfies the urge to engage intimately with a place, and not just be-cause of my own Lovecraft-inspired yen for Providence in particu-lar. Not just because attending WaterFire is the opposite of locking yourself in the house, watching TV, and growing ever more fearful of public life and public space. And not just because the combination of water, fire, and music operates on some basic mammalian pleasure center that doesn't get enough stimulation from the routines of city living.

Those reasons all matter, but I come back for this one: As I work my shift on the boat, and as I walk along or sit by the river, I am seized by a heightened sense of city-ness—of a great crush of humanity, the living as well as the ghosts of the dead, all gathered in one place by the water, their desires and labors and cares shaped by Providence and shaping it in turn. The upwelling of feeling resonates in the buildings, the bridges, the curve of the river, the faces of the people gazing at the fires. I see that they feel it, too. Everything else that isn't this feeling seems to evanesce and lift away, like wood turned to smoke.

Someone Else's Chicago

AS I DRIVE A RENTAL car toward the Loop on the expressway from O'Hare Airport, every hometown instinct is telling me that in half an hour I can be sitting on a bar stool at Legends, the club in the South Loop owned by Chicago's premier virtuoso of the blues guitar, Buddy Guy. I know exactly how it will be: peaceful in the indoor twilight, the dwindling change from my first twenty growing damp on the bar, bent notes from a guitar playing slow blues getting me right there under the heart. Later on I will call people I grew up with, and we'll go south or north to another blues club and so on into the night. The routine has not changed much since my high school years, significant portions of which I misspent at Guy's old place on the South Side, the Checkerboard Lounge. When I come back to Chicago I usually end up in a blues club.

I am, of course, not alone in this habit. The blues business, having gradually relocated in the last 40 years from the working-class neighborhoods of the South Side and West Side to the redeveloped North Side and downtown, has become part of Chicago's official culture, especially its tourist industry. The city seems like a giant theme park designed to shunt visiting fun-seekers along a path of least resistance from airport to hotel to blues club, guided every step of the way by brand managers reminding them that they're in the Home of the Blues. Many locals feel that Chicago blues lost its way and its heart, collapsing into an unending series of blazing guitar solos that

Original publication: *Washington Post Magazine*, March 7, 2004.

never fail to wow the non-cognoscenti, when it made a devil's bargain to capture the tourist audience that now largely supports live blues in the city. Some of this criticism amounts to no more than bluesier-than-thou snobbery supercharged by the usual foolishness about music and race, but it's also undeniably true that, on the whole, Chicago blues has grown more predictable and less musically vital as it has settled into its role as the city's official theme music.

In the blues clubs, they're playing "Sweet Home Chicago" yet again, the guitar player's taking yet another extended grimacing solo, the snugly seated audience is congratulating itself on having found its way to a real Chicago blues experience—it's all enough to make even the most devoted blues fan wonder what else may be out there in his home town, enough to inspire me to remove myself with a painful jerk from the path of least resistance and deny myself a visit to Legends. There has to be more to Chicago than Chicago blues.

I figure there is nothing unbluesier than polka, the primal 2/4 chug that came out of Eastern Europe to take the nineteenth century by storm (one-two-three *and*, one-two-three *and*, as Anna explains to the King of Siam). Seeking out polka will take me into Polish and Mexican music scenes and neighborhoods that I do not know at all, turning me into a tourist in my own city. In the Chicago in which I grew up, the South Side in the 1970s, the tavern musicians played blues on the electric guitar, and the jukeboxes were flush with the voices of Z. Z. Hill, Lou Rawls, and Teddy Pendergrass. Nobody in my Chicago would ever get into a barroom fight over, say, the relative merits of Li'l Wally Jagiello and Frankie Yankovic. But there are Chicagos other than mine out there, resonant with the sound of the accordion, the antiguitar, instrument of taverns with sawdust on the floors and atmospheres ripe with the cooking, accents, and music of faraway places. I assume that in exploring these other Chicagos I can take a break from guitar heroes and guitar solos, too, since somewhere I have imbibed the notion that polka is usually played on an accordion and never on a guitar. This conventional wisdom is not always accurate, it turns out, but that's part of what I stand to learn.

———

Which all explains why, as Friday afternoon fades into evening, I find myself dancing strenuously with a woman many years my senior named Irene.

I am at the Baby Doll Polka Club, almost as far out on the Southwest Side as you can go and still be in Chicago proper. Across the street from the club looms the forbidding wall that encloses Midway Airport—the city's mom-and-pop airport, dwarfed by O'Hare. Planes take off and land with a swelling roar, leaving a tang of jet fuel in the air. A traveler could plausibly stop over at the Baby Doll for a drink and a polka on the way to and from the airport, which would make for happy travelers. The Baby Doll has a reputation as a welcoming party place where hard-core polka types and curious first-timers can both have fun.

There is no live music this early on a Friday. Inside, it is calm and dim; the decor is Early Midwestern Chalet, the jukebox well stocked with tunes by Frankie Yankovic, Eddie Korosa, Eddie Korosa Jr. and his Boys from Illinois, Brave Combo, and the Polkaholics. Irene Korosa—former wife of the late Eddie Sr., mother of Eddie Jr., proprietor of the Baby Doll, and at the moment bartender as well—offers only general advice to first-time dancers of the polka. She says, "It's peppy, happy music," and refuses to get much more specific than that. Don Hedeker, leader of the Polkaholics and my guide for this afternoon's tour of polka joints, leans in to volunteer some additional detail: "Follow the drum, change your feet with each beat, watch other people, and remember: Polka people are not gonna have any bad feelings if you don't do it right. There are no wrong steps."

I get to test out the efficacy of their advice when Irene gives me a lesson. We have the Baby Doll's small but fabulously lit dance floor to ourselves. A few bemused patrons look on from their bar stools; they have to wait until she's done with me before they can have another drink. Light on her feet, surprisingly strong, Irene back-leads me with great kindness and firmness. I can foxtrot and waltz a little, but I have never tried to polka, and I am not doing very well until I remember that I always did best in French class when I consciously tried to talk like Pepé Le Pew. When I start performing what feels to me like a broad parody of what she wants, politely manhandling her in half-circles and throwing in a periodic lurching hop, she beams and says, "Better!"

Back at the bar, we fall to talking about the lost golden age of polka in Chicago. "This place is nice," Irene says, "but you should have seen the original Baby Doll. We opened it in 1954, at 73rd and Western. It held 500, we had music six nights a week, we had a hundred tables, the bar sat a hundred—it was the longest bar in Chicago. Eight waitresses, six bartenders, two bouncers, we had a radio show, a TV show. Everybody played there. Li'l Wally, Frankie Yankovic, Marion Lush, my husband. Yankovic was the king"—of the Slovenian-rooted, ac-cordion-centered Cleveland style of polka—"and my husband was the prince." But the age of kings and princes did not last. Tastes changed, and younger people fell away from their parents' and grandparents' traditions, the crowds abated, the neighborhood changed. "I sold it in 1980," she says. "Already it was a slow time for polkas. I bought this place in 1981." People come in here all the time, she says, and tell her that their parents or grandparents met at the old Baby Doll.

————

I have been hearing versions of Irene's story all afternoon. The Baby Doll is my last stop on a swing through the West Side. Don Hede-ker has already taken me to a senior citizens' polka dance at the Pol-ish Highlanders banquet hall on Archer Avenue; the International Polka Hall of Fame (where one dusty framed document proclaims, "Whereas the people of Minnesota enjoy polka music all seasons of the year . . .") at Polonia Banquets, another hall on Archer; and the combination liquor store/music store/recording studio of Eddie Blazonczyk Jr., scion of one of Chicago's leading polka families. At each stop, everybody has been talking about a shrinking and aging fan base, reduced circumstances, failed attempts at crossover into the mainstream, golden age and decline.

Everybody, that is, except Hedeker, a devoted student of Chi-cago polka and the lead singer and guitar player of the city's only self-avowed punk polka band. (See? You go in search of something new and you learn that there's such a thing as punk polka.) The Pol-kaholics' feedback-rich power-trio sound can shock traditional sen-sibilities, but their self-evident respect for polka usually wins over even the most skeptical crowds. Hedeker, an optimistic visionary, aspires to bring together the participatory vigor of the polka scene and the novelty-seeking energy of the rock scene. If the blues can be-come tourist music, and if lounge music can become cool again, why can't polka—aerobic, nonjudgmental, beery—find a new audience as well? "We play rock clubs," he says, "but we also play gigs with regu-lar polka bands at polka clubs, and people like it."

Hedeker's band explicitly shuns the accordion, but he may be the perfect guide for my purposes. A gently fanatical fellow in his mid-forties with extensive sideburns and impeccable taste in thrift-shop clothing, he presents a ripe combination of local elements. The son of immigrants from Czechoslovakia and the Crimea, he grew up in Gladstone Park on the Northwest Side, made his way through the public schools to the University of Chicago on the South Side, and is now a professor of statistics specializing in longitudinal data analysis at the University of Illinois–Chicago, which lies just southwest of the Loop. He did not grow up on polka—"a little oompah music and Lawrence Welk on TV, that was my knowledge of it"—and he took up the guitar rather than the accordion, but after many years of playing in rock bands he started coming across polka records during his visits to thrift shops.

He became curious, then hooked. "Polka opened up the city for me," he says. "I found some of my best stuff in thrift shops in Mexican neighborhoods. Because when the older Polish people who still lived there, when they died, their stuff goes to the thrift shop, and nobody in the neighborhood wants it." Why did *he* want it? "Partly it was a childhood ethnic connection, but partly it was something else." Rock was beginning to feel like a rut, and he wanted to find a roots music in which he could immerse himself. "Iggy Pop once said something like, 'I gotta find my own blues,' and I felt the same way. I couldn't see myself doing it with blues or jazz, and I had this Eastern European background, so I got into polka. And then I discovered that it was good. I said, '*This* is my blues.'"

———————

Chicago is not only a big city but a long one. The three-stop itinerary for Saturday night calls for 62 miles of driving. Hedeker has a gig tonight, so I have no guide. After dinner, I head southeast on the interstate almost all the way to Indiana. Down there on the East Side, Chicago's starkest quarter, truncated slices of neighborhood are wedged between wide stretches of industrial landscape, much of it going back to prairie. I am on my way to the Club 505, which faces train tracks and a vast Ford assembly plant. Inside the club, there is a largish rectangular room for bands and dancing, also a darker barroom featuring a jukebox stocked with Al Martino, Santo and Johnny, and the Ampol Aires' "Hot Pants Polka." This is Hegewisch, a neighborhood named for a nineteenth-century industrialist whose company built rolling stock for the railroads. It lies twenty miles southeast of the Loop, but still within the city limits. Rarely if ever has any booster urged visitors to the city to make their way to Hegewisch, but if you want to hear accordion music in its native habitat, try the Club 505 on a live polka night.

The Ampol Aires are playing tonight. The band has been around for half a century (as its pitch-perfectly '50s name will attest), and with fewer personnel changes than you might expect. Uniformed in dark blue pants and blue-and-white checked short-sleeve shirts, the six band members overspill the narrow raised stage as they crank out a pleasingly rattletrap sound. They lope and clunk with easy precision, doubled horn lines weaving confidently over and under the melody of "Honky Tonk Polka," "Stevens Point Oberek," "Sparkling Eyes," one brisk tune after the next. Tom Kula, a founding member of the band, serves as frontman. His concertina playing, like his singing and his teasing between-song patter, balances just enough roughness against just enough lilt.

The Saturday night crowd is thin. Where is everybody? Home with a video, out doing something more up to date, at the casinos in nearby Gary and Hammond—or maybe they are just resting up for Sunday, the big day for polka exertions in banquet halls and Elks lodges. Some idlers trickle in from the bar, and a few dedicated polka people do show up. Most are old-timers: a trim, straight-backed lady named Janina; a codger in an outdated suit who gets up to push Janina around the dance floor with boozy courtliness; a guy with a face straight from the old country who waits his turn and then takes Janina for a jolting, stamping spin on a fast number.

But not everyone is an old-timer. Dan and Jen, a young married couple from the southwest suburbs whose on-the-beat timing and precise moves suggest that they have taken lessons, swing around the floor with long-stepping formality on an oberek (an uptempo waltz) while an older couple provides counterpoint with a loose, busy shuffle that manages to be in time without ever being anywhere near the beat. Two little boys, one white and one black, run around and have a terrific time, interrupting a game of Little Pig to briefly polka together. Their flashing-lights sneakers seem to wink on and off in 2/4 time.

The band knows its business, the Club 505 feels extra-cozy when you picture the dark acreage of overgrown rail spurs and silent industrial buildings that begins across the street, and American currency will get you a beer—so all seems good here. But those few in attendance cannot bring the room fully to life. As one of the Ampol Aires puts it during a break from the bandstand, "This is basically a paid practice for us." Tomorrow they will play a banquet hall packed with a sizable crowd; tonight, the huff and grind of Tom Kula's concertina sounds a little forlorn, bouncing off the walls of the half-empty club.

————

I get in the car and head back toward the heart of the city. Exiting the expressway, I roll past the big turreted prison at 26th and California and pass under a banner that says "Welcome to Little Village." This is one of the neighborhoods where Hedeker shopped for records in thrift stores. Formerly Polish and Czech, it has been almost entirely Mexican for more than a generation. Bungalows and walkups, immigrants and aspiration—it hasn't changed much. Neither has its music. Polkas and waltzes suffuse Mexican music, descending in part from nineteenth-century musical styles brought by the French to their one-time colonial possession and to what is now Texas by Germans and Czechs who settled there.

At Los Globos, a rambling no-frills barn of a dance hall in Little Village, I walk past the impassive tough guys minding the door and into a blast of Mexican polka. Onstage, wreathed in smoke-machine smoke, a band called Pensamiento Negro is working hard. Its music, and that of other local bands playing tonight, sounds like a blend of traditional ranchera genres—norteño, banda, mariachi—but punchier, giddier, like the buzz from drinking too much champagne too quickly. The hoarse, harmonizing singers race one another to the end of the chorus, keyboards do most of the work of a horn section, and drummers define the beat with bass drum, cowbell, and a high-hat played caveman fashion by holding the detached top cymbal in one hand and bashing it down on the lower one, which is fixed to the bass drum's frame. Nobody is playing accordion at the moment, but an accordion would fit right in, and I have hopes.

People in the United States know this music as Durango style; back in Durango, in northern Mexico, it is known as Chicago style. More urban-cowboy disco than folk music, it has lately been winning an ever-larger following. Grupo Montez de Durango, a Chicago-based band with roots in Durango, has led the way to nationwide prominence with hits on the Latin music charts, and local bands in Chicago seek to follow it to the big time.

There is no celebrated out-of-town band to pack the house at Los Globos tonight, but even so a good turnout of perhaps 300 is on hand, mostly young and Mexican. The men, like the bands, wear cowboy hats, dress shirts, new jeans, and boots; the women wear dresses or tight pants, heels, plenty of makeup. The dance of the moment is an appealingly frantic, hip-swaying, ultraclose partner dance called the "Pasito Duranguense," the Durango Step. It seems a little goofy at first, but it looks like fun, and even the most initially skeptical people discover that once you start you can't stop. It has been catching on across the United States, thanks in great part to the success of Grupo Montez.

I have been keeping an eye on a hatless fellow in a white suit whose recently shaven head makes him easy to spot in the crowd. He came in alone and has been hanging on the sidelines among minky-mustached young men who drink beer and scan the room under their hat brims. Many of them are not much more than five feet tall, if you subtract boots and headgear. I lose sight of White Suit for a while and then he reappears, doing a do-si-do step with a game-looking young woman with long blond hair. During the next tune, a smeary waltz, the dancers all do a jerk-leg hesitation step. White Suit and his partner perform a hitch so pronounced that they appear to be play-ing freeze tag on the crowded floor. Other dancers, impressed, clear away from them and they find themselves at center stage: a "Saturday Night Fever" moment, white suit and all.

I become aware that while I've been watching the dancers I have been hearing a squeezebox. Turning back to the band, I see that one of the keyboard players has produced a white, red, and green but-ton accordion, which he manipulates enthusiastically while singing harmony, now and then dropping one hand to add a blast from his keyboard. At least to my ear, the accordion cuts through the clamor like a soulful singer; all the other sound seems to coalesce around it. People often compare a band playing in the Chicago-Durango style to a calliope, but to me it sounds like an outsize accordion played by a tireless, many-handed, bibulous giant. After a couple more tunes, Pensamiento Negro's accordion goes back into its case, but the ghost of the instrument's voice stays in the air.

———

Los Globos looks like it will be going strong straight through to clos-ing time, but the Polkaholics are playing a gig at a North Side rock club, the Bottom Lounge. When I arrive, the band is holding forth in front of an enthusiastic crowd of 100 or so, most of them at least semi-hip, younger than the Club 505 crowd, and older than the dancers at

Los Globos. Some polka expertly, some inexpertly; others just do your basic rock-club nod-and-bop; most of them are smiling. Hedeker produces an impressive roar from his guitar by rubbing the strings on the head of a fan who has approached the stage for that purpose. A lot of beer has been spilled on the floor.

The Polkaholics, sweating like stevedores, are in fine ironic form, decked out in white shoes, black pants, white ruffled shirts, and stunning leopard-print vests with matching oversize bow ties. All wear thick-framed glasses, and anyone standing anywhere near the stage can smell the torrent of Old Spice with which they douse themselves, Method actor style, before a show. They do not play polka versions of rock tunes, an ill-advised crossover strategy that has produced far too many bizarre novelty songs by polka bands. Rather, they play original songs and well-chosen polka covers that make use of rock sensibilities, winkingly sampled classic-rock phrases, and bursts of the jet-engine guitar whine common to certain forms of punk and heavy metal—all undergirded by drums and bass playing straight-ahead, hurry-up polka rhythms. Hedeker handles the vocals with cheerful inattention to niceties of pitch; the other Polkaholics occasionally join in for a chorus in heroic beer-hall unison. The hits keep coming: "Wild and Crazy Polka Fans," "She's Too Smart for Me," the thunderous "Kiss My Polka" ("I wanna polka all night and eat kishka e-ver-y day!"), "Stopped for a Beer," "Cleveland, the Polka Town." The finale, "Polka Can't Die," is both a heartfelt plea and a sendup of a formula especially widespread in country music and rap: the anthem in defense of its own genre.

At one point Hedeker harangues the crowd about guitars and accordions. He explains that Frankie Yankovic popularized the notion that polka means accordions. "The Cleveland style often requires *two* accordions," he says, a gigantic mock sneer spreading across his face and voice, "and that's two too many. You don't *need* an *accordion* to *polka*!" Then he throws a fist in the air and launches into the signature riff of Blue Oyster Cult's "Godzilla," which serves as the opening of a catchy little polka titled "Gamera of Gladstone Park."

I am back in guitar-land. My night on the town, my accordion-seeking weekend in someone else's Chicago, has ended in a no-accordion zone. And I have returned lakeward, toward the circuit of neighborhoods and music venues that constitute the path of least resistance within Chicago's musical nightlife. But coming the long way around to get here, through parts of the city and musical scenes utterly new to me, seems to have refreshingly reversed my musical polarity:

the Polkaholics' hokiest blues-rock riffs and guitar-hero moves now strike me as beguilingly strange in this context, while my 36 hours in polka-land have made their Frankie Yankovic covers and waltzes feel reassuringly familiar. In the city's thrift shops and its inland neighborhoods, where Eastern European and Mexican traditions sustain old forms and produce new ones, Hedeker found his blues. He believes that polka can be flexible and fertile roots music in the way that Chicago blues used to be, generating new styles and not just preserving tried and true formulas. There may be no accordion onstage at the Bottom Lounge, but Hedeker and his bandmates had to make a long journey through multiple Chicagos echoing with accordion music in order to get here. Me, too, and that's a weekend well spent.

––––––––

Sunday morning, driving out to O'Hare just as polka people are waking up and beginning to ready themselves for their big day of partying, I pick out the Eastern European-language stations and Spanish-language stations on the AM dial, crowded among the usual news, talk, and sports stations. I have to depart from the radio's preset buttons and fiddle with the tuner to find voices speaking Polish or Spanish, and often I can't tell what they are talking about, but every once in a while I hear an accordion in 2/4 time making the music of someone else's Chicago.

The Dogs of South Shore

ONE OF MY EARLIEST memories is of my grandmother's German shepherd, Beba, coming out from under the bed on which my uncle was taking a nap to bite the hand of my older brother, Sebastian, who had burst into the room just ahead of me, yelling and waving a light-blue plastic toy pistol. I can call up the solid bone-and-meat crunch of the bite; then the dog's sad, serious face looming suddenly in front of mine; then the rush of the long body going past me, out the door, and down the stairs, leaving me unbitten and strangely incomplete. When my brother got back from the hospital, his hand wrapped and his arm in a sling, he stood at the top of my grandmother's stoop, looking out at the yard and the street beyond, contemplating the day's revelations. I ran through the house to the storm door and shoved it open, driving its sharp lower edge deep enough into his heel to send him back to the hospital for more stitches.

I remember the second crunch of the metal going into his foot, and I remember thinking, to my own horror, that hurting Sebastian with the door completed an opaquely logical sequence, somehow making up for my not having been hurt by the dog. My father and my uncle fell out in later years for reasons that had nothing to do with this incident, but in my mind that trouble, too, somehow flowed in through an opening created by the dog. My grandmother lived in Queens, New York, but my early memory of Beba's attack on my brother sets the theme—dogs as totems of strong feeling and openers of portals to advanced trouble—on which the dogs of my neighborhood in Chicago, South Shore, played variations for years to come.

The nameless dog in a corner yard on 72nd Street a couple of blocks from my house on Oglesby Avenue would lie in wait and then hurl itself in a rage against the high chain-link fence that enclosed it. I passed that corner on my way to the supermarket and the South Shore branch of the public library. No matter how mightily I swore to be forever on guard when passing the dog's yard, I always forgot, sooner or later, and slipped into the natural distracted state of childhood, so that the next slavering rush, the crash of the body against the fence and the furious wet barking wrinkle-lipped muzzle seeking a way through to me, came as a terrible surprise that stopped my heart and loosened my bowels.

In the backyard next door to my own on Oglesby was a crimson-eyed albino dog named Bigot. When Bigot barked and growled at me and jumped stiff-legged at the chain-link fence that divided her yard from ours, the lady of the house—she was Canadian and white, her husband was American and black—would come out on the back steps, trailing cigarette smoke, and say "Bigot" in a low, flat voice that calmed the dog for a while. Bigot chased with cartoon-villain futility after a rabbit that lived in a thick tangle of bushes in the back of her yard, where a wood-slat fence separated yard from alley. This rabbit was a veteran of urban life, a big mottled bruiser I saw only in pavement-colored blurs as it darted to and from sanctuary with the dog in pursuit. I have manufactured a fancifully detailed memory of the rabbit, though, as if it had stood, swell-chested, for a portrait: one-eyed, broken-eared, haunches pocked with BB shot, flanks scored by long transverse scars.

My brothers, Sebastian and Sal, and I played with two boys from the family next door that owned Bigot. The younger of them, Alfred, who was exactly my age, wore beige corduroy flare pants and executed scrapingly punctilious hook slides on the pavement when we played Running Bases on the sidewalk in front of our houses. I once got into a fight with him over a disputed call. In my stroboscopic memory of it I advance confidently on him, his face takes on a look of intense concentration, and then a fist suddenly fills my vision and a terrific shock surges through my head and down into my body; I get up off the ground and go at him again, a little more warily this time; his face takes on that look again as he tips back away from me, shifting his balance, and then a giant shod foot swoopingly eclipses my vision for a flash of a moment before plunging down into my chest, from which an even more terrific shock spreads throughout my body; I get up off the ground and try him once more, even more carefully, but also with a certain satisfaction, believing that there must be merit in fighting a boy who can deliver a real kung fu kick from a standing start. We shook hands afterward, and that seemed to square it. Alfred and his brother had a kind of formality, a touchy properness. Shaken on, the fight became an affair of honor. Alfred went to Tuskegee, and died at thirty-one: he was working weekends as a bouncer at a bar in Minneapolis, he tried to break up a dispute, and somebody shot him.

When my family moved a mile west from our bungalow block on Oglesby to Euclid Avenue in the Highlands, South Shore's big-house district, the dogs next door were Lady and Clem. Steely rather than angry, they shook squirrels to death with matter-of-fact professionalism, stretching their victims' necks to grotesque lengths and leaving the bodies wherever they fell. Coming upon one of the X-eyed, slack-tongued corpses in the grass gave me the same jolt of weakness that had shot through my vitals whenever the nameless dog in the corner yard at 72nd and Oglesby caught me daydreaming. I thought of Lady and Clem as country dogs, possessed of hunting habits and death-lore foreign to the city. I thought of their owners as country, too. They had split-rail fences around their house, owned an irate goose named Pong who lived in the garage, and buried their dead animals in their backyard. Not shying from dead things was of a piece with knowing how to fix machines. Their white van was often up on blocks in their driveway. The parents were Irish Catholics from elsewhere, places where they understood weather and animals; the six adopted kids, three boys and three girls, all at least part American Indian, were from a different elsewhere.

My parents were city people but they were from elsewhere, too. Foreigners, they moved to South Shore when other white people were getting out as fast as they could. As children, they'd both taken shelter while bombers worked over their hometowns; New World social turmoil and a spike in street crime didn't seem like that big a deal to them. My parents, land-hungry immigrants with sons to raise, full-time jobs, and graduate degrees to pursue, saw houses for sale at irresistible bargain prices within a reasonable bus ride of a good school. Some of our black neighbors in the Highlands had a lot more money than we did, among them the families of Jesse Jackson, Walt Frazier, and Ramsay Lewis. But the trouble-seeking kids who came into the Highlands looking for somebody to mess with didn't discriminate. They just saw kids who lived in big houses and owned bikes worth stealing.

A couple of doors down on Euclid was Prince, a big shaggy German shepherd. Prince was sullen, even morose, and never barked or even growled, but it was widely understood among the kids on the block that Prince would kill you dead if he thought you were messing with his owners or their property. We all gave him wide berth. Chris, the boy whose family owned Prince, had an air rifle that he tenderly burnished and oiled and kept in perfect working condition. On the rare occasions when he brought it outside he would impose all sorts of conditions before letting the other kids on the block hold it for even a second. If one of us left a fingerprint on the gleaming blue barrel, he would snatch it away, breathe open-mouthed on the offended spot, and polish it up with a shirttail.

Once—I remember it as a slate-gray fall afternoon—a couple of strangers came along up the block, walking the trouble-seeking walk: mock-limping mock-aimlessly, looking everywhere and nowhere. They crossed the street to approach Chris, who was standing a little apart from us, holding his air rifle. The strangers were our age, or a little older. One of them said, "Hey, man, let me see your gun." Chris astonished me by saying nothing more than "Be careful with it" and handing it over. The stranger sighted down the barrel at the ground, turning it this way and that, inspecting it, and said, "Your mama's white, right? And your daddy's black?" Chris nodded. The stranger said, "So, what are you? Plaid? You plaid. I'm just playing." Laughing, he jammed the barrel into the muddy patch of curbside grass at his feet, twisting it hard to work it deeper into the ground. No longer laughing, he brought it back up, worked the pump action a few times to charge it, pointed it at Chris's midsection, and pulled the trigger. A moist plug of grass and mud fell out of the barrel. There was a pause. Chris took the gun back from him with an oddly polite gesture, proprietary but diffident. The strangers walked away down the block.

Strangers were always coming along up the block. In memory it's always afternoon or evening when they come, their shadows long and disjointed behind them, crossing the street on the diagonal, saying their lines: *Can I get a ride on your bike? You got a transfer? Let me hold a dollar.* Sometimes the talk led to action. I can still see the pattern of horses' heads on the pajama top worn by a boy who broke a length of broom handle over my head, and I can still call up the papoose bulk and skin-smell of my baseball glove as I curled up around it and held on while he tugged at it for a long futile moment and then suddenly was gone, driven off by Sebastian and Chris and other kids on the block. But usually it was just talk. Once, the strangers were a grown man and woman. I had just come outside to call my brothers in for dinner, and the man came up to me and said, "Say it again." His voice had an odd catch in it, a hint of a sob that promised passionate meanness. I looked at him without speaking, my usual policy when faced with superior force. He said, "Say, 'Come on and get your supper.' Say it." He stood over me, waiting. He wasn't exactly weaving, but he gave off an impression of unsteadiness. I remember that my brothers drew closer, one on either side of me, but we were probably unsure of what we could do, even all three together, against a grown man. The woman said, "Just say what you said. He wants to hear it." After a while I said, in a monotone, "Time for dinner." He stood over us for another moment and then they went away.

Stray dogs came down Euclid Avenue in packs on trash night. In memory, in dreams, they come in a sidelong trot, mouths slightly agape, tongues slyly peeking from between their white teeth, noses in the wind, hard bright eyes missing nothing. I carried my own length of broom handle and kept a watch for them as I rolled the big plastic bins out of the garage and down the driveway to the curb, then, my duty done, hurried back up the driveway in the dark to the back door and the safety of the kitchen. The stray dogs lived in the wilder stretches of Jackson Park, we were told, but I thought of them as coming more generally from beyond the borders of the neighborhood, from elsewhere: from the desolate park, or across the Illinois Central tracks from the neighborhoods to the south of us, or they came from the west, perhaps from far to the west, way out across Stony Island Avenue, where, I had heard, there were neighborhoods with tribes of white people in them who were so pissed off about what had happened to their home countries back in Eastern Europe that it wouldn't do me any good to be white if I wandered onto their block by mistake.

When I was in middle school a friend's family on the next block hired me to walk their broad-beamed, hip-sprung, long-haired Golden Retriever, Barney, when they went on vacation. Barney smelled like pipe smoke and dog food and backed through doorways, having had a door slammed on his nose when he was a puppy. He faced down other dogs by barking loudly and slowly, an old man repeating his point until his adversary gave up. He let me put the collar and leash on him and in a spirit of detente we would go up Euclid a block and a half to the edge of the park, but when we got there we often disagreed on the direction and length of the rest of the walk. His owners indulged him in longer walks than other dogs got, and he wanted to follow his usual route, which I didn't know; I wanted to fulfill the letter of my agreement with his owners as minimally as possible and get in out of the cold. Barney was stronger than I was, and if I pulled too hard on the leash he could remove the collar with a practiced dip of the head and swipe of his paw, so we were prone to stalemates.

On the last day of his owners' vacation, as a cold afternoon gave way to an even colder evening, Barney and I stalled with particular finality at the edge of the park. He yearned toward the chain-link fence and the tree line beyond; I refused to take him. Finally, I tied the leash to the green-painted slats of a bench and sat down. Barney sat on the sidewalk next to the bench and looked at me, his eyebrows twitching irregularly. He barked for a while, steadily, patiently, but I ignored him. It grew darker. I had ample time to reflect on dogs and people wanting what they want: those who have less want more; those who have more want to keep it. It seemed like something to bear in mind. The cold spread upward through my body from the bench under my thighs and the sidewalk under my shoes. I untied the leash and tried to take him home, but he wouldn't come. I retied the leash to the bench and sat down again. The cars passing on 67th Street had their lights on; their tires hissed on the cold, dry pavement. It was evening now, night falling fast. A great mass of darkness bulked in the park behind us, swelling to the verge of the glow cast by the streetlights along 67th. The few pedestrians who passed by, walking fast and high-shouldered, plainly wondered why I was sitting there, exposed, on the edge of South Shore at such an hour. I wanted to just go home and leave Barney where he was, if he wouldn't come, but I was responsible for him. He was, at least temporarily, my dog. It was getting late, though, and somewhere out there the strays, trotting sidelong, were already on the move.

Into South Shore

THE RAILROAD TRACKS REACH back to South Shore from just about everywhere I've ever been: on an Amtrak train crossing the Hell Gate Bridge on the approach to Penn Station in New York City; on an airplane passing over sidings and spurs on the descent into Pittsburgh, Barcelona, or Wuhan; in my apartment in Brookline, Massachusetts, from which you can see and hear the D Line trains running behind the houses across the street. All the tracks connect to all the other tracks, and if you know the way you can ride them back to Bryn Mawr Station, 71st and Jeffery, and home.

I get off a southbound Illinois Central train at Bryn Mawr and walk the wrong way, west, to the end of the raised open-air platform that just ends, with no stairs leading down to street level. Everyone else who got off the train walks the other way, east, through the doors into the station house that in cold weather smells of steam and piss, and in hot weather of dust and sun-heated wood. The arriving passengers will go through the turnstiles in the station house and outside again through another set of doors, down the stairs, and into the middle of the intersection. That's the way out, the way you're supposed to go. My way, the wrong way, the secret way, feels to me like the way *in*—into the landscape, into South Shore.

The boards of the platform give a little beneath my sneakered feet. The wood has weathered unevenly—dry and splintered in some places, wearing into moist bluntness in others. Reaching the west end

Original publication: *City*, 3 Book Publishing, 2006.

of the platform, I lean out for a moment to make sure there's no north-bound train coming. Then I turn around, squat, put my palms on the edge of the platform's floor, lower my feet halfway to the tracks, and drop. It's not far, maybe chest height for a grown man, but I'm not full-grown yet; it feels far.

It also feels vaguely historical to drop from platform to tracks, like dropping into a seam in time. I'm old enough to know that the neigh-borhood, the city, has a history, but I know that history in only the vaguest terms. Once upon a time there were white kids in knickers and newsboy caps (for some reason, I see them picking up stray pieces of coal along the tracks), and before that there was prairie, like the high grass growing in vacant lots you can see from the windows of an IC train taking the turn at 71st and Stony Island. There's something unnameably industrial, and, behind that, something even more un-nameably and remotely rural, about dropping to the uncertain foot-ing of the wooden ties and weedy gravel bed between smooth rails that go out to the East Side, where the steel mills are, and extend beyond there all the way to Gary, the Dunes, the Mississippi Delta.

I squint up at the sky, a bug crawling along the neighborhood's spine. You're not supposed to linger on railroad tracks, but they're seductively intimate, private, even though they're right there in pub-lic view in the middle of 71st Street. Still, you could get mashed flat. I step over the far rail, watch for a gap in traffic on 71st, and cut across on the diagonal toward Euclid Avenue, my street. Before me, I think, there were kids who did the same thing, kids who knew the secret.

———————

If not a train, then a bus. I get off at 69th and Jeffery. It happens only rarely that junior gangsters in pea coats and sideways Pittsburgh Pirates caps are waiting at the bus stop to mess with kids like me, kids who live in the Highlands, South Shore's high-rent district. But I like to be ready every time: to disappear or run, if practicable; to fight, only if I absolutely have to; or, as I prefer, to simply walk on, projecting dull purpose drained of both challenge and acquiescence, and never, ever stop, no matter what. When they come asking for a transfer or a dollar, anything to get you to stop and give in to them, you say no without breaking stride, going around them if you have to. They might walk along next to you, craning in close to your stu-diously blank face, double-checking—"You saying no to me, boy? What's your problem?"—but you keep going and don't bother saying it again. That's usually enough. We're all just kids, after all; I don't carry much worth taking, and they're not real gangsters yet. If you slide through, refusing to play, most of them will let it go—"Hey, I'm just playing with you"—and wait for the next candidate, the one who'll stop, which makes it more fun; the one who'll apologize when he says no, which means that he's ready to give up what he's got. You don't have to be a tough guy; you just have to seem slightly more inertial, slightly less worth the trouble, than whoever comes before or after you.

Still, there are days when I get off the bus a block or two early, or ride past my stop and get off a block later, just to mix it up and keep them off balance, to reduce traction so I can keep sliding through. It's not necessary, but I've got nothing but time to spare. I don't have anywhere I need to be.

This time I get off at my regular stop. Nobody's waiting there to mess with me. Walking home on 69th Street, I pass a garage door with a couple of gouges in it. My next-door neighbor Joe, who is a few years older than me, put them there one night. The guys on the next block, the last pack of white stoners left in the neighborhood, had a beef with Joe stemming from words exchanged one afternoon when he provoked them by swerving too close on his purple spider bike with yellow flames painted along the chain guard. They all wanted to see Joe get beat up but none of them wanted to fight him, so they brought in a ringer, a big black guy named Pierre from another part of the South Side. Joe, an American Indian adopted by Irish Catholics, was wiry and compact, hard-built from doing situps and push-ups and pullups in his slant-eaved attic bedroom with the squirrel-infested closet. That night, we watched him go down to the corner to meet Pierre, walking with a pent-up prefight bounce and fitted out for battle: oily faded flare jeans, denim vest, no shirt, long black hair parted in the middle, a doubled length of heavy-duty chain held in one hand and draped over his shoulder. Joe disappeared from view in the dark, and a few seconds later everybody on both blocks—ours and theirs—heard a hoarse shout and then the dull chunk-chunk of his chain hitting the garage door and perhaps Pierre's body. Pierre did not stick around for an extended beating. He fled into late traffic on Jeffery, a Hector-for-hire refusing to face the Achilles of the 6900 block of Euclid.

That's Joe, not me. But the marks on the garage door offer a reminder: you don't have to slide through; you can take the hard way. In later years, after Joe loses a kidney when he and his father get shot up by home invaders who they nevertheless repel with their bare hands, Joe runs off somewhere—to a reservation out west, I hear. The police ring our doorbell and tell us that if he ever turns up in the neighborhood again we should bolt the door and give them a call; they want to talk to him about a string of muggings. But he's long gone. The hard way.

———

My way home, most days and nights, goes through Jackson Park, the South Side's grandest and loneliest park. I'm looking out the window of a school bus grinding down Cornell Avenue, the park's main north-south drive, turning on Hayes Drive and passing the Golden Lady, the statue standing with arms upraised, copying a long-lost big sister's gesture of benediction over a city that vanished. I'm pedaling along the sidewalks in slapstick fast-motion that grows less comic, more controlled as I grow older and stronger and move from the sidewalks out into the park drives, farther from the bushes from which bike thieves can spring in ambush. But I'm increasingly on foot, having grown into a reedy, dreamy teenager who prefers to walk.

It's the end of another night of hanging around in Hyde Park, where most of my high school friends live, and it's time to go home. Crossing wide, empty Stony Island Avenue at 59th Street, I approach the dark tree line, choosing a place to enter the park. Beyond, deeper within the greater darkness of the park, the glow of streetlights lining the drives pinkens the sky. I pick my way through lightless groves, navigating by keeping the lights of Stony Island in view on my right and those of Cornell on my left. I hurry across Cornell, momentarily exposed, and continue south and east in woodland gloom again. I skirt the parking lot where guys cruise around in cars, sometimes with women in the passenger seat or in the back, looking for business or trouble or something else I can't provide.

Once across Hayes Drive, the Golden Lady behind me, the park feels darker, denser. I'm in long-haul rhythm, covering ground, firmly thumping my heel down on the turf with every step. I cross unlit stretches of grass and cut through narrow gaps between patches of brush, still keeping off the paved ways. I pass the locked-up marina, wondering, as always, if boats get stolen just like cars, and if joyriders crash them or bring them back. Then I cross Marquette Drive and enter the homestretch, my feet finding and following the path worn across the golf course by cross-cutters like me.

I see golfers in the daytime, and I understand that they enjoy walking around and hitting the ball and not being at their jobs, but I don't understand why there's a golf course here. It has something to do with the marina and the Golden Lady, I assume. They're historical, too. I'm grateful, in any case, for the expanse of grass and trees and water on the northern border of my neighborhood, the open territory where nobody lives, the way home.

The path crests a small rise, drops, and runs across a flat stretch to another rise. At the far edge of the golf course, I put my hands on the top of a chest-high chain-link fence and vault over, leaving the park and continuing across 67th Street on the diagonal and down Euclid, under streetlights once more. The stately dark houses of my neighborhood, spike-fenced and grilled and burglar-alarmed, resemble a chain of frontier forts.

When I get to the peak-roofed brick house with no front door on the 6900 block of Euclid, I will remember to disarm the alarm before I unlock the door, and to rearm it once I'm in. I will find something in the refrigerator and see if there's anything on late TV, padding around the sleeping house, snug inside the castle with the drawbridge pulled up. But, really, walking down Euclid with the tight-shut houses of South Shore on either hand and the street all to myself, a freight train calling on the IC tracks in the distance, I'm already home.

Lessons

Un Clown Biologique

WHEN I WAS GROWING up in Chicago in the 1970s, a story persistently made the rounds in the usual way—it had happened to somebody twice removed from you, or somebody once removed from you had seen it happen—that a kid had cursed out Bozo the Clown on TV. It made sense to me. When you're too young to put down childish things and too old to continue enjoying them on their own terms, your choices narrow: cultivate ironic detachment, take up precocious dope-smoking (did I mention that this was the '70s?), or rail against fate. Cursing out a prominent clown in front of hundreds of thousands of witnesses would be an excellent example of option three.

The orange-fringe-coifed, blue-suited Bozo had a long-running live show on WGN, Channel 9, which prided itself on being Chicago's family station and sought an audience of small children, old people, and those in between who would rather be one or the other. WGN's programming included Cubs games in the afternoons, Sunday reruns of *The Adventures of Robin Hood*, and *Bozo's Circus* at noon on weekdays. Bozo's show meandered through rudimentary clown routines—"Well, if you forgot to put water in the bucket again, then there's no reason I shouldn't turn it upside down over my head like *this*!"—and an eleven-dollar cartoon (I see an animated Bozo on a scooter against a de Chirico backdrop, then my memory whites out) before arriving at a shattering climax in the form of the Grand Prize Game, in which contestants would stand behind a line on the floor

Original publication: *The American Scholar*, Fall 2004.

and try to pitch a little ball into a row of six buckets extending away from the tosser.

Even though the ball was prone to dubious aerodynamics and disappointing bounces, landing it in even the farthest bucket appeared to be absurdly easy, especially if the tosser leaned over from the waist. That's why the show's producers tended to pick little kids, too short or uncoordinated to manage the more distant buckets, to compete for the Grand Prize. Every once in a while, the selection process went awry and they picked a kid by mistake who was just too big, too competent. It made you feel slightly sick to watch a proto-adult nail the buckets one after another with the tight, swift certitude of a pool player running the table with money on the line.

One day, the story went, they picked a kid who was clearly too old for the Grand Prize Game. I pictured him as small for his age, which would have made him especially testy about being mistaken for a little kid, as he may have been by the producers. Once he had been picked, though, it was too late; there are no do-overs on a live show. As he descended from the stands to the stage and toed the line, it was obvious that the game would be beneath him. All he had to do was drop the ball in one bucket after another, like putting something in the trash. But he short-armed a toss and missed a bucket, and not the sixth one, either; more like the third or fourth. Once you missed, you were out. He muttered an audible expletive: "Shit," in most versions of the story. Different versions disagreed as to whether the next line, "That's a Bozo no-no," was delivered by Bozo himself or by his capon-like sidekick, Cooky. All versions agreed on that precise wording, and on the fact that the kid addressed his response to Bozo, but they disagreed about the exact nature of that response: "Shove it, clown," or "I got your Bozo no-no right here, clown" (with index finger pointing to his own crotch for emphasis), or, as most had it, "Fuck you, clown." I can't remember what, if anything, happened next in the story, but I picture auxiliary clowns arriving onstage to give the bum's rush to the kid, who sags in their double elbow grip, the bitter vigor having gone out of him all at once.

It all seemed plausible—the kid's mortification at having failed at a younger child's game, his anger at having to play out this humiliating scene with what poor grace he could muster, and perhaps his shame, too, at having secretly burned for the fleeting celebrity accorded a conqueror of the buckets. He had probably spent the previous week fantasizing about winning the first ovation of his young life. Perhaps he could not admit this ambition to his friends, or even to himself, but the clowns had brought the hidden load of feeling to the surface, as clowns will.

Plausible, but untrue. I am reliably informed that the story is a much-repeated urban legend, with distinct variants reported in Chicago, Boston, and Southern California, each of which had its own live Bozo show, its own Bozo. Two pieces of evidence purporting to confirm the truth of the story turn out to be false: somebody recorded a fake version of the episode for a compilation of TV bloopers (the kid says "Cram it, clownie"), and an unconvincing liar has come forward on the Internet (imagine that) claiming to have been the foul-mouthed kid. Even when I first heard the story, when I was ten years old or so, I probably knew it wasn't true, but—like a lot of other people, which is what leads to urban legends—I consented to believe it was true. I *wanted* it to be true because it spoke of feeling little and big at the same time, of being two things at once, itchily sharing space within a single changing skin.

––––––––––

Back then I had a friend, Tom C., who seemingly bypassed adolescence and young adulthood entirely, emerging fully formed at the age of twelve—beefy, hirsute, with a taste for pipe tobacco and a nascent smoker's cough—as a parodic knockoff of the sort of 52 year-old character who publishes poetry in obscure quarterlies, shows his paintings at galleries owned by his cronies, and adjuncts in theater arts or creative writing at local colleges. Tom C. lived on the next block, and we used to take the same bus home from school sometimes. In junior high he went through a phase in which he would walk a few blocks along the bus route after school to a bookstore, where he would set himself up on the sidewalk by the front door and thump on a small bongo drum while declaiming original verse—the whole performance intended as a friendly mockery of such things more than as an earnest instance of them. He began with a croaking singsong invocation: "Play the bongos of love! Play for love!" I liked riding the bus on those days. The driver would open the doors in front of the bookstore and Tom C., having bewildered passersby with his bongoing and declaiming, would get on and become just another kid on his way home from school.

Tom C. cultivated a morbid fascination with clowns. Instead of merely doodling in class, he created obsessive dossiers of clown types: the savage Jester, the crocodile-teared Sad Clown, the enigmatic Bowler

Hat, the rare Plume Clown, the annihilating Whiteface. He practiced different stylized ways of saying the word *clown*—drawing it out, barking it sharply, stretching his rubbery features to make a demented face while he said it, adopting a strangled or a booming voice—as if he could figure out what was hiding in the word by turning it inside out. He drew up clown scenarios and composed clown ditties, and invented ancient traditions to which they belonged. He tried to figure out if it would be worse to wake up one night to find a clown at the foot of your bed or to think you had dreamed it and then find a deflated balloon in your room the next morning. Once, at a street festival, we spent hours fleeing a clown on stilts who, Tom C. felt, was after him.

"This is freaking me out," he would say at such times. "I'm freaking out because this is a freak-out." He maintained a Freak Out Box at home, filling it with images he had found or made, masks and other bits of costume, scraps of poetry, and his masterpiece: a drawing known as "The Be-At," featuring a Jester rampant on a field of diamond shapes, executed according to an original perspectival system of Tom C.'s own devising that made everyone who looked at it afraid. Tom C. trained himself to wake up in the night and tape-record descriptions of his clown-filled dreams while they were fresh in his mind, and he kept his dream tape in the Freak Out Box, but one day he decided that listening to the tape might do him irreparable harm, so he destroyed it without ever playing it.

During freshman or sophomore year of high school, our French teacher assigned us the task of writing a short story; nothing special, just a narrative written in French. Most of us dutifully cobbled together something semigrammatical that a child one-third our age might find tedious—"*Il était un chat qui s'appelait Henri . . .*," etc.— but not Tom C. He penned a stark little postmodern fable about an investigation into the murder of a clown, the kind of thing that Robbe-Grillet and Borges might have thrown together while listening to "Houses of the Holy." All I remember of it with any certainty, besides that the French was high-flown and mostly wrong, is the final scene. The Inspector orders one of his assistants to remove the dead clown's makeup so that the decedent's identity can be ascertained, but the assistant reports back that it is impossible to remove the makeup because, as the story's last line puts it, "*Il est un clown biologique.*" My familiarity with the collected works of the young Tom C. encourages me to assume that there had been an earlier scene in which the hyper-rational Inspector staked his reputation and his very sanity on the notion that penetrating the whiteface to discover the clown's true identity would allow him to solve the case. I wonder what our French teacher thought when she read it. It being the '70s, chances are she told her husband that this clown story her student had written was freaking her out, then took chemical steps to get mellow.

Twenty-two or twenty-three years later, the April 9, 2001 issue of *The New Yorker* featured a short story by Michael Chabon entitled "The God of Dark Laughter." In that story, told with pitch-perfect command of the portentous mock-scholarly style appropriate to the form (in which phrases like "certain sacrificial artifacts pertaining to the worship of the proto-Urartian deity" serve the same function as compulsory figures once did in ice skating competitions), an improbably erudite small-town district attorney in western Pennsylvania investigates the murder of a clown. During the course of the investigation, much of it conducted by reading arcane books, the DA stumbles upon an ancient cult of clown-worshippers whose own clownish appearance is not just the result of makeup but of inbreeding that has produced hereditary natural whiteface. A coroner's report theorizes that a depigmentation disorder known as vitiligo might have caused the white patches of skin he found on the dead clown's nape and throat (the rest of the face being unavailable, as the murderer had peeled his victim's head with a long, sharp knife). "Let the record show," the DA adds, "that the contents of the victim's makeup kit, when it was inventoried, included cold cream, rouge, red greasepaint, a powder puff, some brushes, cotton swabs, and five cans of foundation in a tint the label described as 'Olive Male.' There was no trace, however, of the white greasepaint with which clowns daub their grinning faces." In other words, *il est un clown biologique.*

How to reckon with this congruence of tales? (In addition to the *clown biologique*, Chabon's story also features a baboon, a scholarly charlatan, a clown-obsessed intruder who pays a dreamlike nighttime visit to the hero, and other figures who would be cozily at home in Tom C.'s oeuvre.) I can see how two writers of the same generation, sharing not only some of the same esoteric interests but also perhaps the same fear of clowns, might have arrived separately at the same idea and given it similar expression, one in precocious adolescence, the other in the early middle period of a distinguished writing career in which he has lately turned for inspiration to childhood enthusiasms like comic books and coulrophobia. I can even entertain the possibility that *les clowns biologiques* might actually exist, and that Tom C. and Chabon might have separately encountered them—knowingly or not—and rendered the encounters in fictional form.

Then there's this: Chabon is married to Ayelet Waldman, who attended Wesleyan University in the 1980s, where in her freshman year she lived on the same hall as one Wilson "Bob" McDermut of Chicago, whom I have known since nursery school and who has known Tom C. almost as long. Bob remembers telling her about Tom C.'s French story at some point during that freshman year of college, so it may be that the *clown biologique* traveled by word of mouth from Tom C. to Bob to Waldman to Chabon, who would, according to the practical give and take of the storytelling trade, be welcome to make what he could of it. We cannot compare the texts in greater detail because the only copy of Tom C.'s story has been lost, presumably destroyed, and neither he nor I can remember much about it—other than that it was written in a crabbèd script and employed certain curious usages and spellings of an arcane nature which have long since passed from the knowledge of humankind. I do feel obliged to observe, though, that the story of the *clown biologique* really loses something if you don't read it in the original French.

I guess I do not honestly believe that Tom C. influenced Chabon. But I like to think he did, because it would please me to know that the precocious aesthete and poetaster with whom I grew up persists as a literary subtext, even if the adult Tom C.—an insurance man and financial planner with a disused PhD in early modern German intellectual history, who has not drawn a Plume Clown or tossed off a rhymed couplet in many years—no longer bears much trace of the kid who believed it incumbent upon a thinking person to maintain a well-stocked Freak Out Box.

———

Phil, another hulking childhood friend from Chicago, actually became a clown in adulthood (which would make him *non-biologique*, of course). After years as an actor and improv comedian, he moved to Toronto and began studying with Sue Morrison, who apprenticed under Richard Pochinko, Canada's great clown teacher, who died in 1989 and still commands a worshipful following in certain pratfall-taking circles. Pochinko studied with Jacques Lecoq, a French red-nose classicist, and with an American Indian clown sensei known as Jonsmith. Pochinko-derived clowns abound in Toronto, exploring variants of the master's synthesis, which trails centuries-deep roots in the commedia dell'arte as well as in Old World and New World folk traditions.

The Pochinko school places therapeutic emphasis on finding your inner clown and ideological emphasis on tricksterish truth-seeking, neither of which necessarily subsumes itself to the showbiz priority of making 'em laugh. Pochinko clowning can get itchy with the tension between different imperatives coexisting in one greasepainted skin. Phil told me a distinctively Torontonian war story about a soiree held at the performance space operated by Mump and Smoot, a duo known as "Canada's Clowns of Horror," who are Pochinko's most successful students and—not coincidentally—his most practically showbiz-minded. Phil was slated to go on late in the show, which made for a trying backstage wait. "You have to be in your clown before you go onstage," he told me, "but it's hard to be in clown backstage for an hour; it's too tiring. So you don't get into your clown, you just sit around, and you're just you. Meanwhile, everybody else who's on before you is in their clown, and they're messing with you, because they're *clowns*. And you're like, 'Okay, Jingles, whatever you say.'" The emcee clown for the show, an unpredictable fellow who prized his sense of himself as an edgy performer, took a break offstage during the first half of the show. During this break he reported a sudden inspiration: Phil, whose clown was a gentle stooge named Bunce, should come onstage just before intermission and hit him with a folding chair. Phil was hesitant, but the emcee insisted that it would work brilliantly, pulling together certain dramatic threads that had developed in the show's first half. There was no time to explain further. They hurriedly rehearsed the chair routine before the emcee had to rush back onstage again.

When it came time to do the chair stunt in earnest, they missed connections and Phil-as-Bunce ended up whacking the emcee flush on the temple, rather than conking him lightly across the back. The audience gasped as the emcee went down like a steer under the stunner's tool at a slaughterhouse. "I go offstage," Phil told me, "then I come back a minute later—I'm still Bunce—and check him out. Under my breath I ask if he's okay. No answer. The audience is freaking out. So I signal for intermission." A few minutes later, with concerned clowns grouped around him, the emcee leaped up and exclaimed, "That was great!" as if he had been playing possum the whole time. But, Phil told me, "I think he was out cold for a while—I felt it when I hit him—but he tried to play it off like it had all been part of his idea." The moral of the story? "A little more Mump and Smoot would have been good there. More theatricality, more rehearsing, not so much going by the seat of the pants for a big moment of psychological truth, or whatever he was after."

A few years ago, when I was playing hooky from an academic conference held in Toronto, Phil took me to a party hosted by Sue Morrison. After visiting the refrigerator to get myself a beer and poking around the house a bit, I suddenly realized that everybody there except me was a clown. I had known there would be clowns present, of course, but an evening in bars had somehow distracted me from considering that there would come a moment when I found myself among them. In street clothes they looked like graduate students, and they seemed self-consciously arty, like actors in experimental theater or serious mimes. (I figure Bozo or Cooky in mufti, by contrast, would act like a plaid-jacketed Rotarian.) Still, they were clowns, and they talked shop. Somebody was saying that he had done a turn at a children's show that had gone especially well because he had experienced a breakthrough onstage, a cathartic reversal of inner polarities—terror and joy, innocence and experience. The therapeutic triumph seemed to be the point of the story, although he did not fail to make clear that the kids had in fact loved him. "I killed," he said. "I totally killed."

Where was Tom C. when I needed him? Writing second-to-die life insurance policies. I could have used the Van Helsing–like assistance of the inventor of the Freak Out Box earlier that day, too, when Phil scared the hell out of me by putting on his nose. "Check this out," he said, and turned away to fit it over his face. It was just a hollow red plastic ball on a thin white elastic, but when he turned to me it had transformed him. His features grew opaque and still, rearranging themselves around the nose. I was struck by the sudden quiet; we were in his apartment, and I could hear traffic sounds outside. The clown before me, a giant stranger who had devoured Phil, gave me a "What next?" look, distressingly full of possibility. If his tongue had unfurled sixteen feet out of his mouth while making an *ah-ooga* sound, or if his head had swiveled all the way around and then sailed off his neck at a crazy jack-in-the-box angle, I would have been frightened but not particularly surprised. Phil always liked softball, I was thinking, so I could probably find a bat somewhere in the apartment. Would aluminum or wood work better against a clown? It gets cold in Canada, so they might have a fireplace, and if there's a fireplace there ought to be a poker. Or perhaps a steak knife from the kitchen. Or garlic—no, garlic doesn't work against clowns. Nothing works against clowns. Then he took off the nose and he was almost entirely Phil again.

The Two Jameses

I GOT TO KNOW Boxing James, who used to manage fighters and promote fights, because he called me at home one day out of the blue to discuss a book I'd written about boxing. Our conversation led to a several-times-daily email correspondence, which eventually expanded to include a number of other fight people and boxing aficionados. When he's in town, we have dinner. Ascetic, musical, bookish, committed to the avant-garde credo that a true artist in any form revolutionizes the very language he employs to say whatever he has to say, Boxing James makes for an unlikely recovering gangster. But anybody who does business in the fight world has to be a gangster at least some of the time. He has also worked in music, loan sharking, and "the skin business," as he calls pornography and prostitution. He says he's done with all that now. As far as I can tell, he has become a post-lowlife bodhisattva. Remarried to his first wife and profoundly in debt, he eats one meal a day, spends rigorous hours at the piano (he played jazz before he became a manager of heavy metal bands), and has given up exploiting other people's weakness for profit.

James tells a story about a promising heavyweight prospect, a young Dominican who seemed to have it all: he was physically gifted, well-schooled as a boxer, good-looking, personable, and fluent in English. James, who managed him, thought he might just have the next big thing on his hands—the first Hispanic heavyweight champion of the world. After the prospect won his professional debut, James took a

Original publication: *The Believer*, April 2007.

tape of the fight to Al Braverman, who was Don King's director of boxing, a kingpin who could make things happen for a rising star. The prospect had won his debut easily, but they had watched no more than a minute or so of the tape before Braverman remarked, "Got a little muttski in him, doesn't he?"

It came as news to James that his golden prospect was a quitter, a coward—by the unforgiving standards of boxing, that is, since by any normal standard he was uncommonly brave. We've all got at least a little muttski in us, but fighters can't afford to be like everybody else. Braverman told James, "Don't worry, we'll build a wall around the kid," meaning that they would handpick his opponents and try to put off the day when they had to put him in against a fighter shrewd enough to find his soft spot.

Six years and seventeen fights after Braverman pronounced on him, that day came. James's fighter was matched against another contender in a bout that would determine which of them continued on to a shot at a heavyweight title. The other contender's sharp-eyed trainer saw what Braverman had seen. Before the opening bell, the trainer looked James's fighter in the eye, pointed to his own chest while shaking his head, and said, "No heart. You got no heart." Everybody in the ring knew he was right. James's fighter, the more talented of the two, was finished before the bell rang to open the first round.

Spend enough time around fight people and you acquire their habit of sensing weakness in others. It radiates from some people like a skunk's musk, from others like the faintest indefinable odor. James cultivated his faculty for sensing it for so many years that now he can't turn the faculty off. James, who left home early and never did get much of any other sort of education, at least in the formal sense, regrets that he can't stop perceiving desperation in others, especially the desperation brought on by money trouble.

He works on cultivating a more humane perspective, though. There's a street in the neighborhood where his wife works that's lined with iffy businesses and menacing hangers-out. Even once he was out of the lowlife, James would drive down that street and see only business opportunities. He says it took years for him to see *people* on that street—poor people, people in trouble. He can still see their desperation, but now that he sees the people, too, he's less tempted to strike instinctively into the openings it creates.

Corresponding with Boxing James and our circle of mutual boxing acquaintances can sometimes get me in trouble. A while ago, a fellow academic was giving me a hard time, threatening me with an ugly public squabble. I sent him an e-mail inviting him to either do as he threatened or give it up; you didn't even have to be a fight person to sense the weakness coming off of him in waves, like an aura. Rereading my e-mail to him, I can see now that James and company were in my head. "We can do this or not do this" is the tipoff line. The guy's return message ran to well over a thousand words, most of them devoted to a detailed analysis of my ethical and intellectual distress, but he might have saved himself the effort and just written "We're not going to do this," because we didn't.

The fact of his weakness was not, all by itself, reason to exploit it. But there it was, like a slow opponent's left glove held several inches too low, so I counterpunched into the hole. Next time I'll think first; after all, I still have to work with him. Boxing James, who knows about these things, gave me a useful piece of advice about how to fix the situation so it's less of a bother. He counseled me to throw the guy a bone by contriving to reveal a minor soft spot of my own to him—an invented one, of course, since you don't want to be giving anybody an edge over you if you don't have to—which would ease the tension by appearing to even the ledger of vulnerability between us.

James can be dispassionately clear-minded about transactions like this because he treats human imperfection as a purely technical matter. True fight people do not regard the fact of weakness, whether it proceeds from a glass chin or insufficiently mastered fear or some other source, as a good or a bad thing. It's simply part of human architecture, there to be perceived and then exploited. For fight people, human weakness is like market weakness: not a moral category, but merely an occasion for technique.

I call Boxing James by that name to distinguish him from Business James, the other scholar of weakness in my life. (By the way, although they do have the same first name, it's not James.) If Boxing James is an artist who used to be a gangster, Business James is a political philosopher who exploits market weakness for a living. I couldn't tell you exactly what he does, but it involves finding underpriced companies and using money collected from a crew of impossibly rich investors (I picture them as near-miss finalists for the role of James Bond villain) to make offers the companies' owners can't refuse, then managing those companies and buying up other companies to combine with them until they're profitable, then selling them and renting a fleet of dump trucks to deliver the money to the bank.

Business James, an old friend I first got to know in college, is a Howard Dean man and a big donor to the Democrats who spends much of his time making beautiful financial music with Texas Republicans in the oil business. He's a Darwinian pessimist committed to the premises of the welfare state, a money man who reads, a reading man who happens to make money. He makes a running joke of tracking the leading indicators of imminent apocalypse, everything from rising sea levels to the behavior of some older pro-Bush business associates whose secret bearishness on America has reached the point where they're quietly moving significant elements of their fortunes offshore. He jokes about his own doomsaying, but he's also not kidding. He owns high ground up north, far enough from Boston (where we both live) to afford his family pleasant weekends away from the city, but not so far away that he can't get them there quickly in an emergency.

Business James spends his days brooding on the imminent unraveling of life as we know it while he does the business equivalent of shoving serried towers of chips into the pot and surveying the blanched faces around the poker table. So he tends to think in terms of weakness and strength (or maybe it's the other way around: he found the right job for a person who thinks that way), and he tends to scare the people with whom he and his wife socialize—the hypereducated, rich, dutifully liberal progressives of greater Boston.

You could make the mistake of thinking that Business James hates these people, who are of course his people. After all, he calls them the Irrelevant Class, complaining that they have all the credentials and pretensions of a ruling class but none of the will, the strength to stand up to those who really run the country—like the oil men with whom he makes money. But you'd be wrong. He doesn't hate his people. He wants them to wake up, sense the danger, and rediscover their strength in time to fight back against the gathering forces of doom. When he terrorizes them at dinner parties with half-ironic talk of melting ice caps and dissolving social order, it reminds me of the climactic scene of *Blade Runner*, in which the superhuman replicant Roy pursues Harrison Ford through an abandoned building, apparently trying to kill him but really trying to show him what it means to live.

Nothing drives Business James crazier than the quality of education at the school his young children attend. Not that it's a bad school. It is in fact a lovely school, staffed by decent, committed educators. It's exclusive and widely admired and expensive, and parents in his—our—social circle angle vigorously to send their children to it. But James believes that the school's educational philosophy, enthusiastically supported by the parents, emphasizes gentle sensitivity to the exclusion of efficacy. "The end of an age is coming up fast in the rear view mirror," he wrote to me recently, "and they can see it, but they're utterly baffled." In their uncomprehending bafflement, they continue to value above all else the tantric soul-smoothing function of a post-'60s finishing school that turns out sweetly vague, tolerant, well-intentioned, unambitious, underequipped copies of their parents. "They're slow-running deer," he wrote, "with targets painted on their foreheads." They're going to get slaughtered, in any contest for power and resources, by the righteously selfish children of the oil men, the upwardly mobile children of the immigrant strivers James employs as analysts at his capital fund, the children of all those people out there who know that gentleness without strength amounts to abject weakness.

———

On a cool, drizzly, slate-gray October afternoon, I took my kids to this school's annual fair, where we ran into Business James and his kids. The fair, a fundraiser, was as well attended and competently organized as you would expect from a community of lawyers, doctors, professors, architects, editors, money handlers, and other professionals with good connections and good taste.

The Irrelevant Class was out in force. The mothers knew something about art and clothes, the fathers knew something about wine and music, and they all knew something about money—although not the way James did, since they didn't play for keeps the way he does. They all thought *Sideways* had been hilarious, and *so* well acted. They voted. They nodded grimly when reading Paul Krugman's column in the *Times*. They had owned the Buena Vista Social Club CD ever since it was featured on *All Things Considered*; their kids knew some of the lyrics, even though they're in Spanish. Educated, lean, and cultured, these people were not wholly deluded in admiring themselves and each other: slow-running deer with targets on their foreheads, pausing to check out their reflections in the water while hunters gather nearby.

At the pony ride, I had a small epiphany when my daughters took their turns astride the plodding little mounts. Yuan, the little one, compact and cheerful, looked like a two-year-old Sancho Panza as she was led around in a circle by the attendant. When Ling-li, the big one, a four-year-old built like a flexible blade, came around the circle and caught sight of me, she smiled—almost a smirk, really, the outward sign of an inward dawning of command, another thing she could do, another stone added to the rising cairn of her purpose and self-reliance. She was wearing a purple fleece jacket with the hood up, the drizzle having picked up as the afternoon deepened toward evening. Holding the pommel with both hands, she slouched familiarly in the saddle, swaying easily with the pony's motion. Smiling that ancient smile, she looked for all the world like a veteran of many campaigns passing through a village of harmless, well-intentioned souls, making a mental note to come back sometime with her sister-in-arms and sack it.

Now, Ling-li is scared of all kinds of things: pirates, thunder, even the fake pop-up snakes in the school fair's ultramild haunted house. I have not yet found a kids' movie so innocuous that it won't freak her out at some point. Even the Muppets disturbed her at first. But she'll never back down from anything scary that's real—not a doctor with a needle, not a snarling dog, not five boys messing with her sister. She'll look over at the five boys and say, musingly, "I'm going to charge them," as if she weighed considerably more than 33 pounds and had sharp horns growing from her temples.

Maybe I'm wrong, but I don't worry about my kids ending up as slow-running deer. My wife and I—educated and liberal enough to qualify for the Irrelevant Class, but not rich enough, and not operating under the delusion that we matter—are not raising the girls in some special weakness-expunging way, but they seem to have come to us already inclined to self-assertion. Maybe they were born that way; more likely, a year in a kind-but-spartan orphanage gave each of them an early education in the exercise of strength. They lead pleasant middle-class lives that only rarely call upon them to use that strength, but very occasionally I give in to the thought that, should the science-fiction era of chaos that gun-show Christian survivalists call The Coming Times of Economic Collapse actually come to pass, I'm fairly confident my kids would do all right. In a Hobbesian free-for-all, they could get what they needed by taking it away from the children of the Irrelevant Class, their friends and neighbors. Some people just have that inbuilt strength, and no amount of countertraining can entirely change them. Nor would I want to entirely change them if I could. If you strip the drama from Business James's worldview, you get something that looks a lot like mine.

————————

Over dinner, I told Boxing James about the school fair and Business James's impatience with the Irrelevant Class, and he said, "Have you ever thought of them as evolved, rather than weak?" I confessed that I had not. I mean, some of *them* think of themselves as evolved, but I've always regarded that as a fairy-tale self-conception they pick up at Pilates or Princeton. Boxing James went on, "Look, they may not be able to protect themselves, but the fact is that nobody *is* going to come along and take their shit. It's not going to happen. They don't need to protect themselves because they're protected, they're insulated, and things don't change that fast or that much in this country. Maybe the way they are is a rational response to the life they have." Maybe it's false rigor to insist that they cultivate in themselves, as a class, a strength they won't ever be pressed to use. Maybe their gentleness constitutes a kind of triumph.

Business James, had he been there, would probably have argued in return that they should regard exercising meaningful influence over the political and cultural direction of their country as part of their shit, and that they better wake up to the fact that somebody already did come along and take it from them (while giving them tax breaks that further insulate them from noticing or caring). I spent Election Day 2004 going door to door with him though suburban subdivisions in New Hampshire, getting out the vote for a candidate we both despised. It was another thing to hold against Bush: he obliged us to support Kerry. When we were done, we drove back down to Boston, listening to early projections on the radio. Most had the election too close to call, and we permitted ourselves to believe there might be a small chance that things would come out all right. We stopped by a party, thrown by friends of Business James, for people who had worked for the campaign. The well-appointed house, a place of unimpeachable decorating decisions that communicated wealth and ease in the understated Boston manner, was filled with informed people of good will. They drank wine and exchanged cutting bons mots, radio-ready snatches of policy analysis, and rumors of promising electoral news from across the country. More than one of them expected that a Kerry administration would come calling about an appointment in Washington—a chance to make a difference, a nice new item for the CV. There was nothing wrong with these people or with the party, but when I walked in the door I knew all at once and for sure that Kerry was going to lose. Weakness pervaded the house like the plague in "The Masque of the Red Death." Business James felt it, too. He swiftly drained a few drinks, then went to sleep on the thick rug in the den in front of the television. The Irrelevant Class buzzed ineffectually around him, waiting for Peter Jennings to bring them good news that never came.

———

My wife and I have a running conversation about the difference between judging and accepting, between getting things done and digging beauty. You can see the world as a set of opportunities to accomplish something, to exercise your will upon it, or you can see the world as a set of opportunities to appreciate how it works, how it is. Everybody strikes some kind of balance between these opposing principles, but most people don't strike it right down the middle. My wife, for instance, leans toward judging and accomplishing, while I lean toward accepting and appreciating. The two Jameses help me seek a balance between the beauty-digging toward which I naturally incline and the exercise of will I accept as necessary to making a way in the world.

Business James woke up on the morning after Election Day in 2004 and started planning how to perform a backbone implant on the Democrats in time for 2008; from time to time, he gives me updates on his progress. Rather than inspiring him, however, the Democrats' victory in the midterm elections of 2006 seems to have sent him into a funk, as do the presidential candidacies of Hillary Clinton and Barack Obama, which have inspired a false optimism in the Irrelevant Class about an imminent return to proper relevance. "I'm planning on eight years of McCain and a lot more damage," he says. "Then we'll see what we can do with what's left. Things have never been worse than they are now." He lies awake at night thinking about what currently inhabited parts of the world will be underwater and when.

Boxing James, like Business James, sees trouble coming. "I don't recall any time during my lifetime that the world was in as rough shape as it is presently," he recently wrote to me in an e-mail. Were he still in the business of exploiting others' misfortune, Boxing James would be enjoying a boom that shows no signs of letting up. "Things are now irrevocably fucked up enough that, Democrat or Republican government holding sway, there'd still be crack houses in Brockton or Santo Domingo where I could get some work done," and he could count on an inexhaustible supply of "poor women who needed to be hookers, poor suckers who wanted to be pop stars, and poor black guys fresh from prison who were willing to be opponents for my slightly better stable of fighters."

But, unlike Business James, Boxing James expects that the Coming Times aren't coming for anybody except the poor. Trouble won't touch the Irrelevant Class. "The protection and privilege provided to it remains virtually untouched by our political system," which means there's no reason for the Irrelevant Class to cultivate atavistic virtues like strength, toughness, or force of will. It doesn't matter how slow the deer run. "The jungle has changed a lot. We outsource shit now, including having people who are stronger, more intuitive, sharper, and meaner handling our business for us. Those qualities are now not much more than service-industry skills." The Irrelevant Class can therefore carry on refining its beauty-digging skills and shed any vestigial aptitude for the jungle. "The toughest aren't the ones who survive. Even the smartest aren't always the ones who survive. The new survivors mostly consist of those who are, for a multitude of reasons, the least attackable. And, to my mind, the least attackable are the most evolved."

One night I took a break from writing this essay and went to the fights at the International Brotherhood of Electrical Workers Hall in Dorchester. Most of the bouts were terrible mismatches, typically featuring a locally based Irish guy with a winning record throwing thunderously amateurish punches at a black opponent with a good body and a bad record who had been recruited from out of state to lose. Sitting at ringside while the combatants heaved and strained before me, I told myself, as I always do, that this is what life looks like when you take off the cover and inspect the works. Fighters need all their resilience and potency, all their scary competence in locating vulnerability and striking into the gap, because they are the least protected, the most attackable, the weakest of the weak.

Three Landscapes, with Gamblers

Water-Gazers

I was idling at Pier 11 in Manhattan on a breezy weekend morning, waiting to take the Seahorse Express boat down to the racetrack at Monmouth Park on the Jersey shore. It was the day of the Haskell Stakes, a day of big races and bright July sunshine, and I was eager to get away from the routine of postcollegiate life: office work, bars, playing house with my girlfriend. Seagulls called in the narrow, pot-holed streets that surrounded the deserted pavilions of South Street Seaport. I had intended to give the racing form a thorough reading while I waited, but the play of sun on water distracted me.

That made me a water-gazer. In the first chapter of *Moby-Dick*, Ishmael marvels at the pull exerted by the sea on New Yorkers: "There now is your insular city of the Manhattoes, belted round by wharves as Indian isles by coral reefs—commerce surrounds it with her surf. Right and left, the streets take you waterward. Its extreme down-town is the Battery, where the noble mole is washed by waves and cooled by breezes, which a few hours previous were out of sight of land. Look at the crowds of water-gazers there. . . . Posted like silent sentinels all around the town, stand thousands upon thousands of mortal men fixed in ocean reveries. Some leaning against the spiles; some seated upon the pier heads"—as I was—"some looking over the bulwarks of ships from China; some high aloft in the rigging as if striving to get a still better seaward peep." They are all, Ishmael re-

Original publication: *TriQuarterly* 121, 2005.

minds us, "landsmen; of week days pent up in lath and plaster—tied to counters, nailed to benches, clinched to desks." What he wants to know is, "What do they here?"

Most of the water-gazers waiting for the Seahorse Express were in their sixties or older, outfitted for leisure in brightly colored sweats and other loose attire that snapped like sailcloth in the waterfront breeze. The gambling crowd, especially the more modest players, is an older crowd. This was in the late 1980s, before the opening of Indian casinos in Connecticut and upstate New York provided convenient places to warehouse those persisting in the interval between retirement and death, but even then Pier 11 formed part of a regional landscape of legalized gambling traversed by thousands upon thousands of retirees. Grandmothers loitered outside corner stores, waiting for the bus to the Atlantic City casinos; grandfathers crowded into smoke-yellowed Off-Track Betting outlets; in grocery stores, you patiently cradled your milk, sixpack, and Daily News while somebody at the front of the line tried to parlay grandchildren's birthdays into a lottery winner.

Playing slot machines, the lottery, or the ponies is like gazing out to sea at what looks like more life. You feel yourself to be at the verge of some other dispensation that begins where the materials of the everyday come to an end—the lath and plaster of work, family, neighborhood, doctor's appointments, Social Security checks. The unremarkable money you wager, which you earned while nailed to one kind of bench or another, mixes promiscuously with more glamorous money from places unknown, money which a few hours previous was out of sight of land. When you lose, all you get is a taste of salt air and the slightly dazzled feeling of having looked out to sea. If you get lucky and win, your money brings home some of its new seafaring acquaintances, although the exotic charm of such winnings never lasts. Sooner or later, it's all just money again, burning a hole in your pocket. Most casino and racetrack gamblers who win do not even manage to get their winnings home: they throw away house money even more heroically than their own, seemingly hell-bent on leaving the premises dead-even or broke, already recharging the capacity for longing that will draw them back to the water's edge tomorrow.

Gambling as it is done by most people—fitfully, with studied inexpertise, betraying a quasi-religious impulse to lose—proceeds from a willingness to treat one's money as somehow tainted by the work that produced it. In the bewildering logic of "gaming," one disposes of that sweat-stained cash as swiftly as possible, replacing it, ideally, with magically fresh and exciting money one has acquired through play. Ishmael knows better. Recognizing that "there is all the difference in the world between paying and being paid," he goes to sea as a working seaman "because they make a point of paying me for my trouble, whereas they never pay passengers a single penny that I heard of." This is not strictly the case on land, since casinos often give passengers on charter buses their fare's worth of coins to dump in the slots as a preliminary to dumping their own money in the slots, but Ishmael has a larger truth in view: if going to sea, like gambling, feels like throwing off the bonds of drudging routine and reaching for more life, remember that the workaday round of salaried labor gives form and meaning to any attempt to escape from it.

The Seahorse Express got out into the harbor and passed through the Verrazano Narrows, a moment that always seems full of promise. The great bridge soared overhead, we passed a line of ships arriving from far-distant ports, the open sky was full of sea birds. We took in lungfuls of ocean air edged with the tang of Patagonian distances. A trim, white-haired woman wearing a Members Only jacket over sweats came down the rail toward me. She had a folded racing form in one hand and a pencil in the other. "Tell me, son," she said, "who do you like in the fifth?"

Perhaps because I never did manage to give the racing form my undivided attention, relying instead on blind and progressively more drunken inspiration to guide my bets, I hit a couple of long-odds exactas and came home to Brooklyn that night a big winner. I took my girlfriend out to dinner to celebrate. We ordered pricey wine and became hilarious on the subject of my transformation from policy analyst to high-rolling horse player. The long day of heavy drinking, convulsive eating, sunburn, dehydration, and the unfamiliar motion of boat travel caught up with me late that night, and I threw up my meal. It went down the toilet and, after making its way through the sewer system and a waste treatment plant, proceeded into the bay and perhaps eventually out to sea.

Atlantic City

I was introduced to Atlantic City in the late 1980s by a married couple who went there too often and lost too much when they did. The husband—let's call him Ken—worked with me at a sort of think tank (at least partially a CIA front, I came to suspect) in midtown Manhattan. Ken was a few years older than me, but we were both postcollegiate flunkies, writers of memos and occasional speeches, ill-paid because it was understood that we would soon quit because we were ill-paid. His rudimentary helmet haircut spoke of cost-cutting rather than hipster minimalism, and he had a bowling-ball potbelly of which a man twice his age could be proud. Billowy shirts only partially concealed the gut, and, like clouds wreathing a mountain peak, they had the effect of rendering it more impressive. Ken wrote outsider-art crime stories, among the pleasures of which was violently forced exposition that clanked like a rain of safes and anvils: "Jack said, 'Hey, isn't that the same woman who saw us with our masks off right after we committed that bank robbery last year?'" The more I talked with Ken the more I understood that his daily life, even his writing life, amounted to marking time between trips to Atlantic City. Think of three concentric rings: on the outside, his job, easily done and forgotten; inside that, writing, at least two hours a day every day at a desk in his apartment in Sheepshead Bay, Brooklyn, patiently submitting stories and filing the rejections when they came in the mail; and, in the inmost ring, Atlantic City, its lighted towers rising up between the bracketing darknesses of the ocean and the lowrise city inland, offering action all day and all night, and prefab grandeur you could put your fist through.

Lisa, his wife, was tight and dark-haired where Ken was slack and fair, but she had the same air of initial nondescriptness incompletely masking a quality to beware of. Like Ken, Lisa did some kind of low- to midlevel office work, but she made a little more money than he did, their agreement being that she would contribute more to the household in the short run while they waited for his writing to pay off in the long run. The Atlantic City problem seemed to grow between them. Maybe they would have been immune to it if they had not been married to each other, but, since they *were* married to each other, they could hold off for no more than a week or two, careful not to jinx the run of self-control by talking about it too much or too little, before eventually breaking down and heading south once more. I pictured them returning home from work, first Ken (we never worked late at the think tank) and then Lisa, both uncomfortable in their bargain-basement office wear after a long subway commute, and the inspiration striking them all at once: let's change clothes, let's go to the bank, let's gas up the car, let's go. From Sheepshead Bay, they could cross the Verrazano Narrows Bridge to Staten Island, then a second bridge to New Jersey, and be in Atlantic City in two hours. Listening at lunchtime to Ken's latest account of how his closely theorized blackjack system had run afoul of an unlikely turn of the cards, I would imagine them giving in to their weakness, rushing down to Atlantic City, losing all their money, driving home broke and regretful, suddenly realizing—adrenaline coursing through them, despair at the fact of it right behind—that they could lay their hands on more cash, turning around and making the long drive down from Brooklyn again with a fresh bankroll to fritter away.

I went to Atlantic City with them once. Driving down, leaving the orbit of New York City and passing through the indeterminate spaces of south central New Jersey and then approaching Atlantic City as the sun finally disappeared, Ken and Lisa began to sweat. In the car with the windows down it was a comfortably cool summer evening, but their clothes grew dark at the necks and armpits, they shifted in their seats to unstick themselves, and from the back seat I could see shiny drops hanging in the hair on the backs of their necks. It looked like the kind of sweating that begins in anxiety but proceeds into relief, the initial heat and chills giving way to warmed-up looseness. They knew themselves to be weak and bad, but whatever was wrong with them was wrong with both of them, which made it part of what held them together as a couple.

My trip to Atlantic City with them was also the first time I ever went to a casino. This was back when casinos were still concentrated in Las Vegas and Atlantic City and not yet generally regarded as a viable alternative to the welfare state. I had some notion (I still do, every time) that the anthropology of it would be engaging, that I would hang around and place a wager here and there between stretches of observation and a turn or two on the boardwalk in the sea air, that we would drive home to Brooklyn in the morning with a long session of light misbehavior and inquiry into the human condition under our belts. Within two minutes of our walking into a casino, Lisa was inspired to make a relatively large bet at long odds on a spin of the wheel of fortune, the most dull-witted game of chance imaginable. (The wheel was positioned as a sort of toll booth to collect a first round of losses that a gambler would barely notice in the excitement of scanning the vast room full of light, sound, and surging humanity. If the gambler happened to win, he or she would certainly not stop there, at the threshold of big fun, but would instead take those winnings further into the casino, where the house could reclaim them and get at the gambler's own money.) The wheel, improbably, stopped exactly where Lisa wanted it to, and she raked in a pile of winnings that probably exceeded their monthly rent payment. She turned to her husband—eyes wide, a line of fresh sweat droplets starting in the near-invisible down above her upper lip—and said, "I want to go home. Now." It was a lot of money, and they needed it. Having with the evening's opening move beaten the house, Atlantic City, and herself, for once, she was desperate to get out of there before the thrill of gambling with house money overwhelmed the thrill of going home a winner.

But Ken had not even begun to gamble, and of course they had a guest to think of. There was a hurried and mostly silent marital confrontation. Lisa, who rapidly passed from beseeching to accusatory surliness, tried to keep her face in front of Ken's while he smiled thinly and looked around the room, unable to meet her eyes. He tried to counterfeit the air of a reasonable man who must be patient with his wife's moods, but it was all he could do to restrain himself from hissing at her to do whatever she wanted and bolting for the gambling tables, where dealers and croupiers awaited him with appraising looks that said, "Look, pal, why not cut to the chase and just give us all your chips right now? And bring your wife's money while you're at it." At the end of the standoff, Ken headed for the tables—the inevitable result, as they both knew all along—and Lisa said she would find something to eat and then rejoin us to reconsider our options. Ken assured her, as he fled, that there was a chance we might all decide to go home then.

An hour or two later she found us at a low-rollers' roulette table, where we were betting twenty-five cent chips—winning and losing, winning and losing, holding even for the moment against the house's advantage in odds. Roulette is not much more challenging than the wheel of fortune, and even the casino staff affects to look down on low-stakes roulette as a bottom-feeder's pastime. Ken had not yet begun to gamble in earnest; he was just getting loose in preparation for long, stultifyingly systematic hours of blackjack. Lisa, looking pale, hauled Ken off to one side for an urgent negotiation. When finally he brought himself to look her in the face, which she insistently held up to his as if demanding that he inspect fresh damage, he could see that his wife was in trouble. Only a complete animal would have obliged her to suffer further.

When they rejoined me a few minutes later, Ken announced that they were going home. Lisa hung back a bit, hugging herself in the chill of casino air conditioning, unwilling to join the group. Because they were leaving me to take the bus home in the morning on my own, Ken felt obliged to explain that Lisa had managed to lose, in some unspecified way, all of her winnings and then most of the money she had brought with her from Brooklyn. Piling losing bets one upon the other—first, I could imagine, to mark time amusingly until she could go home with her profits, then in an effort to turn dwindling good fortune into a great killing, finally in a desperate attempt to salvage her triumph—she had turned a moment of unlooked-for good luck into a night of memorable failure and weakness. Especially now that her winnings were gone and she had missed her chance to do the prudent thing with them, the strain of cutting her losses imparted a martyred gauntness to her. It took all her strength to resist the urge to complete the evening's logical sequence by throwing away the rest of the money she had brought from home. When Ken was done explaining and apologizing, he and Lisa disappeared into the crowd.

Had Lisa scooped up her much-needed winnings from the wheel of fortune, cashed out briskly, and headed for the door, the whole thing would have been over in about five minutes. When she hesitated, she gave herself and her husband a chance to let her down. Perhaps, though, the ensuing cascade of disappointments only infused her memory of that visit to Atlantic City with more of what mattered: an insight into the character of her marriage, a sense of her own and her husband's strength and weakness, a feel for the push and pull between will and fate. She and Ken did leave early, if not early enough, and what they gave up in additional gambling thrills that night by leaving early they may well have gotten back many times over in the form of an episode to revisit, a small disaster from which proceeded understanding and mystery like quarters pouring from a slot machine that has come up lemons, lemons, lemons.

Powerball

I had a professor who used to say, "People aren't stupid; they're crazy." He meant that we should seek complexity in our fellow humans, a form of giving them the benefit of the doubt. If you can't understand why people do something, especially something you don't like, assume it's because their reasons are complicated and obscure to you rather than simple and contemptible.

I try to keep his advice in mind when I encounter yet another instance of Americans' willfully futile engagement with the gambling industry. I do not mean recreational poker with cronies or an outing at the racetrack, and I don't mean what professional gamblers do (even if they're almost all doomed to failure over the long haul):

I mean consistently betting to lose, which is how most of us pursue satisfaction in casinos and lottery outlets. You want to dismiss such behavior as just plain stupid—*this* is why you wanted a tax cut?—but just plain stupidity doesn't explain the peculiarly self-flagellant quality of most people's poor gambling technique. Let's assume they are crazy instead.

Once, in the mid-1990s, I got stuck in a massive traffic jam on northbound I-95 caused by New Yorkers driving up into Connecticut to buy lottery tickets. While still in the Bronx I was already socked in, rolling forward a few feet every minute or so and then hitting the brakes again, and the radio traffic reports assured me that the jam extended ahead for many miles. It was a blindingly hot Saturday afternoon, my car was threatening to overheat, and I was impatient to get my business done in New Haven and continue on to Boston, where my wife was waiting for me. I was stuck because I had run afoul of a temporary folk migration set in motion by a Powerball jackpot in the $200 million range. New York did not offer Powerball among its various schemes to rook its citizens, so New Yorkers were heading for the ordinarily sleepy convenience stores of southern Connecticut, where Powerball tickets could be had.

People aren't stupid; they're crazy. I was repeating that to myself, trying not to succumb to contempt for those who would be inspired by news of an extra-large jackpot to leap into their cars, rush to the ATM, get on the highway, and spend their Saturday sitting in traffic and then standing in line to throw away their money on the longest shot imaginable—if in fact one can even imagine what it would mean to win against odds of scores of millions to one. They had screwed up my day in pursuit of a prize as close to unwinnable as any prize could be. So, I told myself, eyeing the engine temperature gauge as it swung to the right of the L in NORMAL, let's assume that people did not cast a long, calculating look at the odds and say to themselves, "It's worth a shot. I've got a good enough chance of winning that it makes sense to invest my day and whatever cash I can get my hands on. After all, I could win." Let's assume that nobody, or almost nobody, on the road that day was that dumb.

Let's believe, instead, that ticket-buyers did not expect or even hope to win, but were rather taking a ritual opportunity to register dissatisfaction with their lives and express hope for a better life somewhere. People who buy lottery tickets at all tend to buy lots of them, spending hundreds and thousands of dollars a year on them, which seems like an extravagantly self-defeating thing to do with money. I can only begin to sympathize with such behavior if I understand it as a diversion of precious resources to erect a kind of monument to the yearning for something better, sort of a secular, nihilistic parallel to pinning bills to an icon as it is carried by during a Catholic street festival—as opposed to thinking that one can actually invest toward and perhaps achieve a better life by buying lottery tickets, which would be just plain stupid. I would like to believe that the people around me in traffic had found a coded way to express dissatisfactions and hopes that they could not afford to confront directly for fear of disrupting the attention to mundane detail you must sustain to perform the daily slog. They were acting crazy, in other words, because their lives made them crazy, which strikes me as reasonable.

I was encouraged in this line of thinking by the fact that Powerball's larger jackpot and longer odds had inspired the great rush northward, as if all of a sudden the usual $20 million or $30 million state lottery jackpot at the usual inconceivably long odds were a mere pittance beneath notice. I hope this means that Powerball's attraction resided precisely in the greater chance of *not* winning a bigger prize, in the more dramatic opportunity to ritually immolate one's time and money. Powerball offered a chance to build a more expensively grotesque monument to dissatisfaction and hope—thus the appeal of the drive to Connecticut, the waiting in line, the expenditure of money better spent on almost anything else. It was a kind of mortification of the flesh. I felt better about the traffic jam to the extent that it had been produced by the rich, tangled moral intelligence of humans, albeit an intelligence expressed indirectly and in a death-seeking fashion.

By the time I got into Connecticut my car needed filling and I needed emptying. I pulled into the first roadside service area. So, apparently, had everybody else. Workers in orange vests waved the overflow of cars around to emergency parking areas in the back, and a great mob had converged on the building that housed bathrooms, restaurants, and a convenience store that, of course, sold lottery tickets. The line to buy them trailed through the building and outside into the sun. The prospective ticket buyers looked as if they had been waiting for hours. Parents dozed with kids in their laps; fast-food runs were arranged; people wondered aloud how much longer it would take; a man exasperatedly checked his watch, exhaling noisily, as if he had a right to be outraged. It could have been any crowd of people waiting for anything—concert tickets, jobs, evacuation.

Right then, once we were all out of our automotive cells and face to face, I found myself beginning to feel surprisingly good about the whole episode. In part, I have to admit, it was because I knew the road ahead would be clear now, but it was also because looking at the faces in a crowd, almost any crowd, makes it difficult to remain completely impervious to the claim other people make on you. Even if you have contempt for the crowd's collective behavior, you find it harder to sustain contempt for the individuals who make up the crowd. It usually ends up as respect, for the potency of their complicated drives if not for what those drives lead them to do.

I gassed up and pulled out of there. Within a few miles I had the road almost to myself, even though any Powerball-seeker who had thought to keep driving a few more minutes into Connecticut would have found much shorter ticket-buying lines. By then, though, I was ready to regard this further failure of good sense as just more flesh-mortifyingly soulful performance art. I was back up to cruising speed and the temperature gauge had swung back over between the N and the O of NORMAL where it belonged. And I was back to firmly believing that people are crazy—an uplifting thought, in those circumstances.

The Mouse Sled

THE OTHER DAY ONE of my daughters, in a snit at having been sent upstairs for some infraction, knocked my Casio CQ-81 combination calculator-alarm clock off my bureau and broke it. A silver-gray triumph of late-'70s design, with its green LCD screen slanted upward at the same 45-degree angle as the racing stripe on an AMC Gremlin, it looks like a sled for mice. I picture two or three of them, reclining side by side in the angle, squeaking happily as the CQ-81 zooms across the same hilly snowscape that Santa traversed on his electric razor-cum-snowmobile in Norelco's Christmas ads.

The Mouse Sled sat undisturbed on my bureau for years before my daughter got to it, and before that, as I moved from here to there over the past three decades, it sat on other bureaus and desks, on shelves, in drawers and boxes—all the while dutifully telling the time but rarely consulted, almost never used as a calculator and only once in a long while as an alarm clock. It stopped working for a few years, then started again, perhaps because I finally changed the batteries. Now, thanks to my daughter, it doesn't work at all. But its real value has always been as a totem, anyway.

My parents gave me the Mouse Sled for Christmas when I was fifteen, the first of many presents intended to assist me in getting organized and making myself presentable: calculators, clocks, watches, belts, ties, dress shirts, sweaters, jackets. My parents still give me presents to help me look and act like a grown-up, only now they do it with

Original publication: *Washington Post Magazine*, November 22, 2009.

my blessing. In fact, I tacitly rely on them to help keep me supplied with work clothes. But back when I was fifteen, I received the Mouse Sled as a dire portent.

I didn't want a caculator-alarm clock. For Christmas and my birthday I usually asked for war games. These were board-game simulations, with scores or hundreds of little square cardboard pieces representing military units that players maneuvered on a map marked off with hexagons. A new game, unboxed, smelled like concentrated essence of new book. I would punch out and separate the pieces, set them up on the board, and then set about mastering the dense rule book, which featured entries on the order of "5.87: Unlimbered artillery stacked with non-disorganized infantry in a Brigade grouping (see 4.46–49) can be moved at the rate of the slowest infantry unit in the Brigade over clear terrain, bridges, roads, and, at a penalty of two movement points, streams and brooks (see 3.4–7), except in Rainy Weather scenarios, when special conditions apply (see 8.21)."

I didn't try to find opponents. I played both sides, more than two when necessary. I would spread the board on my desk, which my father's father built, and sit hunched over it deep into the night. My principal failing as a general was a tendency to draw out the opening phases in which the opposing armies jockeyed for position before committing to bloodshed. I shrank from the messiness of engagement, and I wanted to prolong the game. The most important thing about war games was that they took days to play. I wasn't just killing the imaginary troops under my command; without consciously having decided to, I was killing time until I could go away to college, when, I vaguely expected, life would begin in earnest.

Like a soccer team that needs only to lose by fewer than three goals to advance to the next round of the World Cup, I spent my high school years kicking the ball out of bounds, making a shabby pretense of hurrying to put it back in play, running time off the clock. I did my school work, I had friends, I didn't curl up in the fetal position, but I committed as little of myself as I could to life, and I never took a risk—social, emotional, or intellectual—that I could safely defer. War games served my purpose, and their intimidating rule books and pieces bristling with numbers and symbols gave them an intellectual aura that fended off parental objections.

Still, my parents picked up on my stalling tactics. I have a memory of my father, still in suit and tie after a long day at the office, pausing at the doorway of my room late one evening. I was at my desk, bent over a map of Borodino or Tobruk, moving pieces and plotting to outsmart myself. After a while I became aware of him and looked back over my shoulder. He said to no one in particular, "Always playing games. He's always playing games."

Now, 30 years later, I can name the unnameable unease that filled me when I unwrapped the Mouse Sled on Christmas morning. As a gift, it was both a gentle smack on the back of the head—*wake up!*—and a firm handshake welcoming a probationary adult to a life ordered by work rather than play. My parents, immigrants who worked like sled dogs and instructed by example rather than preachment, were urging me to take the measure of time: *It's passing, don't fritter it away; use it well by using up what's inside you, harvesting the crop so that more can grow.* Among the most important gifts they have given their sons is an awareness that life is short and work is good for you.

Now I have the Mouse Sled on my desk in the office at home, where I write. One corner is dented and cracked. When I put in the batteries, a hissing noise comes out of the alarm clock's tiny speaker, but nothing appears on the screen. The perp who broke it sneaks covert looks at it when she comes into the office. She can't figure out why she's not being punished. She's only eight; in a few years, especially if she begins to show signs of thinking that she needs only to lose by fewer than three goals to advance to the next round of life, I'll tell her the story of the Mouse Sled. It probably won't ever tell time or multiply again, but it could still wake somebody up.

A Game

EARLY IN THE MORNING, geese forage in the strip of park along Memorial Drive on the Cambridge side of the river. The leaves are mostly down and it's almost cold. A scattering of homeless men sleep on the grass, having spent the night wrapped in blankets, their possessions assembled around them. The Yale band, hauling cased instruments and carryout from Dunkin' Donuts, straggles across the Larz Anderson bridge, which connects Harvard to its athletics complex, business school, and burgeoning real estate empire on the Boston side of the river. One musician, a dark-haired lass, says, "Okay, the party scene here sucks! I was in taxis all night, and we used up all our money." Others commiserate, but they all seem to have found parties that lasted well into the morning. They cross the river, headed toward the high concrete bulk of Harvard Stadium.

—————

If you continue over the bridge to the stadium, circle around behind it, and cut through a parking lot in which the first alumni tailgaters are already setting up, you arrive at a muddy field where the Yale Women's Rugby Football Club is playing its opposite number at Harvard, the Radcliffe Rugby Football Club. The players wear striped shirts and shorts. Their legs look cold, but they don't care.

Original publication: "Youth & Consequences," *Yale Alumni Magazine,* January/February 2005.

The game kicks off at 8:04. At 8:10, a pile of struggling bodies surges across the try line and a blue-and-white arm touches the ball down on the ground: 5–0, Yale. A stumpy little Harvard bruiser has to leave the game, clutching her ribs and smiling apologetically. One of Yale's coaches says, "We're knocking them around pretty good." Phillippa Thompson, Yale's flyhalf, who wears one of those close-fitting caps with ear guards that make rugby players look like medieval henchmen, crushes a Harvard ball carrier and then scoops up the ball, racing far downfield before being tackled. Soon it's 10–0, Yale.

Drums start up somewhere out of sight, a band warming up. The November sun comes out, bright but weak. Harvard mounts its best scoring chance in the game's final minutes, pushing across the try line as time runs out, but the Yale defenders get their arms under the ball and prevent it from being touched down. The referee blows his whistle, ending the game in a shutout. This, it turns out, will be Yale's athletic high point of the day.

———

In the shadow of the stadium, a middle-aged supervisor in a red windbreaker lectures a group of young local jocks who will serve as ushers. They look like regular guys; buzz cuts and Irish faces predominate. The supervisor, who has a ripe Boston accent, is trying to prepare them for the shock of encountering Harvard and Yale types in extremis. He says, "You will see levels of intoxication you've never seen before." This can't possibly be true, but he's speaking for effect. "They're handing out free beer across the street there," he says. The young guys exchange glances: *Free beer! Now that's the place to go to college.* "Another thing. The students run this place. Not the police, the students. This isn't like anything you've seen before. Brown is bad, but this is worse than Brown. And every one of these people has a lawyer on speed dial, you know what I mean? So be polite, keep 'em moving, and if there's trouble just back off and get a supervisor or a police officer." The ushers appear to be wondering what they have gotten themselves into, but they also seem eager to get a look at the exotic animals they will soon be herding.

———

At 10:20, Yale's football team arrives on three Peter Pan buses and files to its locker room like a company about to go over the top in a decisive battle of the Great War—hushed, grimly intent, eyes fixed on the middle distance.

———

Across North Harvard Street from the stadium, at Ohiri Field, which has been set aside for undergraduate tailgating, cops and security guards check tickets and IDs at the gate. You get your wrist tag here, you get your beer there; no money changes hands. Music cranks. Couches and tables have been hauled out onto the grass. Beer pong players hit the game's signature loft shot with gestures of exaggerated care.

Yale students congregate at the far end of the field. The party has built up more momentum here, young men and women already packing in close, talking loud, greeting new arrivals with shouts and hugs as if surprised to run into them so far from home. The visitors always get drunker than the home team's fans. Their greater excitement derives from the root logic of a college road trip: We were *there*, now we're all *here* . . . it's *amazing*. A clever-looking fellow laughs and laughs, staggering, half-slain with mirth. He wears The Uniform— khaki pants, blue blazer, red tie—and holds a torpedo of St. Ides in one hand.

Several Boston police officers and firefighters move through the crowd, impassive and largely ignored. One cop frog-marches a post-collegiate guy in shades and ball cap across the field toward an exit. Every time the cop says, "You *jumped* the fuckin' fence," the guy interrupts him, saying, "I *did* not jump a *fence*." But most of the police and firefighters have nothing much to do. Nobody's going to touch off a riot with a sucker punch or torch a car just to watch the son of a bitch burn.

No matter how much talk there might be about going crazy at The Game, nobody's going to do anything . . . *crazy*. Yes, a few thousand young adults liquor up well before noon, but it's a ritual suspension of norms rather than a burst of spontaneous troublemaking—a carnival, not a mob scene. There are plenty of people, some of them college students, who regularly get drunk and mean before noon and go looking for trouble, but none of them appears to be on Ohiri Field this morning. And crowds, even crowds of college students, do go wild, but not this crowd. Everybody present, including those who have reasons to feel genuinely alienated from their own Ivy status, has too much to lose.

Back on the stadium side of North Harvard Street, where the alumni have set up camp, the atmosphere is quieter, even serene. A swelling hubbub of genial talk, wafts of cooking-meat smells, and crisp November air combine to produce a distinctive tailgate synesthesia. The faces at this party are road maps of life after college, bearing the marks of marriage and divorce, houses, jobs, money management, sickness, success, disappointment, kids, grandchildren. Compared to them, the attractive and accomplished undergraduates across the street seem like the blank pod people from outer space in *Invasion of the Body Snatchers*; they have yet to take on features and become somebody.

———

A hickory-carved septuagenarian in khakis, walking through the tailgate area with a friend, is seized by a coughing fit so violent that he gags and throws up. He tries to catch it with one gloved hand. Tendrils of vomity spit dangle from his fingers and chin. His companion asks if he's okay. "Yuh," he says with a curt shake of his head, wiping it off, ready for more.

———

At 11:40, the Harvard team, in uniform, files from its locker room to the stadium, cleats clicking on the paved path. It's almost game time.

———

Up in the press box at the top of the stadium, reporters and functionaries occupy two rows of seats looking down on the field. There are also a couple of pro scouts. One of them, himself only a few years removed from college ball, says that while Ryan Fitzpatrick, Harvard's fine quarterback, has attracted a lot of attention from the NFL, he has an eye on three Yale prospects: Rory Hennessey, the offensive left tackle; Ralph Plumb, a wide receiver; and Barton Simmons, the free safety. "Guys like this," the scout says, "they got a chance to get to a training camp maybe as a late-round guy, or a free agent. They'll get a look from some teams. They're smart, and smart guys get better faster." Playing on the road, the Yale prospects have a special opportunity to impress the pros today. "It's easy to look good when they're at home in front of five thousand people, but under pressure on the road in their big game, if they step it up and do well here, that tells me something."

————

On the field, Harvard's seniors are being introduced one by one. Almost all of the seniors on both teams will end their football careers today, but a select few will go on to take a shot at the big time. Coming out of Division I-AA programs, seeking to prove themselves against Division I-A stars, those who do take that shot will be underdogs, an unfamiliar position for a graduate of Yale or Harvard. If they succeed, against the odds, in turning a schoolboy pastime into a profession, the consequences of playing or coaching football will deepen for them, the stakes going up as the years go by. You look up and suddenly you're 30, or 40, and the roads you took mean other roads not taken. It gets harder to change your major in life, even if you went to Yale or Harvard.

————

When the game begins, shortly after 12:30, two separate dramas get underway. In one of them, the familiar drama of Yale vs. Harvard, the players arrive at the climax of their seasons and, in many cases, their football careers. Yale can redeem its disappointing 5–4 record with an upset, spoiling Harvard's chance at a 10–0 season. In Ivy League sports, silver linings abound and character formation trumps statistics. Yale can't win the league title this year, but with a victory it can still win the Harvard-Yale-Princeton title, avert a four-year sweep of its Class of 2005 by Harvard, and deny Harvard perfection. Or, if Yale loses, its players can take solace in striving nobly in defeat and knowing that Yale is still fifteen wins up on Harvard in their long-running series. One way or another, no matter how bad the losers may feel at the moment the clock runs out, everybody wins. Nothing that happens in the game will prevent any of the players from running for the Senate in 30 years or so.

In the day's other drama, a handful of prospects show their wares to the scouts, antisentimentalists who do not hold office hours at which you can ask them to reconsider a grade. The dramas will occasionally intersect—when a prospect makes a game-changing play, for instance—but they are about different things. One is about college; one is about the world beyond it.

––––––––

On the third play of the game, Ralph Plumb catches a pass in the flat for a first down. The scout says "Plumb" and makes a notation on his game program. Plumb catches another ball for a first down before the offense stalls and Yale has to punt. "He moved the sticks," says the scout, nodding. Asked about Rory Hennessey, who blocks with his usual Herculean aplomb, the scout says, "Won't know about him until the third or fourth quarter." Let's see how consistent he can be in a big game, after the initial burst of adrenaline gives out.

On defense, Barton Simmons plows like a bighorn sheep into guys wearing red and looks for a chance to make a big play. Late in the first quarter, Ryan Fitzpatrick hangs a pass up in the air too long and Simmons almost intercepts it, reaching the ball at the same time as the receiver, but they bump each other and it falls incomplete. Early in the second quarter, Fitzpatrick misses a receiver with a pass and Simmons gathers in the ball just before it hits the ground, but the referees rule it incomplete. Simmons gets up and gets back to work, ballhawking, hitting, trying to read Fitzpatrick and make him pay for mistakes.

––––––––

Harvard scores three touchdowns in the first half—on a run, a punt return, and a disastrous error by Yale's quarterback, Alvin Cowan, who, after guiding his team to the goal line, throws the ball directly to a Harvard defender who runs it back the other way 100 yards for a touchdown. Yale manages only a field goal in response. At halftime, it's 21–3, Harvard.

––––––––

By halftime, the scout has written next to Plumb's name the follow-ing laudatory notes: *catch—turned for ball, catch over middle, catch in crowd over middle,* and *inside guy.* There is also one demerit, a *drop,* which seems unfair, since the ball in question was thrown into the turf at Plumb's feet. Next to Simmons's name he has written an ap-proving *Big Hit.* Next to Hennessey's he has written *Beaten off edge pressure*, an instance of stern grading. Hennessey blocks well throughout the first half, but on just one play he allows a Harvard defender to fight past him and hit the quarterback after Cowan has thrown a complete pass to Plumb. Hennessey is Yale's leading prospect: 6'4," 300 pounds, and his coaches claim that he has not allowed a sack in his entire collegiate career. But he allows himself a single lapse in the first half, a lapse that doesn't even hurt his team, and that's all the scout's notes have to say about him.

From the press box, if you turn away from the stadium field and look into the distance through the rear windows, you can see the rugby pitch, where the games continue: Yale men vs. Harvard men, Harvard alumni vs. the current Harvard teams. There are no prospects on display. Most major cities have club teams, but there's no professional American league to aspire to. Ivy League women and men play rugby for love of the game, for the exercise and camaraderie, for the bracing jolt of sporting collisions. If they continue to play after graduation, those same reasons will have to do, because there aren't any others.

The sun goes away behind a thickening overcast and does not come back. Seagulls and pigeons circle above the open bowl of the stadium. A potent chill spreads upward from concrete seats into bodies in which alcohol is dying a slow death.

In the second half, Ryan Fitzpatrick settles into a heroic groove, making unimpeachable decisions with the ball and improvising shrewd, twisting runs for first downs. The game rapidly moves out of reach for Yale, which fights hard on defense and gains ground on offense but cannot stop Harvard or get into the end zone. At the end of the third quarter, Harvard leads 35–3.

It's *Stover at Yale* time. In the great American college novel of 1911, a halftime pep-talker addresses a Yale team that's losing badly to unbeatable Princeton. "You can't win," he says. "You never had a chance to win. But, Yale, you're going to do something to make us proud of you. You're going to hold that score where it is! Do you hear me? All you've got left is your nerve and the chance to show that you can die game. That's all you're going to do; but, by heaven, you're going to do that!"

And, by heaven, they do. Yale doesn't score in the fourth quarter, but neither does Harvard. Barton Simmons angles in to nail ball carriers, trying to force a fumble. Rory Hennessey keeps his man away from Cowan. Ralph Plumb catches every ball thrown to him, and one that wasn't.

The note-taking scout may see all this, or he may not. He and a colleague representing another team leave the press box at halftime and never return. Maybe they move to a different spot in the stadium, maybe they call it a day and make for the nearest Hooters. Whether or not the pros notice, Simmons, Hennessey, and Plumb play out both the *Stover at Yale* scenario and the prospects' drama to the bitter end.

When the game ends, some fans jump down from the stands and run around. Mounted police ride onto the playing field. Premature evening descends, and everybody starts thinking about what comes next: more tailgating, traffic, the evening's round of dinner and parties, life after football.

At the postgame press conference at the Varsity Club, Yale's coach, Jack Siedlecki, sits with three of his players at a table. The players have not yet changed out of their game gear; their cleats leave disk-like clods of mud and grass on the red rugs and polished wood floor. The players slump deeply in their chairs, vacant-eyed. They may well believe that they are inconsolably desolate, but they are impossibly young—the tenderness of fresh hurt accentuates it, making them look like enormous twelve-year-olds whose dogs have died—and they will recover quickly. The coach, an intense bald man whose nightmarish day at the office appears to have put new lines on his taut face, will take much longer to get over it. He praises Harvard's team and his own players' effort, his voice thickening when he says, "I'm disappointed in the team, but not in individual performances. They're great kids, they're going to go on and do great things, and I'm proud of them." But he can't resist revisiting his quarterback's one big mistake, which led to an interception and a Harvard touchdown. Yale was about to score to close within seven points, then suddenly Harvard was up by 21. "That put us in a hole," says Siedlecki. "Big-time hole."

Alvin Cowan, sitting at the table with the coach, manfully takes responsibility for the ill-advised throw. He also notes that Yale has been running that particular play at the goal line all year, perhaps suggesting that Harvard knew it was coming. It could be that a little tension moves under the surface of both men's comments. *If Mister Hotshot Quarterback hadn't made that dumb throw . . . If Mister Offensive Genius Coach hadn't called that predictable play. . . .* But they both try to do the right thing. Mustering their will at its lowest ebb, they rise above the temptation to squabble in defeat.

Dink Stover would approve. "He went out, head erect, back to meet his college, no longer shrinking from the ordeal, proud of his captain, proud of his coach, and proud of a lesson he had learned bigger than a victory."

In the margin of his program, in no obvious proximity to the name of any of the prospects he was observing, the scout wrote *Bad decision.* Perhaps he referred to Cowan's goal line throw, or one of Fitzpatrick's two long passes that Simmons nearly intercepted, or something else—a blocker's error, a defender's misreading of a formation. Oops. Sorry, coach. Won't happen again.

Bad decision. Ideally, collegiate athletics creates situations in which young people must make decisions, must act and be acted upon in character-shaping ways, without external consequence beyond the course of the game and the school's rah-rah fortunes. It doesn't work that way, of course. What happens on the field can shape budgets, application yields, professional futures. Still, a bad decision in even the most important Division I-AA football game seems almost without consequences when compared to bad decisions like marrying the wrong mate, choosing the wrong job, getting behind the wheel of a car after the fifteenth drink. Ask the homeless people who spent the night camped on the grass along the Cambridge side of the river.

Actually, maybe you shouldn't ask them. Maybe you should ask the alumni at the tailgate. Most people feel, rightly or wrongly, that their lives are shaped by what the world visits upon them, rather than by what they choose to do. But, rightly or wrongly, most people who graduate from Yale and Harvard feel that they hold the course of their lives in their own hands, that good or bad decisions matter more than good or bad fate. Part of what draws alumni to the Yale-Harvard game every year may well be nostalgia for a feeling of cozy distance from the consequences of one's own decisions—nostalgia for a long-lost undergraduate moment of insulation from the fact of an increasingly irrevocable life course already beginning to form beneath the surface of classes, parties, and games.

Ralph Plumb and Rory Hennessey were invited to some NFL training camps but never made a regular-season roster. Barton Simmons, who did not try to catch on with an NFL team, became a football reporter, broadcaster, and scout. As of this writing in December 2011, Ryan Fitzpatrick, in his seventh season in the NFL, was the starting quarterback for the Buffalo Bills. Yale was ten wins up on Harvard, 65–55–8.

Playing in Time

SETH ARENSTEIN, A 42-YEAR-OLD editor of cable industry publications and amateur trumpeter, had always played from sheet music. He had shied away from jazz, and especially from improvisation. Not that there wasn't any improvisation in his life. Putting out a magazine, plus a daily update known for its barbed acuity, required a certain ability to be creative within the structure imposed by journalistic form and deadlines. But when it came to music, his first love, he had left the improvising to his younger brother, Michael, a 40-year-old otolaryngologist who was also a gifted jazz pianist. Seth played and listened to classical music, mostly. He had had a solid early musical education in childhood lessons and school bands, then he had put down the trumpet in his twenties as he embarked on his career, but he had taken up the instrument again in his late thirties to join an amateur orchestra. He had returned to his first love as a hobby, but it was more than that: He lived more deeply, more vividly, in music. When he could not play, he listened; when he could not listen, there still was music in his head—phrases, fragments, bits and pieces of beauty sounding in the mind's ear.

On a Thursday evening last summer, Seth found himself on the stage of Kilbourn Hall in front of an audience at the world-famous Eastman School of Music in Rochester, New York, with a moment of truth upon him. He was part of a small jazz group churning through "Autumn Leaves," a standard. The preceding soloist played his clos-

Original publication: *Washington Post Magazine*, June 30, 2002.

ing notes, the crowd applauded and subsided, the rhythm section drove into the start of another chorus, and there came an expectant pause into which it was Seth's turn to step. It was either a dream come true or a sheet-music player's version of the actor's nightmare. He considered for a long moment, trumpet raised to his lips.

Seth and his brother, both of whom lived near Washington, DC, had arrived in Rochester the previous Sunday for a week at the Tritone Jazz Fantasy Camp. Michael, a veteran player and a soulful improviser, was looking forward to studying with accomplished teachers and to a good vacation. Seth, though, described himself as "a blank slate" when it came to improvisation. Four days of master classes, theory classes, small combo and big-band rehearsals, open-mike jams, lectures on jazz history and style, recitals by the professional musicians who taught at the camp, practicing, late-night hanging out, and conversation about jazz with teachers and fellow campers had inscribed on Seth some principles to follow. He was anxious about playing a solo, but trying to improvise no longer made him feel—as it always had before—as if he were adrift in a trackless desert of jazz spontaneity, where the very possibility of pursuing your inspiration in any direction made it almost impossible to get your bearings or go anywhere at all.

Now, soloing, he departed from the melody into unfamiliar territory. He played a simple figure, repeated it, varied it, easing without hurry into an understated, Miles Davis-inflected solo that was plain but musically correct. He had not memorized it in advance, and it was different from the one he had played in dress rehearsal; he had improvised it. The solo lasted no more than 40 seconds, but it formed the climax of an important week in his musical life.

———

Fantasy camps have flourished in recent years, serving intertwined impulses especially well developed among men of the baby boom generation: to revisit one's youth, spend disposable income, and mount a brief excursion along the road not taken. The most numerous and established camps are run by sports teams; staffed by coaches and retired athletes, they often feature cameos by active players. Baseball fantasy camps came first and still dominate the field, but there are others for basketball (including those for women run by WNBA affiliates), football, hockey, and other sports from motorcycle racing to luge. There have been music fantasy camps for marching band, rock, guitar playing, guitar making, country music, folk, and being Christina Aguilera or someone closely associated with her. There have been camps dedicated to pro wrestling, cooking, brewing beer, monster trucks, bull riding, radio. At covert ops camp, mild-mannered regular folks make document drops and stage hostage rescues with paintball guns.

Besides offering amusement and a vacation spent *doing* something—rather than idling expensively in a less than satisfying way, as so many hardworking people do during a much-anticipated week off—fantasy camp can provide an occasion to consider what it would be like to have taken another road in life. For example, Michael Arenstein, the ivory-tickling ear, nose, and throat doctor, might have scratched out a living as a musician had he been willing to risk steep downward mobility. In other cases, the camper engages in pure fantasy, playacting an alternative life without any supporting evidence of potential or aptitude for it. Either way, having spent a week living a dream, the camper can return, satisfied and perhaps even relieved, to the home, career, and security of real life. That dynamic of departure and return helps to give fantasy camp its double-edged atmosphere of possibility and regret.

———

"I'm Bob DeRosa, pseudo-musician." The Sunday evening assembly that opened the Tritone camp had come to order in a big rehearsal room and recording studio in the Eastman School's main building. Returning campers had hugged one another and their teachers, then found seats; first-timers fidgeted expectantly. DeRosa, a big, friendly bassist from Rochester who passed his workdays as a vice president of marketing for American Fiber Systems Inc., was in charge of introducing the campers to one another and to their teachers. Starting a jazz fantasy camp was DeRosa's idea, which he brought to Fred Sturm and Jim Doser, professional teachers of music at Eastman. The three friends founded Tritone, which, in its fourth summer, offered two week-long sessions: one at Eastman, one at a resort in Wisconsin.

As a first order of business, DeRosa introduced "some real musicians," the camp's teaching faculty, who took up their instruments and launched into Thelonious Monk's "Well You Needn't." They were pros—not stars, but respected teachers (most of them on the Eastman faculty) and first-rate players who could hold their own in fast company. They knocked off a short set of standards, crackling with expert musicianship but not showing off. The campers looked impressed, scared, excited. After a while the band stood down and Janet Planet, the voice teacher, came on to sing a couple of showstoppers, accompanied by Gene Bertoncini on guitar. The singers bent toward her in their seats like sun-seeking plants.

Of the 47 campers, who each paid $650 in tuition for the week (room and board was an additional $360), about half had been to Tritone in previous years, and perhaps two-thirds were from out of town. Among the campers, there were two guidance counselors, a college administrator, two students; various business people, from small-business owners to corporate executives; three government officials, a judge, an FBI agent; two journalists; a handful of physicians, a speech pathologist, a psychologist, a psychotherapist; a chemist, a "gizmologist," a software engineer, other sorts of engineers; and two artists. There were also several retired people, finally free to devote themselves full time to music; most of them would spend the rest of the week walking around with beatific expressions on their faces. Each camper (except the singers) was assigned to a small combo and a larger ensemble. Combos would give a concert on Thursday evening, ensembles on Friday. They had four days to get ready.

––––––––

Fred Sturm had more than half of the campers in his ensemble, a very big band that included most of the beginners and few of the top-level players. Three rows of horns, rotating crews of pianists and drummers, a small civilization. Much of his task would be to convince them that they could play together at all. At the first rehearsal on Monday, Seth Arenstein looked around from his seat in the third row and thought, "My God, this is going to be impossible. The band's too big, we only rehearse an hour a day, and we've got less than a week."

"I've got an ambulance and a nurse ready," said Sturm, raising his hands to cue the first number. "So here we go. We go 'til we crash." As the band roared into the head, he called out, "Watch your key signature, everybody, or I'll *kill* you." His smile caught and spread throughout the room, so that soon almost everybody was wearing a goofy, triumphant look.

Having taught all manner of students, from hell-bent Eastman School preprofessionals to hormone-occluded middle-school band members, Sturm has a special talent for getting musicians who have good cause to be unsure of themselves to deliver their very best. He soon had the ensemble loosened up. When he finally called for volunteers to take a solo, a couple of camp veterans went first, then first-timers began taking the plunge. As each soloist played, the big band vamping gigantically in support, Sturm sought eye contact with the next prospective soloist.

He made an expectant, encouraging face at Seth, who, still playing with the rest of the trumpet section, looked up from the sheet music to shake him off with a regretful grimace that managed to communicate a whole thought: Not yet, but thanks for asking.

––––––––

When he was younger, Seth thought he would pursue a career in music. He was president of his junior high school band, first trumpet, soloist, he even conducted. He and his brother regularly won the school band's awards for best instrumentalist. Their parents had always encouraged them to play—their father, in fact, had told them when they were little boys that they had to take lessons for at least a year before they could decide for themselves whether or not to pursue music any further—but when Seth reached high school his parents told him that he was not gifted enough to play professionally. It's a good hobby, they said, but it's not a life, it's not a career. He might have a good ear and nice tone, he might be as competent and as committed as his band teachers could wish for, but that would never be enough for him to make a living from music. Seth had to start thinking about college and the prosaic business of getting on in life.

Michael, though, had a gift. From an early age, he could sit down at the piano and play what he heard. "I knew pretty early that there was a certain amount of innate talent he was blessed with," says Seth, "and I wasn't. It happens. You have to face up to that. I knew enough about music to see that he was so good that he could even fake out his teachers, just play by ear instead of learning the piece." So Michael went two steps further in music than his older brother could. Even though he already had medical school in mind, Michael majored in music at college, and he played professionally full time for a year before settling into a doctor's life without too many regrets.

––––––––

Also on that Monday, in a small room high up in Eastman's annex building, Gene Bertoncini's combo had its first rehearsal. These were some of the camp's best players, guys who could play gigs for money all the time if they wanted to. Warming up in a loose circle, waiting for the drummer to get ready, somebody started fooling around with the melody of "Out of Nowhere" and others picked it up. Bertoncini, a short, gray-haired Bronx Italian guitar genius with an old-fashioned stoopside manner, said, "Yeah, let's play something, let's play that tune," and they were off at a moderate swinging pace. A trumpet-playing Canadian engineer took a robust solo, then a music teacher from Fayetteville, New York, took a flashier one on tenor saxophone, laying on the fancy runs and effects. A deputy administrator in the Federal Insurance and Mitigation Administration from Silver Spring, Maryland, played a complex, chordal guitar solo. Then Michael Arenstein took his turn.

Michael's playing was not as imposing as the music teacher's or the federal actuary's, not as busy; it was more relaxed, more direct, more elegant. The word for that quality is "musicality," a kind of command that sounds like sophisticated ease rather than heroic strain. A key in the piano's high range was broken, producing a tinny clunk when touched, but Michael played it anyway, smiling at the ugliness of the noise, making it all into music.

They sounded good, not like dabblers trying to get through it but like musicians making music. When it was done, Bertoncini said, "Yeah, let's take it on the road," and the campers smiled and nodded, trying to be cool about how pleased they were.

Then Bertoncini got down to business. "We played that pretty good," he said, "but all—most—of us had trouble with one chord change. Let's work on that." He had the soloists, except Michael (who had gotten it right), go at it again, patiently moving from one to the next until each of the offenders had worked out a solo line that engaged the detail rather than glossing over it. Bertoncini urged them to remember their solutions. "It's no sin as a jazz player to look at the changes and work out a lick," he said. The music teacher, who had fudged the change the first time under cover of a frilly run, said contritely, "If you have chops, you can fool people on the changes, but I want to *play* the changes, not fool people."

The evening open-mike jams took place in a cool, green, glass-enclosed atrium across the street from Eastman. The sun set in the windows behind the bandstand; campers trickled in, dispersed themselves among the chairs and tables scattered about the space, and unpacked their instruments. A trio struck up "Take the A Train." A retired engineer played dense, forceful piano, turning out thick ropes of notes as he rolled from side to side on the bench like a ship in heavy seas. A college-age drummer and a retired corporate executive on bass formed the rhythm section. After a couple of choruses, a rock-jawed FBI agent straight from central casting joined in on tenor sax and took a solo. He timed it perfectly, strolling from the margin to the center of the room and leaping into the little pause between choruses.

A new crew came on to play "Blue Monk." A sales assistant from Tokyo took an appropriately Monkian piano solo. A black-bearded psychiatrist from Ottawa, who, in white shorts and black socks, resembled a sorcerer on his day off, played a sinister clarinet solo, fearless and original, if not always in tune. An 87-year-old tenor saxophonist named Carle Porter, bent at mid-back so near to double that the nether curve of his instrument almost scraped the ground when he played, took an enthusiastic turn in the center of the room.

Seth Arenstein, watching from a seat at the back of the room, muttered, "I gotta get in there," but his trumpet stayed in its case. He told himself that he wasn't ready, that it was still only the first day of camp. In his mind's ear, along with the musical phrases he could have been playing at that moment, sounded a saying he had heard somewhere: Remain silent and you may be thought a fool; open your mouth and remove all doubt.

———

All kinds of people walk around all day with music in their heads: snatches of recordings, idealized versions of their own playing, half-formed harmonic and melodic ideas. Most such people hold jobs that have little or nothing to do with music, which obliges them to reach an accommodation with their internal jukeboxes in order to function in the workaday world.

The stakes in this bargain—the amateur musician's version of the professional musician's struggle to balance aesthetic satisfaction with earning a living—can be high. Music can make life worth living, but it can make you crazy, too. Just ask the two campers, a psychiatrist and a psychotherapist, who treat the anguished psyches of musicians as part of their practices. "I went to see the 'Messiah' one year," the psychiatrist said, "and there were fifteen people onstage I'd treated," a chorus of the musically afflicted.

Several campers said they have had to resist the musical urge at work, deferring it until later in the day, later in life. John Barrett, a trombone-playing lawyer known to all at Tritone as The Judge, used to be a town justice in Webster, near Rochester. "I wore robes, sat in court," he said. "I tried to keep a sense of humor, but sometimes you have to be serious, because people make serious mistakes and they have to pay for them. I had to push aside music to do the job." Charlie Rath, who went to the University of Notre Dame with Gene Bertoncini before embarking on a corporate career, also shoved aside the music in his head when he was at the office. "I tried to suppress it," he said. "I had to get some work done." Rath rose to the position of executive vice president for marketing at Wendy's International before retiring to a comfortable bass-playing existence that has allowed him to let music take over his life, rather than distract him from it.

The Arenstein brothers are still in their early forties, far from the age when they can think of retiring to make music all day long. Michael forbids himself to listen to jazz when he performs surgery. "Good music in the operating room is no good," he says. "I get too into it, I pay too much attention to it." Seth, who hears trumpets in his head, says that music always threatens to take over, even when he is far from both the office and his instrument. "It can even interfere with your golf game. When I get ready to swing I have to clear my head. The last thing in there is usually a piece of music."

If all those who hear music in their head could devote themselves to it as they devote themselves to their job, the world would be a more perfect place for them. But, the world being considerably less than perfect, most members of the music-in-the-head tribe have to work hard to find time for music in lives ordered by other priorities. And, since they cannot develop their musical gift as fully as they might like to, they have to learn to be content with making music at all.

That, in a way, is what Fred Sturm was talking about when he said to his big band, "Kids don't know how much fun it is to play in time. One of the simple pleasures of playing jazz as you get older is playing in time, just loving time." He raised his hands to conducting position to cue another try at a rollicking passage that was not yet tight enough. "Okay, at number 36," he said, "and think time, *love* time."

———

On Tuesday morning, Mike Kaupa, shepherding his combo through a practice run on "Autumn Leaves," called on Seth Arenstein to take a solo. The FBI man and a bearded fellow known as Smoky had just taken their solos. Seth paused to collect himself, then delivered one. Nothing exceptional, but it would do. A few choruses later, taking his turn at trading solos with the drummer, Seth came up with a simple, melancholy phrase. When trading again with the drummer on the next tune, he tried a laughing effect at the end of a run. Kaupa said, "Hey, great. Never played jazz before, and you're doing it."

"Inner voices," John Harmon told his master class of advanced pianists on Wednesday morning, "that's where all the fun is. It's always the things in between that create interest beyond what's already there. You want to pick up every rock and see what's underneath it." Harmon sat at a piano; Michael Arenstein and three others sat at desks, taking notes now and then.

Harmon was talking about the subtle textures and tone colors found in the middle notes of chords, where, he said, the essence of a song often resides. "The trickiest part," he said, "is getting from one chord to the next in a musical way." Beginners and midlevel noodlers, trying to play the right scale over each successive chord, tend to produce choppy, dutiful music that sounds like a series of exercises arranged side by side. Listening to a song's inner voices, and improvising melodic and harmonic lines around them, would help Harmon's charges resist that tendency.

"Take chances," Harmon said. "Get out on limbs and find your way back."

———————

After dinner on Wednesday, the Arenstein brothers took stock of the week so far. Seth said he was learning a great deal about instrumental technique, about how to practice, about jazz. He was excited and daunted by the prospect of improvising in public on Thursday and Friday evenings, but he did not want to let that excitement make him lose sight of what mattered most: learning to do things properly. "The actual moment of the solo is not the point," he insisted. "The next six months is." He planned, when he got home, to "look for people who want to be serious about playing jazz—not just get together, but people who'll say, 'We'll play these ten tunes in these keys.'" Being equipped to get serious like that, rather than the spirited attaboys he might receive from fellow campers after fumbling through a solo in concert, would be the best thing about having spent a week at Tritone.

Michael, too, was holding back from plunging into the summer-camp melodrama of the climactic talent shows. "This camp is really good for people who don't get to play with other people much," he said. "I'm using it differently. I have people to jam with at home. I'm using it to learn." Gene Bertoncini and John Harmon, especially, were showing him "how to construct more interesting music, form-wise: how to build an introduction, a middle section, not just blow through." They had inspired Michael to set his sights higher as a musician. "Maybe I'll do a little arranging, maybe even composing."

Both brothers were having a good time at Tritone, perhaps even a life-changing good time, but they wanted to concentrate on doing things well, rather than on sentiment. They wanted camp to be about being a jazz musician rather than about acting like one for a week.

––––––––

The beginners in Fred Sturm's combo—including a kindly but formi-dable retired teacher on trumpet, a pair of gentle flutists, and the ancient Carle Porter on tenor sax—did not feel ready to perform in public, but Sturm assured them they would be fine. On Thursday morning they picked gingerly through John Coltrane's "Mr. P. C.," with Sturm help-ing out on trombone to keep them together. "Just a couple of things when we get out there onstage," he told them afterward, projecting optimism. "If you're going to take two choruses on your solo, you want to keep interest. Think about the architecture a little. Ramp up. Start with slow rhythmic values, quieter, and then you're getting higher, busier." Most of his charges looked as if taking two choruses was the last thing on their minds. They would be happy to get through one chorus without having a stroke, or to forgo soloing altogether. Only the eternally game Porter, bent over his horn, did not seem scared. He looked as if two choruses might not be enough for him.

Sturm hurried off to grab a sandwich for lunch, then returned to meet with his other ensemble, the big band. He was still recruiting soloists for their Friday evening concert. "Anybody else who hasn't gotten around to volunteering?" he pressed. "Anybody? I won't name names, like Seth. How about it, Seth? Do you want to take a solo?" Seth Arenstein said, "No," smiling but emphatic.

––––––––

Kilbourn Hall, august and plush, holds some 450 people. Campers, their friends and families, and curious locals half-filled the hall on Thursday evening for the combo show.

The audience's preconcert hubbub fell away, and the pregnant hush that followed seemed to stretch and stretch—until Carle Porter's voice carried into the hall from offstage, calling out, in mock anguish, "I can't go on!" Smiling devilishly, he led Fred Sturm's combo onto the stage a moment later. He took the first solo, too, mistakes and all, honking and growling.

Sturm's teaching and optimism had paid off. The beginners played their very best, better than they had in practice sessions. Having made it through the first tune, as the crowd applauded them, Porter and the trumpeter spontaneously turned to each other and shook hands; so did the flutists, flushed with joyful relief. Not exactly poker-faced jazz cool, but on this evening who needed it?

The combos came on one after another, progressing from beginners to advanced players. Each played a couple of tunes and offered some nugget of pleasure. Especially at the beginning, most of the concert's charge derived from the drama of people who do something else for a living putting on a show. The crowd applauded them for their pluck as much as anything else, for daring to bare their secret musical lives in public.

Seth Arenstein took his solos, on "Autumn Leaves" and an odd tune called "Farm Fresh Reggae," with eyes and trumpet raised skyward. He kept calm and did not rush, creating a simple figure to explore in one solo and employing a mute in the other. He had a full, round tone and a measured air that made simplicity seem musically direct rather than rudimentary. Thirty years before, when he was a kid, his teachers had made him memorize his chords and scales. He had never really put that knowledge to use until called upon to improvise at Tritone.

The four singers came on, one by one, to do their numbers. They had all worked hard with Janet Planet to temper their Broadway and operatic training with jazz technique, and the lessons had taken, at least in part. One camper's "I'm Beginning to See the Light" had more jazz in it than it did on Monday, for instance, but when she arrived at the last "light" she gave it the big opera treatment from which Planet had been trying to dissuade her all week.

Bertoncini's combo came out to close the show. Michael Arenstein took a masterful solo on their brisk, coolly rephrased "No Greater Love," telling a story in chord colors and long, twisting lines. The pleasure of the concert had changed. The more advanced groups were good enough that one could stop worrying about catastrophes and enjoy the free music.

After the concert, in the lobby of Kilbourn Hall, Seth took back what he had said about the relative unimportance of his first public performance as a jazz player. "No, it's a big deal," he said, smiling broadly, relieved and proud, storing the evening to take out and reconsider later.

———

At the big band's dress rehearsal on Friday, when Fred Sturm asked one last time for volunteers, Seth sheepishly raised his hand, and everybody gave him a cheer. When it came time to take that solo in the evening concert, on a tune called "Follow the Leader," Seth rose from the back row and opened with a surprise quotation from Duke Ellington's "C Jam Blues," which went over big. He kind of got through the rest of it, but, still, he had pulled off a musical witticism onstage, which for a novice improviser took presence of mind and some nerve.

As human drama, the two concerts were satisfying, and sometimes as jazz, too. When the music was good, it was good enough; when it was bad, it was honest and heartfelt. The expression of stunned joy that typically spread over the face of a camper after taking a solo seemed well earned. And when Sturm's big band got going, mostly on the tracks but just a little out of control, the sheer volume of blowing and aspiration carried everyone away with it.

The teachers at Tritone urged the campers to strip down their playing to its essence, rather than anxiously cluttering the soundscape with rote licks and scales. They preached a gospel of improvisational simplicity: the music you wish you could play is inside the music you can already play, not out there somewhere in an undiscovered realm of genius. And, at least during the week they spent at fantasy camp, the campers could believe in the larger application of this message: when you strip away the clutter of living and devote yourself to music, you find that the life you wish you could lead is already there, inside the life you lead now.

Acknowledgments

I OWE A DEBT of gratitude to the John Simon Guggenheim Memorial Foundation, the Mrs. Giles Whiting Foundation, and the George A. and Eliza Gardner Howard Foundation, all of which supported work that went into this book. And I owe special thanks to the editors with whom I worked on these pieces. There's almost nothing better in a writer's life than a good editor, and there's a particular deep satisfaction in working with an excellent editor you've worked with before. My partnerships with David Rowell, Dean Robinson, James Burnett, and Kathrin Day Lassila are all represented by more than one piece in this book. There's just one piece in the book that I wrote for Anne Fadiman, and she no longer runs a magazine, but she's on my list of keepers as well. I have much to thank her for, not least the pleasure I take in being responsible for the first (and, I would think, last) appearance in the pages of *The American Scholar* of the phrase, "I got your Bozo no-no right here, clown." My thanks as well to Robert Devens, another trusted editor I've worked with before; Kailee Kremer, a copy editor with a sharp eye and a sure touch; and their colleagues at the University of Chicago Press. I have been a little surprised by how much it matters to me that this book, like its author, comes from the South Side of Chicago.